Reflections on Life, Death,
and the Constitution

OTHER BOOKS BY GEORGE ANASTAPLO

The Constitutionalist: Notes on the First Amendment (1971, 2005)

Human Being and Citizen: Essays on Virtue, Freedom, and the Common Good (1975)

The Artist as Thinker: From Shakespeare to Joyce (1983)

The Constitution of 1787: A Commentary (1989)

The American Moralist: On Law, Ethics, and Government (1992)

The Amendments to the Constitution: A Commentary (1995)

The Thinker as Artist: From Homer to Plato & Aristotle (1997)

Campus Hate-Speech Codes, Natural Right, and Twentieth-Century Atrocities (1997, 1999)

Liberty, Equality, and Modern Constitutionalism: A Source Book (1999)

Abraham Lincoln: A Constitutional Biography (1999)

But Not Philosophy: Seven Introductions to Non-Western Thought (2002)

On Trial: From Adam & Eve to O.J. Simpson (2004)

Plato's "Meno," Translation and Commentary (with Laurence Berns) (2004)

Reflections on Constitutional Law (2006)

Reflections on Freedom of Speech and the First Amendment (2007)

The Bible: Respectful Readings (2008)

REFLECTIONS ON LIFE, DEATH, AND THE CONSTITUTION

George Anastaplo

THE UNIVERSITY PRESS OF KENTUCKY

Scholarly publisher for the Commonwealth, serving
Bellarmine University, Berea College, Centre College of Kentucky, Eastern
Kentucky University, The Filson Historical Society, Georgetown College, Kentucky
Historical Society, Kentucky State University, Morehead State University, Murray
State University, Northern Kentucky University, Transylvania University, University
of Kentucky, University of Louisville, and Western Kentucky University.
All rights reserved.

Editorial and Sales Offices: The University Press of Kentucky
663 South Limestone Street, Lexington, Kentucky 40508-4008
www.kentuckypress.com

13 12 11 10 09   5 4 3 2 1

Publication of this book was supported by
a Loyola University of Chicago School of Law subvention.

Library of Congress Cataloging-in-Publication Data

Anastaplo, George, 1925-
Reflections on life, death, and the constitution / George Anastaplo.
p. cm.
Includes bibliographical references and index.
ISBN 978-0-8131-2533-6 (hardcover : alk. paper)
ISBN 978-0-8131-9230-7 (pbk. : alk. paper)
1. Law—Philosophy. 2. Constitutional law—United States. 3. Law and ethics.
4. Right to die—Law and legislation—United States. 5. Capital punishment—
United States. 6. Abortion—Law and legislation—United States. I. Title.
KF385.A63 2009
340'.112—dc22   2009010796

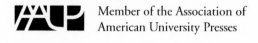

To

the Memory

of

Three Teachers Who Cherished Life

Henry Rago
(1915–1969)

Malcolm P. Sharp
(1897–1980)

and

David Grene
(1913–2002)

Contents

Preface

I strove with none, for none was worth my strife:
  Nature I loved, and, next to Nature, Art:
I warmed both hands before the fire of Life;
  It sinks; and I am ready to depart.
                              —Walter Savage Landor, *Dying Speech of*
                                          the Old Philosopher (1849)

The Essays in this volume draw on my half-century of Great Books
seminars in the Basic Program of Liberal Education for Adults at the University of Chicago and on my quarter-century of Constitutional Law and
Jurisprudence courses in the School of Law at Loyola University Chicago.
This volume of constitutional sonnets includes suggestions (1) about texts
that illuminate enduring issues with respect to mortality and the law, (2)
about United States Supreme Court cases that attempt to deal with such
matters, and (3) about how life-and-death issues might well be regarded
by us. Both public policy and constitutional questions are dealt with in
the light of principles that draw upon long-familiar notions about life,
death, religion, liberty, natural right/natural law, nature, chance, morality,
and the common good. An effort is made thereby to suggest—to legislators, judges, and other citizens interested in the principles and practices
of the Constitution—how to think further about the matters examined
in these Essays.

The Essays developed here begin with reminders of what is said elsewhere (in space and in time) about the matters critical for understanding
the life-and-death issues addressed in American constitutional law. The
first half of Part One mostly recalls the ways that such issues were addressed by gifted authors prior to the emergence of the United States.

After the Declaration of Independence and the Constitution are
drawn on in this context, there is a series of examinations of the modern
efforts to reconcile the attractions of individualism with the demands of

ix

citizenship. Particularly relevant here are the measures considered necessary for the waging of war today.

Part Two of this volume discusses cases in which parties are even more influenced by religious doctrine than may be seen in the cases considered in Part One. Some of the matters touched upon here are considered even further in the projected fifth volume of this series of constitutional sonnets, *Reflections on Religion, the Divine, and the Constitution*.

Life-and-death matters are considered further in the second half of Part Two of this book, leading to a reconsideration of the underlying issues addressed in the opening Essays of Part One. The concluding Essays return to matters developed in the projected fourth volume of this series of constitutional sonnets, *Reflections on Slavery and the Constitution*. (My *Reflections on Freedom of Speech and the First Amendment* listed, on page xiv, the then-remaining volumes of a hoped-for ten-volume series. The three volumes already prepared for publication in this series have benefitted significantly from the informed and meticulous copy editing of Derik Shelor. All of my work in recent years has benefitted as well from the considerable research assistance provided by Charles Fisher and Wendy Wermerskirchen of the Loyola University of Chicago School of Law Library.)

It is intended in my *Reflections* volumes to suggest, again and again, the enduring questions that bear upon how various cases, many of them well known, can be usefully reconsidered. It is hoped that a wide enough range of cases is presented in these volumes to permit the student of law to think usefully about the many other important cases that cannot be discussed here. The student of law also has available several generous reviews of my *Reflections on Constitutional Law* (Milner S. Ball in the *Journal of Legal Education*, Philip A. Dynia in the *Law and Politics Book Review*, and Shawn G. Nevers in the *Law Library Journal*) and of my *Reflections on Freedom of Speech and the First Amendment* (Ira L. Strauber in the *Law and Politics Book Review*). Also generous are the reviews of both books by Joseph Goodman (*The Federal Lawyer*). Even though Howard Schweber's review of *Reflections on Constitutional Law* (in *The Review of Politics*) can identify it as "alternatively delightful and infuriating," he (in his criticisms) does quote or paraphrase enough from my book to permit the thoughtful reader to work out for himself (especially after consulting the six other book reviews acknowledged here) the limitations of the conventional approach to these matters depended on by this reviewer.

Abortion-related issues continue to divide Americans, and understandably so. The volatility of and interest in this subject are reflected in a front-page headline in the January 17, 2008, *Chicago Tribune*:

Abortions at 30-year low
Illinois sees large drop: 19% in five years

Such fluctuations can be expected to continue, especially as contraception and abortion-inducing medications come to be used in such a way as to leave it uncertain as to how things really stand among us with unwanted pregnancies and their deliberate termination. (A Steve Chapman column in the *Chicago Tribune* of January 20, 2008, addressed these issues.) Much of the debate here, for three decades now in this Country, turns around the issue of precisely what is being killed (once there *is* a conception) and the issue of when any killing may properly be done, by whom, and how. We can be reminded, here as elsewhere, of the significance of the law in the regulation of both living and dying. Killing on a much larger scale, and clearly of human beings, may be seen as well in the systematic destruction (by aerial bombardment and otherwise) of civilian populations in times of conflict. Obliteration bombing itself is discussed in Essay Twelve of Part One of this volume.

The perhaps unprecedented campaigns by the Nazis during the Second World War against Jews, Gypsies, and others, as well as the depredations of the Stalinists, have long been notorious. It is suggested, in some detail, in the materials drawn on in Appendix I of this volume, how much such atrocities depend for their "effectiveness" on the victims' law-abidingness and on the general "reliability" of everyone involved in such dreadful programs. Respect for the law did come to be undermined.

The atrocities in Lithuania and in Dachau chronicled in the accounts excerpted in Appendix I of this volume are grim samples of what was happening in much of Europe between 1939 and 1945. (Perhaps the most ferocious version of such crimes against humanity is what the Pol Pot regime did in Cambodia a generation ago.) Particularly telling is an observation by the Holocaust survivor drawn on in Appendix I of this volume, upon encountering respectable gentiles who could see the dreadful plight of their Jewish acquaintances: "That's what bothers me more than anything—that they did not have any pity for us."

We can, in assessing the worldwide responses to such revelations, be reminded of the reliance placed in 1776 by the Declaration of Independence (Appendix A of this volume) upon the judgment of civilized opinion everywhere. It was recognized, or at least hoped, thereby that there are enduring standards—of right and wrong, of good and evil, and hence of better and worse—that it is prudent to expect civilized peoples everywhere to insist upon, and for this we can be grateful.

—George Anastaplo

Hyde Park
Chicago, Illinois
May 2, 2009

Part One

1. On Understanding the Others

I

What can be learned from other "cultures" about life and death? Can the Others truly be known, except by a rough approximation, especially when there are profound differences in language involved that are likely to elude translators? Is it primarily, or most reliably, about Ourselves that we learn when we study Others?

The point of departure, for our purposes here, is the Yukio Mishima short story "Patriotism," which describes what we would call a suicide pact between a Japanese Army lieutenant and his wife. A traditional Japanese mode of suicide is drawn upon by the young officer. Our interest in this story is reinforced by what we know about how the author of the story orchestrated (in 1970) his own suicide at age forty-five.

We move here from this short story to glimpses of the status and modes of suicide elsewhere, ancient and modern. We can be reminded thereby of how difficult it can be truly to *see* Others. Particularly to be noticed are varying insights and assumptions about the nature of the human soul and about the status of what we often call the Self.

II

In Mishima's "Patriotism" much more attention seems to be given to how the couple undertake to kill themselves than either to why they do this or to whether they should do it. The man in this short story insists upon subjecting himself, in full view of his eminently dutiful wife, to a traditional Japanese mode of suicide, the *seppuku* (or *hara-kiri* [belly-cutting]). It is hard to imagine a more painful form of suicide, a form which makes the wife's slitting of her own throat thereafter seem genteel by comparison.

Statements are thereby being made by this couple in the story, statements which are, I have indicated, reinforced (for contemporary readers) by the mode of suicide chosen by Mishima himself in 1970. Mishima performed his suicide in the company of military-style companions, one of whom attempted to provide a merciful beheading of Mishima after the ritual disemboweling had gone far enough. This companion was then killed in turn by beheading, all of which (performed rather crudely) was said to have been done to advance nationalistic principles in postwar Japan.

The Mishima suicide, by an artist who was a serious contender for a Nobel Prize in Literature, created the stir in Japan that was evidently intended. We can be reminded of the differentness of the Japanese from us when we notice that they have many more known suicides than there are in the United States, a country with more than double the population of Japan. Reinforcing our awareness of profound differences from them is the report that Yukio Mishima could be criticized by some of his countrymen for having presumptuously used for himself an elevated form of suicide that was not appropriate for his station in life.

III

It can be instructive to compare the Japanese response to suicide with that of Western Antiquity. That the Greeks tended to look down on suicide is suggested by restrictions placed on burial sites for those who had killed themselves. But someone such as Ajax, as in Sophocles' play, could be provided honorable burial, and others such as Orestes, Electra, and Pylades can (in one of Euripides' plays) contemplate honorable suicides.

For the Greeks—such as Jocasta, Antigone, and Phaedra—suicide was not a "statement" (as it seems to be in the Japanese *seppuku*). Rather, it was primarily a release from torment, as it may also be for Shakespeare's Romeo and Juliet. On the other hand, Socrates' death, which has been regarded by some as suicidal, might instead be regarded as a "statement."

Something "Socratic" may be seen in such Roman recourses to suicide as those of Cato and of Seneca. In other instances—such as those of Brutus, Cassius, and Mark Antony—suicide is the alternative to demeaning captivity as prisoners of war. This may be seen also in the recourse to suicide by Cleopatra, a fellow-traveler of the Romans, who was most "un-Japanese," however, in her researches into the least painful way to kill oneself, researches that (according to Plutarch) included her experimenting lethally on slaves.

IV

Perhaps the most spectacular suicide in the Bible is that of the blinded Samson, who not only put an end thereby to his misery but also destroyed many of his people's enemies in the process. Even more spectacular, of course, is the self-sacrifice of Jesus, with a view to saving (not destroying) others. This, too, is regarded by some as somewhat suicidal.

Christianity, by and large, has condemned all forms of suicide, with Job providing the model of endurance in the face of the most dreadful calamities. This response may be seen in the reservations expressed by Augustine about the suicide of Lucretia, the fatally violated matron much celebrated by the Romans. On the other hand, Augustine can justify what Samson did as having been commanded by God and Dante can honor Cato (despite his suicide) in his *Divine Comedy.*

A perversion of the Christian disavowal of suicide may be seen in the refusal of the villainous Macbeth, even when faced by overwhelming odds, to "play the Roman fool." The fool of fools, it can be said by Christians, is Judas Iscariot, who adds suicide to his other monstrous sins. Furthermore, the traditional Christian antipathy to suicide is reflected in the fact that someone such as William Blackstone can report that the English law regards it as "self-murder."

V

We can be reminded of our limitations in understanding other peoples when we hear of the epidemic of suicide bombings in the Middle East these days. Some of us can recall the shock of the dramatic acts of a few Buddhist monks setting themselves afire in Vietnam forty years ago. Then there were the suicide bombings, which evidently continue, by the Tamil Tigers in Sri Lanka.

But the scope of the suicidal attacks, first in Israel and then in Iraq, has surpassed what the world had been accustomed to. Even so, it should be noticed that the tendency of the Muslims who organize and celebrate these attacks is to call them "martyrdoms" rather than "suicides." This seems to defer to sensibilities shaped by the longstanding Islamic prohibition of suicide.

Although religious doctrines may be drawn upon in these suicide bombings, with unlikely heavenly rewards sometimes made much of, the attacks seem to be primarily "political" in their orientation, and certainly not something done on impulse. Thus, almost all of the Muslim self-sacrificers seem to come (as Robert Pape has pointed out) from territories considered by the relevant organizations as "occupied." Indeed, many of these self-sacrificers can even seem to be spiritual descendants of Samson.

VI

It should be evident, upon examining the spectacular ways of death embraced by others, that we should be cautious in assessing the extremes to which others go in matters of life and death. Questions can be raised here as to what is truly natural. Some may be tempted to wonder whether there is indeed any guidance provided by nature with respect to the most momentous decisions by human beings about life and death.

Modes of suicide differ around the world, with the Modern Greeks, for instance, evidently preferring (as did Sophocles' Jocasta and Antigone) suicide by hanging to all other modes combined. But most of such cases —in Modern Greece as among us—occur among people who can be said to be, if only temporarily, "out of their minds." By way of seeming contrast is what was once evidently not unusual (if not even a tradition) among the Hindus, the act of *Sati*—or widow-suicide-by-burning—and this among a people that has long been recognized as quite cultivated (or "civilized").

Consider, for example, this excerpt from a 1993 account of prominent twentieth-century cases that followed the legal prohibition of *aiding* a recourse to *Sati*:

> The earliest cases of abetment of suicide [that is, being an accessory to suicide] arose out of unfortunate incidents of Sati, which were not uncommon in India at one time and which were forbidden by law in 1833 [evidently by the British rulers of India]. [Consider, for example,] *Ramdial and Others* v. *Emperor*, AIR 1914 All.249 (14 Cri.L.J. 634) . . . , a 1914 case in which the accused were tried for the offense under Section 306 [of the Indian Penal Code] for abetting the suicide of a young widow who committed suicide by becoming a "Sati" on the death of her husband. The prosecution case was that on the death of Ram Lal due to sickness, his young widow announced her intention of committing Sati. Her

family members including [the principal defendant] Ramdial, the cousin of her deceased husband, [attempted to] persuade her not to do so [but] as the widow persisted to put into action her intention, they even sent a message to the police station which was far away. Before the police could arrive, the widow directed Ramdial and some others to take the body of her deceased husband to the funeral pyre which they did. The widow followed the funeral procession. A large crowd of about two thousand people from adjoining villages, having come to know about the impending Sati, also gathered to witness the same. The prosecution witnesses [testified] that the funeral pyre was built and the dead body of the deceased was put on it by Ramdial and others at the insistence of the widow, who on her own thereafter took seven rounds of the funeral pyre, sat on it and placed the head of the corpse on her lap and demanded ghee from Ramdial who gave it to her whereupon the widow poured it on herself and the dead body of her husband and later on Ramdial also poured ghee on her and the dead body. [Ghee is a semi-fluid clarified butter made especially in India.] The wife succumbed to burns on the funeral pyre. [The defendants] admitted [all the] evidence excepting the aforesaid last overt act alleged against [Ramdial], namely [his] pouring ghee on the body of the deceased and the widow. The witnesses had deposed that the pyre was then put on fire but did not say by whom. In fact the witnesses and the accused stated in the court that when the woman demanded fire, the accused refused to give it to her, telling her that if there was any virtue in her, she could produce [fire] for herself, whereupon she whispered into the ear of the corpse and raising her arms prayed to God and shortly after the pyre burst into flames.

The status of "becoming Sati" seems to have been such that not only could this widow proceed without being physically restrained by the community (as distinguished from the police), but also that thousands gathered to watch (if not even to endorse) the spectacle (somewhat as thousands gather among us today for death-defying stock car races). This evidently old-fashioned response to what the widow had insisted upon was countered by the modern (and *we* would say "enlightened") response by the appellate court upholding the convictions in this case:

The High Court . . . held that as regards the part played regarding setting fire to the funeral pyre, there was a conspiracy of silence on the part of prosecution witnesses to oblige the accused which was further clear by the story narrated by the witnesses and the accused of inventing the miraculous theory of spontaneous combustion, and that though the accused initially remonstrated the widow not to take the extreme step, they finally gave way to her determination and intentionally aided her in committing Sati . . . As regards sentences, the High Court held them to be too lenient and enhanced sentences of all the accused to *four years* rigorous imprisonment. [Emphasis added.]

VII

Although there may be similarities between the Hindu widow committing Sati and the lieutenant's wife in our Mishima story, there are profound differences in circumstances. Thus, one woman acts altogether in public, the other very much in private, however public the reports of what has happened are apt to become. Also different may be the motives that are reflected in these two acts of self-sacrifice (but both differ much from that to which we are accustomed).

The lieutenant's wife, it seems, follows the lead of her husband. It seems to be a lead developed as a patriotic response to a crisis, or at least as a reluctance on his part to engage in any military action against comrades. The Sati-embracing widow (even though *her* name is not given, but only her husband's, in the Indian case report I have quoted) acts more on her own, in that she chooses to die at this time, while it is not likely that her late husband had chosen to die when he did, succumbing as he did to a chance illness.

The quite diverse institutions drawn upon, and reinforced, by these two women depended for their development upon centuries, if not even upon millennia, of experience and perhaps glorification. We can be reminded of the stark differentness of both of these sets of institutions from what we are accustomed to when we recall Chaucer's Wife of Bath, who has buried several husbands and is still full of life and hence expectations. However unusual the Wife of Bath may be in the scope of her appetites, she is no more than an extreme (and not an unattractive) form of what we are accustomed to, the notion that each of us has, to a remarkable degree, his or her *own life to lead.*

VIII

The double-suicide in what *is* for us the weird Mishima short story works from a 1936 political struggle in Japan, a struggle that evidently found Imperial partisans deeply divided. Within a decade Japan was engaged in a war with major Western powers, a war initiated by surprise attacks on Pearl Harbor, Singapore, and other prominent bases of the West. However perfidious these attacks were regarded in the West, they were proudly commemorated monthly in Japan throughout the war.

It is far from clear what the Japanese had hoped to gain from conducting themselves as they did in December 1941. Indeed, those initial attacks could almost be regarded as suicidal for that nation, although not as obviously so as what the (sometimes quite reluctant) *Kamikaze* pilots did later in the war when attacking enemy naval vessels. However self-defeating the December 1941 surprise attacks were, they did not seem to have been regarded by the Japanese as dishonorable, any more than were their earlier atrocities in China.

How different the Japanese sense of honor was (and perhaps still is) from that in the West is suggested by their response to the sudden death of Franklin D. Roosevelt in April 1945, at a time when American bombers were steadily pounding the Japanese mainland. The news of our President's death, which was received with jubilation among the Nazi leaders in Germany, was (it is said) dealt with in this fashion among the Japanese:

[Short-wave radio] carried the flash into the heart of Tokyo. An announcer for Radio Tokyo repeated the bulletin to his people and said, to the puzzlement of American monitors: "We now introduce a few minutes of special music in honor of the passing of this great man." But the music did not last long. Japan's new Premier, Kantaro Suzuki, who had heard the news, rushed to the radio station and went on the air himself. Befuddling American eavesdroppers even more, he said: "I must admit that Roosevelt's leadership has been very effective and has been responsible for the Americans' position today. For that reason I can easily understand the great loss his passing means to the American people and my profound sympathy goes to them." (Anastaplo, *The Constitutionalist*, 752)

It should have been difficult, for anyone who knew of these broadcasts, to strike Japan with two atomic bombs a few months later, devastating actions that testified to the depth of the enduring hatred that the Pearl Harbor attack four years before had indeed inspired among us.

IX

Dramatic differences of opinion, with respect to the sanctity of human life, are reflected in various uses of and responses to actions that end one's life prematurely. The most pronounced condemnation of suicide, as a deed worthy of eternal damnation, may routinely be found in the West. But when a terminally ill patient is suffering unrelenting excruciating pain, even the most devout Christian may be willing to see extraordinary measures used to relieve that pain, even if these measures *are* likely to hasten the death of such a patient.

The traditional Western response to these matters (whatever dissenters such as Montaigne, John Donne, and David Hume may say) makes much of that individual soul which is ultimately independent of the community, subject as the human soul is to the Will of God. This may be seen in the willingness of the hero of John Bunyan's *The Pilgrim's Progress* to abandon his wife and children in order to secure his eternal salvation. Underlying one's concern here may be that dread of death as "a fearful thing" expressed so graphically by Claudio to his pious sister in William Shakespeare's *Measure for Measure* (III, i, 119–133):

Ay, but to die, and go we know not where,
To lie in cold obstruction and to rot,
This sensible warm motion to become
A kneaded clod, and the delighted spirit
To bathe in fiery floods, or to reside
In thrilling region of thick-ribbèd ice;
To be imprisoned in the viewless winds
And blown with restless violence round about
The pendent world; or to be worse than worst

Of those that lawless and incertain thought
Imagine howling—'tis too horrible!
The weariest and most loathèd worldly life
That age, ache, penury, and imprisonment
Can lay on nature is a paradise
To what we fear of death.

We can be reminded by such passion of how deeply rooted the desire to preserve oneself may be, a desire that may somehow even find expression in suicidal acts. Consider how Thomas Hobbes, who seems to have grounded his political science on the individual's natural desire for self-preservation, could speak in Chapter VIII of his *Leviathan* of the phenomenon of suicide:

> Likewise there raigned a fit of madnesse in another Graecian City, which seized onely the young Maidens; and caused many of them to hang themselves. This was by most then thought an act of the Divel. But one that suspected, that contempt of life in [these Maidens], might proceed from some Passion of the mind, and supposing they did not contemne also their honour, gave counsell to the Magistrates, to strip such as so hang'd themselves, and let them hang out naked. This the story sayes cured that malnesse.

We can be reminded here of how careful the lieutenant's wife was, in our Mishima story, to make sure that her corpse should be found decorously clothed, which suggests that she (like Hobbes's Greek maidens) *did* want to "die," but not altogether.

2. Life and Not-Life in Thucydides' Funeral Oration

I

It seems to have been customary, for those who delivered funeral orations in our orator's city, to "praise the one who made this [kind of] speech a part of [the] law, saying that it is noble that a speech be delivered over those being buried after falling in war." The orator opened, in this way, his own funeral address, recorded in the account of the Peloponnesian War provided by Thucydides, an address provided (in the remarkable Thomas Hobbes translation) in Appendix D of this volume (but a translation *not* quoted in this Essay). But the orator immediately voiced reservations about the accepted practice here, thereby calling into question the judgment of his predecessors.

For, he argues, "I would have thought it enough that the honors of those who become good men by deed be presented also by a deed—such as you see even now in what has been prepared at the public expense for this funeral—and not that belief in the virtue of many should be risked to one man's speaking well or badly." How well, or at least how carefully, the orator spoke on this occasion is indicated by how he speaks of those who had "fall[en] in war." They had "become good men by deed"—that is, by having succumbed in battle.

We can see here an instance, perhaps even an extension, of the Ancient Greek reluctance to use ominous expressions. *Dying* was not to be spoken of lightly, nor were some names (such as that of the death-connected Persephone) to be used frequently (if at all), of which reluctance we can perhaps hear echoes in the use among us of "passing." These and related observations have been anticipated by Leo Strauss, who noticed, in *The City and Man* (194), something that Thomas Hobbes, as translator of Thucydides, evidently did not notice, that Thucydides made his funeral orator here "avoid the words 'death,' 'dying,' or 'dead bodies': only once does his [orator] speak in the Funeral [Oration] of death, and this in the expression 'unfelt death' (II, 43.6).''

II

Thus, the emphasis in this funeral oration is upon the living. This is evident in the opening remarks, which recognize the accomplishments of the audience's ancestors, but not without going on to acclaim the recent generations, and even more the present generation, as superior. It cannot be said, however, that future generations will be even greater—for, after all, one's posterity are simply unpredictable in their accomplishments, if not in their very existence.

Although the ancestors are questioned, they are still obeyed. That is, the orator, as a law-abiding citizen, will (however reluctantly) provide the required address. There may be seen here a commendable limitation upon the freedom for which this city is generally recognized.

That freedom does depend on the continued existence of the city. That city need neither come nor go, unlike the human beings who make it up. Respect for the endurance of the city is reinforced by the "marginalization," if not by the deliberate suppression, of death even in a funeral oration.

III

There are of course many cities, with several vying (as in this war) for recognition as preeminent. But *this* city is rare, if not altogether distinctive, in that "the same people always have inhabited [this] country." The orator draws thus upon a long-received opinion to the effect that the ancestors of his city had lived there forever.

The eternality of *this* city is thereby affirmed. One can, upon noticing this account, wonder whether the city is even to be regarded as godlike. And this in turn can make the reader wonder about the status of the divine in this funeral oration.

It is only then that one may notice in turn that conventional notions about the divine are dispensed with here. The gods, for example, are never referred to, however much might have been said about them in the funeral rites already performed on this occasion. The city itself may even be said to have replaced the gods in this oration.

IV

Is there something divine, however, in the namelessness of this city? Greece *is* referred to by name, as is Lacedemonia (Sparta), but not the orator's city. Nor does the orator use his name, or that of any of his own forebears—and this reticence we can usefully respect for the time being in this Essay.

But then, the honored dead are not named either. We are not told how many of them there were or even precisely where and when they died. Nor are their families identified, however many of them there may have been in attendance.

All this is to say, still another way, that only the city truly is. Human beings come and go—and their lives are meaningful only because of the city with which they are associated. Very much (if not all) depends, therefore, on the stature of the city with which one is associated.

V

"Our whole city," the orator can assure his fellow citizens, is unique, worthy of emulation by other cities. It is, in fact, "the school of Greece." This assertion constitutes, among other things, a challenge to the traditional opinion that Homer was the educator of Greece.

The orator's awareness of this challenge seems to be reflected in his observation, shortly after his "school of Greece" assurance, "[W]e have no need . . . of praise from a Homer." He, then, in praise of his city's accustomed worldwide boldness, bestows the daring commendation, "[We] have everywhere established memorials of deeds bad and good." The awe of *this* city implicit in this commendation suggests how the Divine, in its Mystery, should be regarded.

Does the orator's endorsement of his city as the "school of Greece" suggest that his own speech contributes to a corpus which would replace Homer? Or is it not the orator, but rather Thucydides, who is Homeric in scope? The patriotic aspect of Thucydides may be indicated in the way he identifies himself politically in the opening words of his account of the Great War.

VI

The orator's city is distinguished not only from the cities of the Barbarians but also from other Greek cities. It is a democracy, very much dependent on an open discussion of public issues. It welcomes foreigners, some of whom were evidently part of the orator's audience.

It is a city that is remarkably tolerant of all kinds of personal lives by its citizens. It is taken for granted by the orator that these diverse lives can be drawn upon, when needed, for the good of the city. The city is not simply the instrument of men and women seeking to preserve themselves and thereafter to serve their diverse interests.

Much the same might be said elsewhere in Greece, of course, about the primacy of one's city. But much more might also be said elsewhere about the gods and the preeminent founders of a city. *Here,* however, there is a nameless city that has "always" been, standing thereby for the primacy of the political order, whatever "history" and other stories may say about origins and about other "things" which may be, or may seem to be, forever.

VII

Thucydides had, at the outset of his grand story, offered it as an account of particularly memorable events. The things which truly endure, he seems to say, are not cities or noteworthy human beings, but rather an occasional work of the mind. He, too, can look beyond Homer, even presuming to correct him about what had happened in the Trojan War.

But Thucydides' own account of the origins of the orator's city is rather prosaic. True, there had not been into that city the kind of movement reported for other cities in what we would call "historical times." But this may have been because the soil there chanced to be so poor that outsiders preferred to invade and occupy other places—and this, we can add, permitted the orator and his fellow citizens to regard their city as having "always" been occupied by the same people.

We have recalled the orator's endorsement of virtually any deeds ("bad and good") that might make a city memorable. But do not even such deeds themselves depend, for their "immortalizing" effect, upon the accounts that do chance to survive? Thus, the city, as city (unlike both the heroes and cities in stories), is as mortal as human beings naturally are.

VIII

Nothing is said by the orator, in this formal address, about the souls of those honored on this occasion. They should be satisfied, it is indicated, with the honor bestowed on them. But then, they are so dealt with that it is not as if they had died.

Indeed, the immortalizing of the unnamed (and hence somehow generic?) city on this occasion is paramount. Death itself, when explicitly spoken of, can be referred to (as we have seen, with Leo Strauss's help) only as "an unfelt death." Death can thus be superseded—or, at least, circumvented.

We can wonder whether the orator's unnamed city is, in principle, unnameable, especially if it is indeed unique in being generic. We can also wonder whether any oration, such as the one assigned to the orator by Thucydides, is remarkably unfeeling for the survivors of the recently fallen. Thucydides himself knows, of course, that the orator who can so artfully avoid mortality even in a funeral oration will himself (because of a plague) unexpectedly (some might even say, justly) end his days on Earth soon thereafter.

IX

We might find it odd that the orator makes as much as he does, at the beginning and at the end of his address, of the expenses incurred by the city because of these dead. This seems consistent, however, with his repeated indications that *the city* should get on with its life, that life which (it seems to be suggested) is the only ground for the meaningfulness of the lives of citizens. Thus, the city as city—not only the orator's city?—is held up here as something to be taken seriously, at least as something that may endure.

The political, it would seem, is ranked higher than the poetic. The *deeds* of this city are more to be treasured than the *verses* of a Homer. But, we have noticed, the deeds that are remembered, and how, can very much depend upon what is recorded (and how that is done).

The *memorable*, we have also noticed, is more to be treasured (the orator suggests) than even the *good*. But does not this argument depend on some sense of the good itself that the memorable serves? And can the good be truly grasped, especially by those dedicated to politics, if human mortality is not seen (and spoken of) for what it is?

3. Death and Resurrection in Euripides' *Bacchae*

I

Euripides, evidently self-exiled in Thrace, included in his final dramatic trilogy, produced posthumously for him in Athens, a play about the unsettling introduction into Greece from the East of the Bacchae (the followers of Dionysus), and particularly their introduction into Pentheus' Thebes. The audience is reminded of what had happened to Semele in Thebes, a generation before the coming of the Bacchae to Greece, while she was carrying the infant Dionysus, fathered by Zeus. It is said of Semele, a daughter of the Theban founder, Cadmus, in the *Oxford Classical Dictionary*:

> Her story consists almost wholly of her relations with Zeus and Dionysus. [Zeus'] association with her aroused Hera's jealousy, and the goddess, disguising herself, advised [Semele] to test the divinity of her lover [Zeus] by bidding him come to her in his true shape. [Semele] persuaded him to give whatever she should ask, and he was thus tricked into granting a request which he knew would result in her death. The fire of his thunderbolt killed her, but made her son immortal. Zeus put the unborn child in his thigh, whence he was born at full time . . .

It can seem odd to us, of course, that Zeus, when he was tricked in effect by his spouse (Hera) into granting Semele a wish, did not foresee what would be asked for. But then, Hera herself had not anticipated the formidable divinity that would in effect be forged (or "confirmed"?) in Semele's womb by Zeus' thunderbolt. The child that Zeus and Semele conceived is recalled thus (along with his cult) in the *Oxford Classical Dictionary*:

[Dionysus] is rarely mentioned in Homer, for, like Demeter, he was a popular god who did not appeal to the Homeric knights . . . His cult was widely spread in Thrace, and the Thracian and Macedonian women were especially devoted to his orgia. The myths of invasion of Boeotia [where Thebes is located] and Attica by Thracians are not to be wholly disregarded. . . . Boeotia and Attica were [the cult's] chief seats; in the Peloponnese it is less common . . . [The cult] swept over Greece like wildfire [and the cause of this] was its ecstatic character which seized chiefly on the women. They abandoned their houses and work, roamed about in the mountains, whirling in the dance, swinging thyrsi and torches; at the pitch of their ecstasy they seized upon an animal or even a child, according to the myths, tore it apart and devoured the bleeding pieces. This so-called omophagy is a sacramental meal; in devouring the parts of the animal the maenads incorporated the god and his power within themselves. . . . Orgia of a milder kind were celebrated in historical times on Mt. Parnassus [near Delphi] by official cult associations of women, and there is a trace of the omophagy in a State cult [in some Greek cities]. The frenzy of the orgia was tamed by Apollo, who admitted Dionysus at his side at Delphi and brought his cult into the gentler forms of State religion.

The *Oxford Classical Dictionary* entry on Pentheus provides, in effect, a summary of *some* of the action in Euripides' *Bacchae*:

[S]on of Agave, daughter of Cadmus, and her husband Echion. When Dionysus returned to Thebes from his conquests in the East, Pentheus denied his deity and refused [as ruler in Thebes] to let him be worshipped. But the supernatural strength of the women who had gone out to worship Dionysus was too much for [him], and he consequently (by advice of a mysterious stranger, the god in disguise . . .) went out to spy upon them. He was detected and torn to pieces, his mother, who in her frenzy took him for a beast, leading the rest. It is possible that this goes back to some ritual killing . . .

We can see here the human passions often at work in religion, powerful passions related to efforts to cope with the natural limitations of human life. We can also see the questions suggested about the locus of piety in the female, with a dramatization of those relations between male and female that are particularly productive of both good and evil.

II

Dionysus, after coming to term in Zeus' thigh, is raised in obscurity, away from the jealous eye of Hera. His upbringing (according to the play) is in the East, which helps account for the non-Greek elements in his worship. Thus, he is not, at least at the outset of his career, part of the established "social order" among the Olympian gods, even though he is a son of Zeus.

Dionysus is associated with the development of the vine for human beings. The gods, it seems, did not need whatever it is that wine offers to an often-troubled mankind. Women, it seems, found the Dionysian way particularly liberating, not unlike what modern feminism sometimes seems to offer.

It should be noticed that the Chorus of Asian women accompanying Dionysus in Euripides' play are far more moderate (as can usually be expected from "established" worshipers) than the possessed Theban women temporarily running wild on the mountainside. Friedrich Nietzsche evidently believed that the Apollonian element in Classical Greek life was necessarily supplemented by the Dionysian element (with which the birth of tragedy is associated). This is not to deny that the Dionysian element might seem outlandish, if not even unnatural, to the Classical Greek purist.

III

By the time of Euripides, the Greeks seem to have become accustomed to a Dionysian worship that was fairly tame in practice. Vestiges of its Asian origins remained—in some of its vocabulary, gestures, and costumes. But, long since, the Greeks had "naturalized" Dionysus, even insisting that he had had a Greek woman as his mother and a "Greek" god for his father.

It can be wondered whether the elderly Euripides had encountered, in northern Greece, a fiercer version of the Dionysian cult than that which had long been established in Athens. Also, had the Peloponnesian War reminded the Greeks of the fierce passions "sublimated" (as we would say) in religious practices that had been tamed? The intensification of life and death issues during the war had exposed to view passions that had been usefully covered over in peacetime, but had not been truly eliminated.

The Dionysian cult had become, in Athens, so tame that it could be trusted to preside over perhaps the most productive (perhaps even the most civic-minded) theater of which we know. The cult's vitality, as well as that of a remarkably sophisticated Athens, may have depended on deep-rooted passions that had long been harnessed, not eliminated. Such harnessing could even take the form of representing a "death" which somehow had the capacity of a "resurrection."

IV

The Dionysian cult has been regarded by some as an anticipation, in critical respects, of Christianity. Particularly significant here perhaps is the considerable reliance on female religious sensibilities. It is significant as well that a mortal female (a virgin before her encounter with Zeus?) helps develop a divinity who will provide much-needed solace for mankind.

There are ancient accounts which have Dionysus dying (if not even being killed), only to be resurrected. In Euripides' play (as in the myth he evidently drew upon), Pentheus is himself, in a way, a Dionysus who is sacrificed. After all, Pentheus and Dionysus *were* first cousins, inasmuch as Pentheus' mother (Agave) and Dionysus' mother (Semele) were sisters.

Dionysus, as presented by Euripides, very much resents his aunts, who had not believed what his mother (their sister) had said about who had impregnated her. The catastrophe of Zeus' thunderbolt could be understood, "naturally" enough by many in Thebes, as divine punishment of Semele for a blasphemous invocation of Zeus. Pentheus seemed to be of the same opinion, an opinion that is very much supported, of course, by ordinary human experience.

V

Pentheus, in any event, does resist the introduction of the Dionysian cult in Thebes. The (temporary) maddening of the women of Thebes obviously disturbs the established social order of the city, somewhat the same way (it could later be said) that the Christian cult did. Indeed, does not the way that Dionysus acts (using Agave and her companions to dismember her son) make Pentheus seem prescient in his vigorous resistance to the introduction of this cult?

Pentheus can be seen, despite his youthful imprudence, as somewhat representative of responsible leadership in a Greek city. He may even be seen as a crude version of the Marcus Aurelius that John Stuart Mill, in his *On Liberty* essay, depicts as the unfortunate persecutor of Christians. Euripides' Pentheus is then, despite his immoderation, a champion of rationalism and of the city as city.

This young ruler, in his efforts to preserve the sovereignty of an established rationalism, does not seem to recognize that "life force" (in himself as well as in the community at large) which has to be accommodated if there is to be social health. He simply does not *see*—perhaps he is not permitted to see—the Asian women of the Chorus (the already-established Bacchic cultists) who are much more moderate than the possessed Theban women roaming the hills. *We* can wonder whether there is anything of the "life force" associated with Dionysus in that *daemonic* thing that Socrates reports (in Plato's *Apology* and elsewhere) to have long been life-preserving for him personally.

VI

The concluding speech of the play has the Chorus saying (in the William Arrowsmith translation):

The gods have many shapes.
The gods bring many things
to their accomplishment.
And what was most expected
has not been accomplished.
But god has found his way
for what no man expected.
So ends the play.

The word translated here as "the play" is *pragma,* or "thing," the word incorporated in our "pragmatic." One can well wonder what the *pragmatic* response should be, especially by the political order, to determined claims of divine revelations.

David Hume's essay on miracles can be instructive here. Certainly, it is understandable that the explanation Semele had given for her pregnancy should have appeared either desperate or presumptuous to her fellow citizens. The pragmatic response of Cadmus, seeking to take advantage of what he considers a contrived connection through his daughter (Semele) with Zeus, is emphatically repudiated in the play.

Still, we can be left to wonder what the status and viability of civic-mindedness are in the Dionysian scheme of things. We can be reminded here of Apollo's challenge to the Furies (who *are* somewhat "Dionysian" in their frenzy?) two generations earlier, in Aeschylus' *Oresteia*. Apollo does prevail *there* in his championing of the restoration of the political order in opposition to the female principle invoked first by Clytemnestra and then by the Furies.

VII

Is it merely a matter of chance that Pentheus and Dionysus are first cousins? Or is there something fundamental, if not even natural, in the way that their deadly antagonism develops within a family? Must the divine, in order to fulfill itself, repudiate the human element in its own being?

Thus, Dionysus can be seen as fulfilling himself by destroying his human counterpart in Pentheus. Is he, in this respect, somehow like Abraham, who undertook to sacrifice his son? Thus, it was not only in ancient Thebes that dramatic episodes could be "celebrated" displaying how vulnerable the most intimate family relations can become at the hands of those serving the Divine.

The most memorable Greek play that dealt with such matters may have been Sophocles' *Oedipus Tyrannus*. That story, too, is very much connected with Thebes, a story which can be said to have suggestive parallels in the account of the relations between Pentheus and *his* mother. Are the peculiar elements in family relations and in the tension between family and city, repeatedly examined in the Theban plays that we happen to have, somehow connected with the origins of some of the Thebans (such as Pentheus' own father) in the fierce harvest after the Dragon's seeds were sown?

VIII

Dionysus can appear to us outsiders as sly and vindictive. He destroys Pentheus spiritually, on stage, before arranging for his physical dismemberment in the hills. The god appears to the Thebans, as the action of the play draws to an end, with sentences for erring mortals that begin somewhat like this:

> [I am Dionysus, the son of Zeus, returned to Thebes, revealed, a god to men.] But the men [of Thebes] blasphemed me. They slandered me; they said I came of mortal man, and not content with speaking blasphemies, [they dared to threaten my person with violence]. These crimes this people whom I cherished well did from malice to their benefactor. . . .

There is no recognition by *this* Dionysus that the Thebans may have been sensible, or at least understandable, in not accepting the accounts of miracles offered first by Semele and thereafter by an enigmatic stranger. Cadmus capitulates: "We implore you, Dionysus; we have done wrong." When Dionysus insists that they had not acted properly when it was the time to do so, Cadmus can protest, "But your sentences are too harsh."

Dionysus then makes what can be considered by the pious as the decisive judgment (echoes of which may be heard in the *Book of Job*): "I am a god; I was blasphemed by you." Cadmus (or, according to some editors, Agave) responds in a way that can be considered Euripidean (if not also Socratic), "Gods should be exempt from human passion." That this response is not without some force is indicated by the defense that Dionysus then falls back upon (the kind of explanation evident also in the Oedipus story), "Long ago my father Zeus ordained these things."

IX

Are we (the audience) supposed to see that there *is* something deeply questionable about the way that Dionysus conducts himself? Are we also supposed to wonder how apolitical, if not antipolitical, those cults can be that are very much moved by the desire to relieve, if not even to deny, human mortality? Is the grief-assuaging wine, kindly provided by Dionysus, part of a response that does not truly face up to the "ineluctable facts" of life and death?

A kind of resurrection is provided by Dionysus in that the sacrificed Pentheus lives on in his divine cousin. Pentheus, like Oedipus thereafter in *his* career as ruler of Thebes, was challenged by a plague threatening the city (with the remarkably long-lived prophet Tieresias warning both of them). These rulers can be understood to have *tried,* despite their profound ignorance about themselves, to do the right thing for the city.

Oedipus, and perhaps Pentheus as well, can also be understood to have illustrated the need to respect a Delphic directive, endorsed by the Classical philosophers, "Know thyself." The emergence in Greece of the Dionysian cult, with its consoling efforts to come to terms with human mortality, can be understood as a precursor, if not even as a contribution, to the Decline of the Classical World. One contribution to, if not fulfillment of, the Dionysian "project" may perhaps be seen, two millennia later, in the project of that notorious (anti-Fundamentalist?) skeptic who, too, was very much devoted to the cause of human self-preservation, Thomas Hobbes.

4. Resurrection and Death in *Everyman*

I

Everyman, from the late fifteenth century, is considered perhaps the greatest of English morality plays. The action of the play begins with Everyman learning that his death is imminent. Death, ordained by God Himself, is exhibited as an inevitable limit on human life.

Although one may "know" of this limit from early on in one's life, death can still appear unexpectedly. If a series of reincarnations on Earth is *not* posited, death is always substantially unexpected in that the human being has never had that experience personally and hence cannot truly know what is coming. Expectations with respect to death can be complicated because of the variety of prevailing opinions about what happens to the soul after death (that variety glimpsed in Appendix E of this volume and in texts such as Plato's *Apology*).

These opinions can include threats to one's eternal well-being because of the condition (that is, the history?) of one's soul at death. Dying, if it is truly the end of one's conscious activities, could be regarded as resembling falling asleep. But the teaching of *Everyman,* which is massively Christian in its presuppositions, can make death appear far more ominous than it may naturally seem to be.

II

If, however, death is part of a natural process, with nothing substantial knowable about one's continued existence thereafter, then nature may guide human beings reliably as to the happiness available to them while they are still alive. That guidance can take uses of property into account as aids to sustaining and enjoying oneself here. Nature may even rank the many ways that human beings enjoy themselves.

Some may be led by nature particularly to esteem worldly accomplishments. Most will be led to enjoy themselves physically as much as
they can—and there *is* something natural about that. A few may be led
to esteem philosophy, or a disciplined understanding of things, above all
other pursuits.

The teaching of *Everyman,* however, deprecates in effect *all* of these
pursuits. Contempt for the world and earthly pursuits (whether high or
low) is made much of. All earthly pursuits are radically diminished by the
immediate prospect of death, with human life itself exposed as something
truly trivial to anyone aware of the immensity of what awaits one after
death.

III

The exposure of goods, pleasures, and fellowship as snares and delusions is, in effect, a repudiation of the everyday concerns that human
beings are likely to take seriously. Such concerns can be identified as usually trivial, promising more than they can reliably provide. They can even
come to be dismissed as dangerous and harmful.

A political order is alluded to in the play, an order with considerable
concern about property. The very existence and operations of property
depend on the political order. Rulers, when most conscientious, attempt
to protect and otherwise to serve the proper material interests of their
subjects.

Paramount among those interests is life itself, that continued existence
of human beings upon which everything else that is cherished by them can
seem to depend. But, Everyman is reminded, there is a Ruler elsewhere,
the God who (evidently because of Adam and Eve) ordains death for all
human beings. Thus, Everyman is obliged to face up to the implications
of his mortality.

IV

Temporal rulers, however useful they may be in serving one's everyday
interests in life and property, are ultimately helpless when one confronts
one's death. Indeed, such rulers may even interfere with the essential services provided by the Church for the sake of one's eternal salvation. The
tension between the religious and the political is reflected in the advice

given to Everyman that he, if he is to be saved, should put himself entirely in the hands of a faithful priest, setting aside his worldly concerns.

The priest provides the means for the confession, penance, and last rites essential for salvation. Good deeds can be useful in helping one to be properly receptive to what the priest, and only the priest, offers. And, it seems, it is the priest (and not any temporal ruler) who can most reliably instruct human beings about what are indeed the deeds that should be considered Good.

Thus, property is put to good use when it helps the poor and the afflicted. The relevant "welfare" programs here are much more apt to be directed by spiritual than by political leaders. Otherwise, the property that is cherished by human beings and protected by the political order is apt to distract and corrupt the propertied.

V

The authority of the Church depends ultimately upon the Crucifixion endured by the Divine in its human incarnation. Death, because of that sacrifice and its attendant Resurrection, has been conquered (as is celebrated, for example, in the Eastern Orthodox Easter hymn). The Resurrection teaches that death need not be regarded as the end of one's existence, that something more (and better) can follow, that the natural limits of life can be transcended.

This teaching disparages, in effect, the significance of earthly life itself, except as a preparatory test for one's eternal condition. This apparent disparagement of what Nature seems to offer challenges, in effect, the Aristotelian observation (in the *Politics*) that there is a sweetness to existence that human beings properly cherish. Also challenged here, in effect, is the Socratic insistence (in the *Republic*) that the Divine is unitary and does not change its form.

One consequence of the doctrines drawn on in this play is that the authority of Nature as a guide for human beings *is* substantially diminished, if not even simply eliminated. Another consequence of the Resurrection is that death becomes far more ominous than it need be when Nature is the principal guide for human beings. Thus, the most comprehensive treatise in antiquity on the moral virtues, Aristotle's *Nicomachean Ethics,* had made do without much concern for what, if anything, happens to the soul after the death of a human being.

VI

Furthermore, Aristotle would have found it odd that Everyman, who was introduced to us as someone who had devoted his life to questionable worldly pursuits, should finally be hailed as a man of exceptional virtue once he is redeemed. This transformation testifies to the authority of the Church, an institution that has its point of departure (as does the play itself) from a Divinity who can suffer and die in order that He may be resurrected to good effect. The unfathomable complexity of such a Divinity is evident in the Trinity that is looked to for authoritative guidance, even down to the closing lines of the play.

It seems to be taught that a saving imitation of the Divine is performed by the human being who sacrifices everything in order to be saved. Such a willingness, if not even an eagerness, to sacrifice all that human beings hold dear can effectively call into question much that the political order takes seriously and promotes. One consequence of this can be to undermine the sense of community which encompasses both the ancestors and the descendants of those gathered in an enduring earthly association.

An additional consequence of all this can be to ignore the diversity among political communities worldwide. All of them are to be subordinated, instead, to a system of ministering to the need of individuals for personal salvation. Another way of putting this is to observe that "the general Welfare" should not be taken as seriously as it seems to be in the Constitution of 1787.

VII

It is assumed in *Everyman* that the salvation depicted there is available to human beings everywhere. But, we can wonder, what is the role of chance in determining what happens to be known about the Christian Way and where? Certainly, there have been billions of human beings who never had meaningful exposure to the teachings and hence to the services of the Church.

Conscientious Christians, aware of this, have promoted missionary efforts worldwide. Some, such as the Mormons, evidently have, in effect, a missionary program that seems to minister even to the unchurched dead. And, of course, plays such as *Everyman* guide the living who happen to witness them, reminding them of what is both essential and available for personal salvation.

The universality of the Christian teaching is suggested by the names appropriated for the Divine in *Everyman*. *Adonai* can be used, as can be *Jupiter*, drawing thereby on both the Jewish and the pagan predecessors of Christianity. Its universality is also suggested by the fact that all of the characters in the play, including the dubious ones, routinely use oaths that presuppose a Christian orientation.

VIII

Thus, the world of *Everyman* is massively Christian. No alternative "world view," except for that of the simply worldly, is evident. Even Satan is barely alluded to, however intimidating may be the fate to be expected by the human soul that is not saved.

Personal salvation, we have seen, requires the help of the priest, not that of the political system. It *is* recognized that there may be, among the cadre of priests, some who are renegades. But political rulers *do not* seem to be relied upon to discipline wayward priests.

The tension between the religious order and the political order (to use our vocabulary) may be testified to by critical changes made in the text of the Constitution of 1787 by the drafters in 1861 of the Confederate Constitution. These 1861 framers, unlike those in 1787, invoke in *their* Preamble the divine favor. Such piety, which in Christian circumstances tends to promote a radical individualism, is accompanied in the Confederate Constitution by the deliberate elimination of any federal concern for that "general Welfare" found in the Constitution of 1787.

IX

An invocation of "the general Welfare" does tend to make more of a community in which all look out for one another. The emphasis in *Everyman*, on the other hand, is upon personal salvation. We remember that this may perhaps be seen most dramatically in English literature in John Bunyan's *The Pilgrim's Progress*, where the desperate hero must leave (in effect, seem to sacrifice?) his wife and children in order to secure his own salvation.

It is repeatedly indicated in *Everyman* that life, when properly conducted, is a pilgrimage. It is the goal of a good death (especially as it provides sufficiently for the afterlife) that matters, *not* the kind of life one leads here, except to the extent that the way one does live here may affect one's ability to take advantage of the Christian dispensation. Human happiness—the happiness of persons or of communities here on Earth—can become irrelevant, if not even a fatal distraction.

It is ultimately inconsequential whether one settles into any stable political community or whether one's memory *there* endures. Constitutionalism and the political order are left by *Everyman* in a secondary state, if not dismissed altogether. Thus, the victory represented by the Resurrection may even leave Nature depreciated and death magnified.

5. John Milton and the Limits of the Garden of Eden

I

The problem of death is very much a concern of John Milton's *Paradise Lost*. The opening lines of this epic anticipate the subject to be explored:

Of Man's First Disobedience and the Fruit
Of that Forbidden Tree, whose mortal taste
Brought Death into the World and all our woe,
With loss of *Eden,* till one greater Man
Restore us and regain the blissful Seat,
Sing Heav'nly Muse . . .

That "greater Man," Jesus of Nazareth, is introduced as a divinity in this poem and is shown, in his earthly form, in Milton's sequel, *Paradise Regained.*

The "loss of *Eden,*" dramatized in *Paradise Lost,* means in effect an imposition of capital punishment on disobedient mankind. Eden itself seems to be given an earthly location, and within it there is a paradisiacal Garden. It is very much a place not only to be enjoyed while possessed but also to be longed for once it is lost.

But, the reader of *Paradise Lost* may be intended to wonder, what are the limits of the Garden? Is life there presented as so good that it would be desirable to have it forever? Or are its inherent limitations, especially with respect to knowledge by human beings of good and evil, appropriate only for the infancy of our species?

II

We confront here a millennia-old question of which Milton was very much aware. It is not only moderns who presume to suggest that Adam

31

and Eve—that is, human beings generally—have been significantly better off because of "the Fall." The limits of the Garden of Eden can sometimes be regarded by us as imposing barriers to the full development of humanity, even though we might grant that such a development could have been otherwise provided for in the Divine Plan if Adam and Eve had, from the outset, shown themselves fit for immediate permanent elevation.

The limits of Milton's epic can usefully be sketched here. It opens, we have noticed, with an announcement of the purposes of the poet, which include that of accounting for the presence of death in the world. But before the fateful events of the Garden are described, there is an extended account (across several books of the poem) of the plight and doings of a vengeful Satan and his multitudes of fallen angels, doings that do not bode well for mankind.

At the other end of the poem is the expulsion of Adam and Eve from the Garden. The gate through which they depart is barred by "dreadful Faces . . . and fiery Armes." Even so, although "natural tears" are shed by them as they leave, the closing lines of the poem do seem rather hopeful in tone:

> The World was all before them, where to choose
> Their place of rest, and Providence their guide.
> They hand in hand with wandring steps and slow
> Through *Eden* took their solitary way.

III

The movement at the end of the poem depicts the human descent into the mortality announced at the beginning of this story. At the midpoint of the poem (that is, at the end of Book Six of its twelve books), Adam is warned by the angel Raphael against an envious Satan. The Satanic motive is explained thus:

> [He] now is plotting how he may seduce
> Thee also from obedience, that with him
> Bereavd of happiness thou maist partake
> His punishment, Eternal miserie;
> Which would be all his solace and revenge,
> As a despite don[e] against the most High,
> Thee once to gain Companion of his woe.

Raphael had already described to Adam, in some detail, how Satan and his angels had been expelled from Heaven. He adds, here, this further warning:

> [L]ist'n not to [Satan's] Temptations, warne
> Thy weaker [Eve]; let it profit thee t' have heard
> By terrible Example the reward
> Of disobedience; firm they might have stood
> Yet fell; remember, and fear to transgress!

And thereupon, early in Book Seven, the poet sums up the warnings that had been given:

> The affable Arch-angel had forewarn'd
> *Adam* by dire example to beware
> Apostasie, by what befell in Heaven
> To those Apostates [Satan et al.] lest the like befall
> In Paradise to *Adam* or his Race,
> Charg'd not to touch the interdicted Tree
> If they transgress and slight that sole command,
> So easily obeyd amid the choice
> Of all tasts else to please thir appetite,
> Though wandring [that is, seeking variety].

The "dire example" is that provided by the career of Satan and his co-horts. A recollection had been provided of the grand rebellion in Heaven and thereafter the cataclysmic eviction of the rebels. Milton, in his prose Argument for Book One, summarizes that part of the action thus:

> [Satan,] revolting from God, and drawing to his side many Le-gions of Angels, was by the command of God driven out of Heav-en with all his Crew into the great Deep. Which action passed over, the Poem hast[e]s into the midst of things, presenting Satan with his Angels now fallen into Hell . . . , a place of utter dark-nesse fitliest call'd Chaos.

IV

The "dire example" provided by the fallen angels, and particularly by Satan, may deal with what can well be, for most readers, the most interesting part of the poem. We learn not only about the great rebellion in Heaven, but also about how the fallen angels reorganized themselves after the Debacle. That is, the Fall of Man had been preceded by the Fall of the Satanic Conspirators.

The Satanic coup seems to have been provoked, at least in part, by the announcement that the Son would have to be acknowledged, by all the angels, as somehow equal to the Father. Particularly galling for Satan, it also seems, was that lowering of himself implicit in this elevation of the Son. What does it say about us that the rebellion that follows, with its consequences, should be the most engaging part of the poem for the typical reader?

After all, the "everyday" careers of the Obedient Angels are not apt to be of much interest to most of us, perhaps because such angels do not really "live." Do we need stories of challenges and strife because of our own limitations as fallen (that is, as mortal) human beings? Certainly, *Paradise Lost* has always been far more popular than Milton's *Paradise Regained,* just as Dante's *Inferno* has always been far more popular than either his *Purgatorio* or his *Paradiso.*

V

We return thus to the question of whether human life was indeed somehow improved because of "the Fall." Certainly, there can be quite a story because of what Adam and Eve did, but should that be the prime consideration in assessing what happened? All this has to be aside, of course, from the motives of Satan in engineering this remarkably "productive" human disobedience.

Perhaps the most startling observation in the poem comes when Adam, "replete with joy and wonder" upon hearing the Archangel Michael's glowing account of the eventual Paradise awaiting a permanently redeemed human race, exclaims (in Book Twelve):

O goodness infinite, goodness immense!
That all this good of evil shall produce,

And evil turn to good; more wonderful
Than that which by creation first brought forth
Light out of darkness! full of doubt I stand,
Whether I should repent me now of sin
By mee done and occasioned, or rejoyce
Much more, that much more good thereof shall spring,
To God more glory, more good will to Men
From God, and over wrauth grace shall abound!

It is this kind of assessment which is evidently reflected in the medieval idea of the transgression in the Garden as a "fortunate fall" (a *felix culpa*). A similar assessment may be heard in the closing lines of *Paradise Regained*, where it is anticipated that "a fairer Paradise [would be available] for Adam and his chosen Sons."

The Archangel Michael's silence, after Adam's exclamation about the future Paradise, leaves us wondering—and it may be considered the basis upon which modern man (if not also premodern man) has concluded that Fallen Man is truly superior in critical respects to any perpetually innocent creatures in the Garden of Eden. Of course, as we have noticed, an enhanced Paradise could have been provided in some other way if Adam and Eve had never sinned. Even so, we, when passing judgment on what happened in the Garden of Eden, may be tempted to invoke the memorable lines from the *Areopagitica* (where John Milton, as polemicist, speaks in his own voice):

I cannot praise a fugitive and cloister'd vertue, unexercis'd and unbreath'd that never sallies out and sees her adversary, but slinks out of the race, where that immortall garland is to be run for, not without dust and heat.

VI

Jesus of Nazareth can also be said to have had "a fortunate fall." It was his Incarnation, with all its trials and tribulations, that allowed him to distinguish himself from the host of other Immortals in Heaven. He alone volunteered for the grim fate said to be necessary for the salvation of humanity: none of the angels, it seems, were up to this sacrifice (just as Satan, alone among the fallen angels, volunteered for a difficult mission).

Thus, Jesus came to "life" in a way that no one else then in Heaven did. It can be difficult for us, when reminded of "the long view" of things that a divine Jesus must have had, to "appreciate" how grim his earthly career was to be. We can be reminded of that grimness by this sixteenth-century poem, "The Burning Babe," by Robert Southwell:

> As I in hoary winter's night stood shivering in the snow,
> Surprised I was with sudden heat which made my heart to glow;
> And lifting up a fearful eye to view what fire was near,
> A pretty babe all burning bright did in the air appear;
> Who, scorchèd with excessive heat, such floods of tears did shed
> As though his floods should quench his flames which with his
>   tears were fed.
> "Alas," quoth he, "but newly born in fiery heats I fry,
> Yet none approach to warm their hearts or feel my fire but I!
> My faultless breast the furnace is, the fuel wounding thorns,
> Love is the fire, and sighs the smoke, the ashes shame and scorns;
> The fuel justice layeth on, and mercy blows the coals,
> The metal in this furnace wrought are men's defilèd souls,
> For which, as now on fire I am to work them to their good,
> So will I melt into a bath to wash them in my blood."
> With this he vanished out of sight and swiftly shrunk away,
> And straight[way] I callèd unto mind that it was Christmas day.

It can also be difficult for us to *feel* the evil that Adam and Eve had done, an evil so comprehensive as to warrant the countless miseries suffered by mankind ever since. Milton, too, it can be suspected, shared our difficulty, for he has "Heav'ns high King" (in Book Five) send Raphael with a renewed warning to Adam, "lest willfully transgressing he pretend / Surprisal, unadmonisht, unforewarnd." What does this suggest, we can wonder in passing, about the adequacy of the warning against willful transgression in the Book of Genesis?

VII

The post-Eden story of the human race is anticipated in *Paradise Lost.* But is it largely a matter of chance—or is it Providence—what inherited series of events we take seriously and are interested in? Other stories about the origins of things—ancient stories not only from Asia and Africa (as well as from the Western Hemisphere), but also even from the Mediterranean world—are apt to be of far less interest for most of us today.

Does our obvious vulnerability as human beings, reinforced by the stories we hear, incline us to wonder about the ultimate meaning of human life? And what should the accounts we now have, about vast spaces and countless galaxies, do to our inherited sense of the specialness of Our Own? Similar questions may be at the root of current concerns about Darwinian evolution, Intelligent Design, and the like.

It is hard to learn much that is reliable about the Others, even when we chance to become interested in them. This becomes evident when we try to understand the constitutional arrangements and political "dynamics" of most other people even in our own time. Especially is this so when we encounter such "phenomena" as those systematic recourses to suicide bombings that do seem to call into question what we consider the natural desire of living things for self-preservation.

VIII

Again and again we are obliged to ask what it is that may be considered truly good. We may even recall here the opening lines of Aristotle's *Politics,* where it is asserted (in the Laurence Berns translation),

> Since we see that every *polis* is some kind of association and that every association is constituted for the sake of some good (for all men do everything they do for the sake of what is thought to be good), it is clear that while all associations aim at some good, it is the one which is most authoritative of all and comprehends all the others that does so in the highest degree and aims at the good which is most authoritative of all and this is the one called *polis,* the political association.

This Aristotelian proposition is put to a critical test, as we shall see further on in these *Reflections,* when the devastating careers of monsters such as Adolf Hitler and Josef Stalin are confronted (as in Appendix I of this volume).

A much earlier test is provided, of course, by the career of Milton's Satan, who *is* often regarded as the most powerfully conceived character in *Paradise Lost*. Is there not, in his rebellious insistence upon equal treatment, something "Anglo-American"? He does present himself, and is acclaimed by his deluded minions, as the preeminent champion of liberty in the universe because of his defiance of what he and his followers condemn as the tyranny of their omnipotent ruler.

It is suggested by C. S. Lewis (in *A Preface to Paradise Lost*) that "Satan lies about every subject he mentions" in the poem. Fundamental to his lying may be the self-delusion, seen in his reluctance to acknowledge that he, unlike his Grand Opponent, is a *created* being. Even so, there *is* something "Anglo-American" in the reliance by Satan and his comrades upon deliberative bodies, as may be seen in the assembling of "that infernal court" in the concluding lines of Book One of *Paradise Lost*:

> [F]ar within
> And in their own dimensions like themselves
> The great Seraphic Lords and Cherubim
> In close recess and secret conclave sat
> A thousand Demy-Gods in golden seats,
> Frequent and full. After short silence then
> And summons read, the great consult began.

IX

The "great consult" might even have conjured up for Milton's contemporaries the assembly of the Barons at Runnymede or, much closer, the assembly that brought down Charles I. For Americans, Milton's account might have anticipated what happened at Philadelphia both in July 1776 and in the summer of 1787. Following immediately upon the lines just quoted is the Argument that Milton provides for Book Two, which begins with this summary of the ensuing action by the Satanic assembly:

The Consultation begun, Satan debates whether another Battel [was] to be hazarded for the recovery of Heaven: some advise it, others dissuade: A third proposal is prefer'ed, mention'd before by Satan, to search the truth of that Prophesie or Tradition in Heaven concerning another world, and another kind of creature equal or not much inferior to themselves, about this time to be created: Their doubt who shall be sent on this difficult search; Satan their chief undertakes alone the voyage, is honourd and applauded. The Council thus ended, the rest betake their several wayes and to several employments, as their inclinations lead them, to entertain the time till Satan return.

We should be reminded by all this that goodness does not necessarily follow from adherence to the forms and processes that are considered "due." Even so, there *is* something distinctively "English," and hence perhaps something somewhat "American," in how these rebels conduct themselves and, even more important perhaps, in how they explain themselves. This kind of talk is not heard in Dante's *Inferno,* although it may be talk that is somewhat in the spirit of Dostoyevsky's Grand Inquisitor.

It has been suggested in our own time that James Joyce's *Ulysses* has replaced John Milton's *Paradise Lost* as "the book which all subsequent books in English take for granted." We can see in the Joyce novel a radical "humanization" of the epic Homeric struggles, a movement (some would say, a marked decline) that makes much of everyday concerns at the expense of heroic undertakings. It is such a fascination with the Self that tends to see the meaning of our ever-vulnerable life in accommodating oneself to the challenges one encounters, something that is implicit in Adam's final speech in *Paradise Lost,* a markedly anti-Satanic speech (to the Angel Michael who had told of Jesus' future career on Earth), which ends with these words (in which the last use of "death" in the poem may be found):

Henceforth I learne that to obey is best,
And love with feare the onely God, to walk
As in His presence, ever to observe
His providence and on Him sole depend,
Merciful over all His works, with good
Still overcoming evil, and by small
Accomplishing great things, by things deemed weak
Subverting worldly strong, and worldly wise
By simply meek, that suffering for Truth's sake
Is fortitude to highest victorie,
And to the faithful Death the Gate of Life;
Taught this by His example whom I now
Acknowledge my Redeemer ever blest.

6. Human Mortality and the Declaration of Independence

I

We are reminded, at the outset of the Declaration of Independence, of the transitory character of our lives. Its initial words, "When in the Course of human Events," look both to events past and to events yet to come. Much is being provided for in a momentous present.

The inherently vulnerable, yet ever resilient, human species is taken for granted. It is evident throughout the Declaration that recollections of what has already happened can provide guidance both as to what to expect and as to what should be done. Among the things to be reckoned with are accounts of instructive recollections and of justified expectations.

Life and death are much in view in the argument developed in the Declaration, with an awareness of mortality illuminating (as well as darkening) many of the matters examined. For some purposes the human species is regarded in the Declaration as worldwide and undifferentiated. For other purposes, and especially for the political purposes immediately at hand, the divisions within that species (however arbitrary they may sometimes seem to be) very much matter.

II

A distinction is assumed, from the outset of the Declaration, between "one People" and all other peoples, and especially that people across the Atlantic with which this People had theretofore been intimately associated. It is this People who can "hold these Truths to be self-evident," Truths that others could hold the same way, if they should be both experienced and civilized enough to do so. The appropriate experience can include instruction by those who have come to see what is evident in the very nature of things.

This People—perhaps this can be said of most peoples—is largely self-identified, as may be seen in the opening words of the Preamble to the Constitution of 1787: "We the People of the United States." It is recognized in the Declaration of Independence that *this* People is made up of human beings who have, across generations, immigrated to this continent. The extent of the self-creation of this People is suggested by the assumption that those "native" human beings who had been on this continent for perhaps thousands of years are not intrinsically or naturally part of the People of the Declaration.

Although most of *this* People may be British by descent, something more than blood is inherited from the Old Country: a political system and the language which that system relies upon. That which has been inherited has been transformed, by geography and history, to provide the basis for a distinctive people. This history includes the array of grievances which permits, if it does not even require, that self-identification-and-separation condemned by some traditionalists as mere rebelliousness, if not even as treason.

III

"The History of the present King of Great-Britain is," the Declaration argues, "a History of repeated Injuries and Usurpations, all having in direct Object the Establishment of an absolute Tyranny over these States." "To prove this," the Declaration continues, "let Facts be submitted to a candid World," a recital to which half of the document is thereupon devoted. What, it can be wondered, prepares auditors to be part of "a candid World," those human beings who are open to reasoned argument?

One should explain oneself, especially if long-established relations are to be repudiated. Petitions and arguments had, for at least a decade, been addressed to those "British Brethren" considered, at least in principle, ultimately responsible for the troubling state of affairs on this continent. It now appears that "Consanguinity," the significant ties of blood and common heritage, cannot continue to be relied upon for the treatment of long-festering wounds.

The standards and related expectations invoked in the Declaration should be familiar to the British. But it is expected that the principles relied upon and *some* of the complaints collected there will mean something to the rest of mankind as well. Thus, that human nature which accounts for our mortality also offers guidance to how we should live, guidance grounded in an awareness of the Good which peoples worldwide can be helped to recognize and to respect.

IV

The point of departure, even when "a candid World" is addressed, is provided by Anglo-American history and institutions. Thus, it is taken for granted that there has long been a "Constitution" which provides some of the basis for assessing what the British have been doing to their North American associates. Much that is complained about would mean little to many of the other peoples of the world, however universal the antipathy to particularly barbarous acts can be expected to be.

At the heart of the Declaration are grievances associated with the development of various Acts of Parliament. Questionable conduct by the King and his ministers has been in the service of efforts to enforce those Acts in North America and elsewhere. Life-and-death issues figure prominently in these grievances, as do complaints about repeated interference with orderly government in the thirteen Colonies.

Although personal human concerns are ultimately appealed to, a proper political order is depended on for a reliably civilized life. Again and again, good government is placed in juxtaposition to tyrannical measures. There are standards both of the Good and of the Bad to be drawn on, standards that peoples worldwide are expected to support despite their varying political experiences, civic arrangements, and social expectations.

V

The Divine ordering of the World (whatever the Divine may mean and however It may be known) is taken for granted throughout the Declaration. The "Laws of Nature and of Nature's God" are invoked in its opening lines, followed soon by the insistence that "all Men . . . are endowed by their Creator with certain unalienable Rights." There are, in the closing lines of the Declaration, both an appeal "to the Supreme Judge of the world for the Rectitude of [their] Intentions" and a "firm Reliance on the Protection of divine Providence."

Such repeated invocations of the Divine suggest that human existence is purposeful, or at least not without enduring meaning. The Nature that is drawn upon throughout the Declaration has, as one vital manifestation, the mortality of human beings. Is the human understanding of the Divine, if not somehow the Divine itself, ultimately limited by human mortality?

Human activities and human ends naturally take that mortality into account. A proper constitutionalism ministers to human needs and makes proper use of inevitably limited resources. Can there be something eternal, or at least something apparently permanent, in the way that transitory, ever-changing things are organized?

VI

We have noticed that there are at the heart of the Declaration those grievances related to Acts of Parliament. We can see here that an established constitutionalism does not guarantee good government for all the subjects of a regime. Particularly revealing, as to who both the principals and the beneficiaries are of a constitutional system, is whether taxes are imposed on a people "without [their] Consent."

Among those who may be said to have been routinely deprived of their property without *their* consent are those condemned in the Declaration as "the merciless Indian Savages," those tribes that it is charged that the British government perfidiously attempts to arouse against the Colonists. Still others are the slaves whose "domestic Insurrections" the British government is accused of improperly exciting. The unhappy condition of these two exploited peoples could even have been used by the authors of the Declaration as evidence for the precarious condition of any people that does not properly rule itself.

The Indians are particularly condemned because their "known Rule of Warfare is an undistinguished Destruction of all Ages, Sexes, and Conditions." Thus, although "all Men are created equal," there are still profound differences among human beings which the civilized recognize and respect. Do such differences reflect varying degrees of susceptibility among us to the brute facts of mortality?

VII

The Authors of the Declaration speak at the outset of "the causes which impel them to [a] Separation" from Great Britain. And toward the end they speak of "the Necessity, which [calls for their] Separation." It is argued, however, that things need not have come to this pass.

That is, it is reported how diligent the Colonists had been in attempting to resolve their differences with the Mother Country. The diligence exhibited here, despite both passive and active misconduct for years by the British, provides guidance to later generations as to the forbearance needed by those nursing from time to time the grievances that flesh is heir to. After all, the incompetence and vulnerabilities of mortal beings *are* such that it is not prudent to change, "for light and transient Causes," governments that are long established.

It can be wondered, of course, how much the necessity exhibited in *this* bid for Independence was due to the chance character and measures of influential leaders both in Great Britain and in North America at that particular time. Could the long-term relations between these American Colonies and the Mother Country have been different, perhaps somewhat like what came to be seen with respect to, say, Canada or Australia? To recognize the workings of chance in such matters may be still another way of recognizing the pervasiveness of mortality in human things.

VIII

Life-and-death issues very much affect human happiness. The political order must be arranged, and continually rearranged, in the light of those issues, issues that it is assumed "everyone" should be able to recognize as paramount. The dependence of happiness upon property is taken for granted throughout the Declaration.

Early on in the document, for example, there may be seen the transformation of the traditional "Life, Liberty, and Property" into "Life, Liberty, and the Pursuit of Happiness." Property, it may even be implied, is useful, perhaps essential, to the pursuit of happiness. Indeed, it can be said, our mortality is due, at least in part, to that physicality of our bodies which is like property in its most tangible form.

Deathless angels (whatever John Milton may have experimented with in *Paradise Lost*) should not have the kinds of grievances catalogued in the Declaration. Thus, angels would not be likely to complain, for example, of being taxed "without [their] Consent." Property, then, is in the service of life here, with death to be kept within proper limits—and certainly not to have its somber domain unnecessarily expanded by the misconduct of governments.

IX

The Declaration concludes with its authors "pledg[ing] to each other [their] Lives, [their] Fortunes, and [their] sacred Honor." To pledge thus is to surrender the Liberty they might have had to conduct themselves otherwise. To refer to their Honor as "sacred" is to seem to enlist in their political endeavor that "Protection of Divine Providence" that is relied upon and in effect prayed for in the Declaration.

Had a similar enlistment of the Divine been seen, at the outset of the Declaration, in having it first come to view as "Nature's God"? This anticipated (I have suggested in the opening chapter of my *Abraham Lincoln* book) that "constitutionalizing" of the Divine which is developed in the series of references in the Declaration to the Divine. In this as in other ways the emphasis *is* placed on ordering matters, including portrayals of the Divine, with a view to the service of life here.

Thus, life is recognized, both at the beginning and at the end of the Declaration of Independence, as the condition of the good things available to human beings insofar as they *are* mortal. The last four grievances leveled against the Government of Great Britain dramatize, in graphic terms, the killings that the rebelling Colonists have had visited upon them by the Mother Country in a way unworthy of "a civilized Nation." It is thus emphasized that the government thereby repudiated is particularly to be condemned for making its subjects even more susceptible to mortality than they are naturally bound to be.

7. Time and the Constitution

I

An awareness of human mortality is evident throughout the Constitution of 1787 and in its Amendments. Such an awareness is implicit in the traditional civic trinity of "Life, Liberty, and Property." The conversion of "Property" into "Pursuit of Happiness," as in the Declaration of Independence, may acknowledge further the transitory aspects of human existence.

The Preamble, in expressing the concern of the Framers to "secure the Blessings of Liberty to [them]selves and [their] Posterity," attempts to build upon the stable elements in our ever-changing lives. To speak of "posterity" suggests that although one may not personally endure forever, at least on Earth, one may have descendants, just as one has had ancestors. The prospect of posterity can make our lives seem more meaningful than they might otherwise be.

A grimmer recognition of human mortality may be seen in the constitutional provisions for dealing with wars, invasions, and insurrections. It may be seen as well in the provisions made with respect both to capital punishment and to the death of holders of various offices. The immortality somehow offered by political bodies can make attempts at political dismemberment particularly disturbing.

II

An awareness of our mortality may be seen not only in provisions for the incapacity or death of office-holders, but also in provisions for their eligibility. There are age and residence requirements for Representatives, Senators, and Presidents. It matters, that is, how long one has had to mature—and where.

These and related changes are reflected in provisions that keep track of and accommodate changes in the populations of the various States of the Union. Related to such provisions are those for the development of new States. The vulnerability of some States is anticipated by the assurance that "no State, without it's Consent, shall be deprived of it's equal Suffrage in the Senate."

Repeated reliance in the Constitution upon the calendar also testifies to human mortality. The lengths of time matter—whether it is the ten days ("Sundays excepted") that the President has to assess bills passed by Congress or the six years that Senators are selected for. Among the efforts to minister to mortal human beings in their earthly existence is the provision for "promot[ing] the Progress of Science and useful Arts."

III

Mortality is, of course, natural—but so may be efforts to cope with it, if not even efforts to eliminate it. The Constitution speaks, in providing for the President, of "a natural born Citizen . . . of the United States." The "natural" spoken of here depends upon those artificial limits evident in national boundaries.

Congress is empowered "to establish an uniform Rule of Naturalization." Thus, immigrants can become, for almost all purposes, as if they had been naturally born as citizens. It is usefully "forgotten," when such matters are dealt with, that no one is "really" (that is, naturally) the citizen of *any* place, unless perhaps the entire Earth is considered.

Political boundaries do matter, in part because of limitations upon the scope of our knowing and caring for one another. Not only must the United States be separated out, for many purposes, from other political entities, but also States within the Union matter for many purposes. Differences among the States are reflected in their names, with their geographical distribution recognized in the orderly manner they are listed (that is, from North to South along the Atlantic seaboard) both in Article I, Section 2, and in the roster of witnesses appended to the Constitution.

IV

Provision "for the common Defence and general Welfare of the United States" is made in Article I, Section 8. This reflects a similar pairing in the

Preamble, an arrangement that the framers of the Confederate Constitution of 1861 dispensed with. The general welfare, it seems, depends upon an adequately sustained political order: life must be reliably preserved (by a common defense and otherwise) if it is to be steadily enhanced.

Forcible interference with a people's way of life has to be dealt with, including threats both foreign and domestic. In extreme circumstances, the ordinary rules of domestic relations may have to be dispensed with. Thus, the "Privilege of the Writ of Habeas Corpus" may have to be suspended "when in Cases of Rebellion or Invasion the public Safety may require it."

It is evident throughout the Constitution that private property is very much respected and depended upon. It may even be regarded by many as the key to effective self-preservation. Such a hedge against the risks of mortality, as well as against the demands of tyranny, may tend to make much of individualism, sometimes threatening thereby the attractions of citizenship and the willingness to sacrifice for the common good.

V

The constitutional accommodations to mortality seen in the citizenship, age, and residence requirements for various officers of government are dispensed with when the judges of the Courts of the United States are provided for. Thus, ordinary political considerations do not necessarily affect *their* qualifications, however much politics may "naturally" influence judicial nominations. The nominally apolitical character of judicial appointments is evident also in their lifetime tenure.

Judges, it seems to be assumed, are to be guided by something other than the constantly changing—that is, they are to be guided by something other than the emanations from a transitory mortality. It can be hoped that enduring, if not even eternal, standards will be brought to bear in adjudicating the judicial controversies that rise "in the Course of human Events." Judges are naturally looked to for guidance beyond that provided by the transitory and the accidental.

The reflections of judges, across centuries, have helped shape the Common Law upon which the Constitution depends. Something enduring, or at least trans-political, may be seen as well in the Law of Nations recognized by the Constitution. Again and again, it can be seen that the Framers, however practical they were in dealing with their immediate circumstances, looked (and not only for the Judiciary) to standards not limited to particular times and places.

VI

However much the enduring and timeless may be yearned for, the immediate and the transitory do have to be respected. Thus, critical actions taken in one State have to be reckoned with elsewhere. And so it is provided, "Full Faith and Credit shall be given in each State to the public Acts, Records, and judicial Proceedings of every other State."

Significant actions may be taken as well in collaboration with other sovereigns. Thus, "the Supreme Law of the Land" includes "all Treaties made, or which shall be made, under the Authority of the United States." These, it should be noticed, include treaties made before the Constitution of 1787 was ratified.

Such provisions remind us that memory does matter, that the inevitably transitory character of human life can be stabilized somewhat, if all-too-often only in appearance. This may be seen as well in the respect shown in the Constitution and its Amendments for the Common Law, which is itself very much dependent both on long-established precedents and on constant reconsiderations grounded in enduring standards. In this way salutary accommodations can be made to the constantly changing circumstances dictated by human mortality with its dependence on time.

VII

Changes in circumstances are recorded most dramatically perhaps in the Amendments made to the Constitution after the Bill of Rights. The Bill of Rights provisions themselves can be understood to have, for the most part, acknowledged long-established privileges and immunities of the English-speaking Peoples. Thereafter, political and social developments are responded to from time to time by constitutional amendments, sometimes ineffectually (as with the Prohibition Amendment of 1919).

That amendments were provided for in the Constitution, and in a much more practical way than had been done in the Articles of Confederation, testifies to the Framers' recognition of their own limitations. Human mortality means, among other things, that chance can be expected to have significant, and sometimes unpredictable, consequences. It may happen, of course, that chance developments might even expose the provisions for amendments as themselves inadequate in some circumstances, as happened when the Articles of Confederation came to be "amended" in 1787–1789.

The 1776–1789 Confederation *is* referred to in Article VI, where *its* debts and engagements are acknowledged to continue to be valid. That the Confederation is to be superseded is anticipated in the Preamble to the Constitution of 1787, where "a more perfect Union" is offered. Perverse testimony to the "reach" of the yearning for the Preamble's "more perfect Union" is provided by the desperate efforts made by some Americans, in 1861–1865, to legitimate a Confederation Constitution which implicitly repudiated (in *its* Preamble) the "more perfect Union" standard of 1787.

VIII

The provisions for amendments is, we have noticed, not the only testimony in the Constitution to the uncertainties related to human mortality. There is also such testimony as that implicit in the provisions for trials, for impeachments of officers, and for the conduct of wars. A grim reminder of how unreliable even longstanding arrangements can be may be seen in the provisions made with respect to the always unsettling crime of treason.

How disturbing treason can be is suggested by the need to limit what may be done about it under the Constitution, recognizing thereby how treason trials had come to be sorely abused in England. "Treason against the United States," the Constitution of 1787 has to provide, "shall consist only in levying War against them, or in adhering to their Enemies, giving them Aid and Comfort." Reforms here include the directive that "no Attainder of Treason shall work Corruption of Blood, or Forfeiture except during the Life of the Person attainted."

Limitations are thereby placed upon the capacity of government to control "history"—that is, to control the prevailing account of the vagaries of developments keyed to human mortality. "History" is also placed somewhat beyond the reach of government with the provisions that neither the United States nor the States shall grant any "Title of Nobility." Each generation, it seems to be understood, should (for the health of a republican order) be substantially on its own, neither privileged nor oppressed because of the deeds of its forebears.

IX

It is natural for human beings to yearn for the enduring even as they deal with the ever-changing. Both the "long-term" and the "short-run" are reckoned with in the Constitution of 1787. This may be seen in the Framers' concluding language:

DONE in Convention by the Unanimous Consent of the States present the Seventeenth Day of September in the Year of our Lord one thousand seven hundred and Eighty seven and of the Independence of the United States of America the Twelfth . . .

Thus, two millennia of human history in the West are drawn upon in which the People of the United States can be "situated" relative to other peoples. Thus, also, a decade of "local" history in North America is drawn upon, during which memorable events have been recorded and built upon. We can be reminded here that the Union *is* older than both the Constitution and most (if not even all) of the States (as States), a reminder that was challenged by Southern Secessionists in 1860–1861.

The reference to "our Lord" can remind us, once again, of the efforts human beings are moved to make in order to come to terms with their mortality. The efforts of the Framers may sometimes seem puny by comparison, but they do draw, in effect, on the Declaration of Independence, to which the birth of the United States is keyed. And in the Declaration itself, of course, there is a reminder of eternal things, with the invocation in that sacred document of "the Laws of Nature and of Nature's God."

8. Fyodor Dostoyevsky and the Modern Project

I

Niccolò Machiavelli can usefully be regarded as critical to the development of modernity in political (and hence in constitutional) principles. At the foundations of even the most exalted regimes, he argued, have been deeds that tend thereafter to be kept out of sight. Two of Fyodor Dostoyevsky's most remarkable characters—Rodion Romanovitch Raskolnikov of *Crime and Punishment* and the Grand Inquisitor of *The Brothers Karamazov*—exhibit a Machiavellian "understanding" of things.

These two characters, though obviously unalike in station and reputation, are yet deeply similar in the killing they are willing to do in order to advance their respective causes. Raskolnikov murders two women (one of them a pregnant bystander) in order to initiate his grand project. The Grand Inquisitor has been executing heretics by the scores, and indicates that he is prepared to execute "Jesus" himself in order to sustain his even grander project.

Each character can help us to see the other better. Each, it may also be said, can help us as well to see better not only the tormented soul of the author but also "the soul" of that modernity which has spawned the characters relied upon by the author. The New World, dramatized by the Protestant Reformation, the American Revolution, and the French Revolution, may be said to be grounded in fundamental reconsiderations of the proper relationship between the individual and the community.

II

Raskolnikov undertakes to murder and rob a pawnbroker of his acquaintance in order to advance the project he might develop. The propriety of killing the pawnbroker is suggested to him by a conversation he overhears. Others, that is, also recognize how reprehensible a human being (even worthy of death) this pawnbroker appears to be.

He had believed he would be frightened on his way, in St. Petersburg, to the murder he contemplates. Instead, his thoughts are otherwise:

> Passing the Yusupov Gardens, he began to consider the construction of tall fountains in all the squares, and how they would freshen the air. Following this train of thought he came to the conclusion that if the Summer Gardens could be extended right across the Champ de Mars and joined to those of the Mikhaylovksy Palace, it would add greatly to the beauty and amenities of the city.

Raskolnikov, upon finding himself ruminating thus, can rebuke himself by saying, "What rubbish!—it would be better not to think at all."

These ruminations had been introduced by the author as "irrelevant thoughts." But is there not something Napoleonic in Raskolnikov's city-planning, which is part of the grand project that is supposed to be initiated by the murder of the pawnbroker? That the innocent sister also has to be killed in the process, lest the murderer of the pawnbroker be exposed and thwarted in his "humanitarian" campaign, can be regarded as the kind of regrettable "collateral damage" that may be inevitable whenever any spectacular reordering of things is undertaken.

III

The Grand Inquisitor of Ivan Karamazov's story is "humanitarian" as well. His project is also so momentous that he, too, is willing to kill the innocent along with the guilty in order to accomplish his purpose. The innocent party here is "Jesus" himself, who appears in sixteenth-century Seville at a time when this Inquisitor is executing many heretics in great public displays.

The appearance of "Jesus" could have been taken as divine reproof of what the Grand Inquisitor was doing. But the Inquisitor protests that the message of Jesus has always been too exalted for the generality of humanity. Something else much more mundane, reinforced by dramatic executions, is needed for the good on Earth of multitudes of human beings—and "Jesus," however innocent and high-minded he may appear to be, will not be permitted to interfere with the Grand Inquisitor's project.

Indeed, "Jesus" himself would be treated by the Inquisitor as a heretic, however much the authority of the Churchman depends upon at least memories of the career of Jesus fifteen hundred years before. It would seem, therefore, that the Grand Inquisitor could not proclaim in public what he says to "Jesus" in a prison cell. The Inquisitor is the only one who speaks on the occasion conjured up here by an erratic Ivan, with "Jesus" presumably limited (at least until the "official" Second Coming) to what he had said and done during his original Incarnation.

IV

One of our "heroes" is still quite young, the other is very old. Is the Grand Inquisitor what a "successful" Raskolnikov could be like in his old age? And would a "successful" Raskolnikov be "obliged" someday to head off a young "Raskolnikov," much as this Grand Inquisitor responded to the untimely appearance of "Jesus"?

The Inquisitor, in his unwillingness to concede the immediate authority of "Jesus," can seem to imitate John Milton's Satan. He is, of course, more humanitarian in his intentions than was Satan. But the Inquisitor is not so humanitarian as to believe (as Socrates did?) that human beings can be truly happy only when they know and can deal with the truth about things.

Raskolnikov, too, if he is to succeed, must depend upon keeping vital truths to himself. That is, the power he seeks depends upon thwarting still another Inquisitor, Porfiry Petrovitch, who is investigating the axe-murder of the pawnbroker and her sister. Thus, the most remarkable character in each of these two novels can be considered an apostle of reason who dares not openly declare what he stands for.

V

Both of our heroes are prepared to set aside accepted, or normal, standards and practices. This they do, it can sometimes seem, on behalf of multitudes. Both act, that is, to save the world.

Grand projects, we can be reminded, are apt to have sordid beginnings—or at least they may require, once established, sordid reinforcement measures behind the scenes. Thus, even those Founders who seek to establish constitutionalism and the rule of law may have to resort to irregular means in doing so. This may be seen in how the Articles of Confederation arrangement was irregularly "amended" out of existence in this Country by proponents of the Constitution of 1787.

That Raskolnikov is heretical is evident enough, living up thereby to his schismatic name, but is not the Grand Inquisitor also deeply heretical, however zealous he has been in executing heretics on a perhaps unprecedented scale? Indeed, the Grand Inquisitor, in the way he threatens an inconvenient "Jesus," can remind us of the sometimes desperate Jewish authorities who found the historical Jesus a threat to the safety, if not even to the continued existence, of the Jewish community in the Holy Land. How questionable both Raskolnikov and the Grand Inquisitor can seem to the commonsensical observer is suggested both by Raskolnikov himself when he attempts to dismiss as "rubbish" his ruminations on the way to the murder and by D. H. Lawrence when he speaks the same way of the Grand Inquisitor story upon first reading it.

VI

Rubbish or not, both Raskolnikov and the Grand Inquisitor consider themselves (at least at times) as out to save the world, acting as they do on behalf of multitudes. All this may be, in each case, only in the mind of an individual. It may be on the part of each a case of individualism run wild, with personal (if not even megalomaniac) fantasies acted upon.

Raskolnikov is obviously "fevered" in the days leading up to the murders. And the Grand Inquisitor may be hallucinating, a condition brought on by the torrent of executions for which he is responsible. After all, he *has* managed to inspire a temporary return of "Jesus" to the Earth.

What is presented as clearly real is the number of executions presided over by the Grand Inquisitor. Does he harbor some doubts about what he has been doing? If so, the "visitation" by "Jesus" can be understood as the Inquisitor's self-examination.

VII

The appearance by "Jesus" in Seville may be, therefore, more than a matter of chance. Rather, it can be regarded as a manifestation of the reservations that the Grand Inquisitor himself should have about what he is routinely doing so ruthlessly. Without such personal reservations, he would be little more than a monster in clerical robes.

Perhaps there is also something like this in the killing by Raskolnikov of the pawnbroker's sister. The sister can be regarded as that aspect of the pawnbroker which should be exempt from "execution." The pawnbroker is, after all, a (somewhat pious?) human being who evidently acts within the law, however avaricious and mean-spirited she may seem to others.

One can be again reminded, by how both Raskolnikov and the Grand Inquisitor regard their "projects," of the Aristotelian proposition that all human actions aim at the Good. We shall see, further on in these *Reflections,* that this is a proposition that can be put to severe tests by the careers of Stalin and Hitler during the first half of the twentieth century, careers that are evident in the recollections drawn on in Appendix I of this volume. But even if all do somehow aim at the Good, the aim of some does seem to be far better than that of others.

VIII

Almost all, if not *all,* that matters for both Raskolnikov and the Grand Inquisitor is life here on Earth. Eternal rewards and punishments do not seem to figure into their assessments of actions called for here. On the other hand, the multitudes ministered to by men such as the Grand Inquisitor can be very much affected by *their* expectations with regard to eternal rewards and punishments.

A recognition of human mortality, and of the concerns aroused by an awareness of such mortality, can be said to be critical to both Raskolnikov and the Grand Inquisitor. This kind of recognition by them can become even more acute than it might naturally be whenever individualism is made much of. In such circumstances the prospect of the deliberate termination by others of one's personal existence here on Earth becomes even more troubling than it might naturally be.

Thus, an emphasis upon individualism can have the unexpected effect of our relying more than formerly upon community campaigns to protect ourselves. And in such campaigns, it can sometimes seem, anything goes. In this way, it can be said, both Raskolnikov and the Grand Inquisitor are moderns not bound by old-fashioned restraints.

IX

Thus, for such Projectors, constitutionalism is too tame, however useful it may be in governing the multitudes for whom they consider themselves responsible. That is, they themselves are not constitutionalists, or even predictably law-abiding. But the people at large are apt to serve their own good when they *are* law-abiding in their inclinations and habits.

The founders responsible for establishing a quite new constitutional system, therefore, are not themselves likely to be routinely law-abiding. It can even be wondered whether they are likely to be respectful of what is right by nature. It can be wondered as well whether they consider themselves bound by the guidance provided by old-fashioned political philosophy, a way of thinking that tends to be dubious about the grand projects that both the ambitious and the humanitarians are likely to develop.

Raskolnikov, we are told by Dostoyevsky, is eventually redeemed, having come to sense (if not to recognize) the folly of his great project. The Grand Inquisitor, we are also told, is redeemed as well, *if* that is how his being kissed by the departing "Jesus" is to be understood. But the path to redemption is littered, for both Raskolnikov and the Grand Inquisitor, with the corpses they have created in their desperate efforts to minister to the limitations that seem to be posed for all of us by human mortality.

9. Public Health and Private Consciences

I

Our lives do not depend solely on our decisions. Certainly, we do not seem to have *any* control over the beginnings of our lives (unless human souls preexist their incarnation on Earth). And control over the termination of our lives also can be significantly limited.

Thus, we are accustomed to attempted restraints by governments upon activities that are likely to cut short human life. Prohibitions of homicide are routine. Also familiar are prohibitions both of suicides and of efforts to assist in suicides.

We are accustomed as well to measures designed to minimize accidental deaths. Highway traffic laws are familiar to us, as are measures aimed at making motor vehicles and their use safer. Again and again we recognize that various factors can affect how and when our innate mortality can make us particularly vulnerable.

II

We are accustomed to public health measures and other programs designed to enhance life, as well as to protect it. The guardians of minors are obliged by law to be sensible in providing for those entrusted to their care. It may not even be enough for such guardians, including parents, to provide for their wards only as much as they provide for themselves.

To some degree all residents in a community can be treated as wards of that community. This is evident in subsidies, goods and services that may be provided for the least privileged members of a community. This is evident as well in efforts to regulate hazardous products and activities, including that done through instruction and persuasion.

These efforts can begin early, with prenatal care and the care of infants being regulated and to some extent supported by a community's laws and programs. A major influence is expected in and through the schools that the young are obliged to attend. Critical here can be the testing to which schools, teachers, and students are routinely subjected.

III

The efforts by communities to make lives healthier and longer can be worldwide in scope. Such efforts include responses to concerns about the environment, about access to proper air, food, and water, and about the control of the presence of contaminants among us. Critical to these efforts are the constant, many-faceted inquiries into what is truly harmful.

Differences of opinion are encountered, of course, as to how far anyone may go in advancing what appears to be his own interest when others seem to be threatened thereby in their well-being. The abortion controversy of the past quarter-century has led to bitter disputes as to whose life matters most. Such a controversy can even be extended to disputes about what it is that nonhuman animals may be entitled to.

Differences of opinions may also be encountered as to what may be exacted from citizens for the good of the community, with the levying of taxes being an obvious instance of such compulsory sharing. Another instance is the use of conscription to supply the military forces of the community. How far this can go may be seen in the reminder, in the Articles of War, that cowardice in the face of the enemy is punishable by death.

IV

The United States Supreme Court case of *Jacobson* v. *Massachusetts* (1905) indicates what may be done to any one of us in the expectation that the community as a whole is likely to be benefitted. Massachusetts law provided that "the board of health of a city or town if, in its opinion, it is necessary for the public health or safety, shall require and enforce the vaccination and revaccination [against smallpox] of all the inhabitants thereof and shall provide them with the means of free vaccination." A penalty was ordained for anyone, over twenty-one years old, who refused or neglected to comply with such a requirement for himself or for an appropriate minor for whom he was responsible.

The power of the State was upheld on this occasion by the Supreme

Court, with nothing said about what would happen if someone resisted vaccination on religious grounds. The Court could have reminded such a protester that changing one's place of residence from one town to another would relieve one of this particular imposition. Whatever the risks were of an epidemic would not likely be lessened because of the religious opinions of those who were exposed to smallpox.

We can be reminded by such considerations both of the dependence of human beings upon their communities and of the extent to which they can be used and directed by their communities. Obligatory evacuations of cities are particularly dramatic illustrations of the authority that a community may be obliged to exercise on occasion. The principle of eminent domain has a much wider application than is usually recognized, not least because virtually all the property we have, use, and dispose of exists pursuant to authority and guidance provided by some community.

V

Community authority extends to the family relations that we rely upon. Thus, for example, who one's spouse is and on what terms usually depends on some law. Allocations of, and duties toward, children may also depend on various laws.

There are in these and like matters better and worse legislative dispositions. The best arrangements, it is to be expected, are those that are most respectful of the dictates of nature. An intended recognition of nature, in the form of eugenics, may be seen in *Buck* v. *Bell* (1927), a decision by the United States Supreme Court upholding the application of a Virginia statute "providing for the sexual sterilization of [only female?] inmates of institutions supported by the State who shall be found to be afflicted with an hereditary form of insanity or imbecility."

The Opinion of the Court, delivered in this case by Justice Oliver Wendell Holmes, includes this description of the woman ministered to:

> Carrie Buck is a feebleminded white woman who was committed to the State Colony [for Epileptics and Feebleminded] in due form. She is the daughter of a feebleminded mother in the same institution, and the mother of an illegitimate feebleminded child. She was eighteen years old at the time of the trial of her case in the Circuit Court [of Amherst County, Virginia].

The Virginia order for sterilization was upheld by the United States Supreme Court in an Opinion which is said (in the *Encyclopedia of the American Constitution*) to be "insensitive." Particularly troubling for critics of Justice Holmes is this passage in his *Buck* v. *Bell* Opinion:

> We have seen more than once that the public welfare may call upon the best citizens for their lives. It would be strange if it could not call upon those who already sap the strength of the State for these lesser sacrifices, often not felt to be such by those concerned, in order to prevent our being swamped with incompetence. It is better for the world, if instead of waiting to execute degenerate offspring for crime, or to let them starve for their imbecility, society can prevent those who are manifestly unfit from continuing their kind. The principle that sustains compulsory vaccination is broad enough to cover cutting the Fallopian tubes. *Jacobson* v. *Massachusetts,* 197 U. S. 11 [1905]. Three generations of imbeciles are enough.

VI

There is, of course, something disturbingly cold-blooded about Justice Holmes's assessment here, especially as he *seems* to accept as routine the execution (if not also the starvation) of the "degenerate offspring" of "imbeciles." It is difficult for many observers, upon encountering such Legal Realism, not to be reminded of the Nazi eugenics programs in the following generation (programs glimpsed in Appendix I of this volume). Some would be inclined to see the same spirit at the heart of the case made today for virtually unlimited access to abortions.

Carrie Buck's attorney on this occasion (I. P. Whitehead) included these observations in his Argument before the Supreme Court:

> If this Act be a valid enactment, then the limits of the power of the State (which in the end is nothing more than the faction in control of the government) to rid itself of those citizens deemed undesirable according to its standards, by means of surgical sterilization, have not been set. We will have "established in the State the science of medicine and a corresponding system of judica-

ture." A reign of doctors will be inaugurated and in the name of science new classes will be added, even races may be brought within the scope of such regulation, and the worst forms of tyranny practiced. In the place of the constitutional government of the fathers we shall have set up Plato's *Republic.*

However dubious the closing comment about Plato's *Republic* may be in this Argument, the concerns expressed about racial and other improper discrimination are not without merit. The spirit of Justice Holmes's Opinion must have made Mr. Whitehead feel somewhat vindicated in his concerns (especially if he noticed the Holmes reassurance that the kind of sacrifice to be exacted of Carrie Buck was "often not felt to be such by those concerned").

We, in turn, can wonder—knowing what we know not only about the Nazi eugenics programs a half century ago, but also about the sometimes ruthless Chinese one-child-per-family policy at this time—what a government may properly do to limit its population. Is it *not* the objective that would be questionable but rather the methods used to achieve it? Certainly, one can imagine circumstances in which it would be suicidal for a people *not* to try to keep its population within the bounds that can be supported by its resources.

VII

A different kind of collective suicide may be seen whenever the population of a community steadily declines. Old-fashioned restrictions upon abortions and even upon birth control devices may be considered called for in such circumstances. Other measures, including even some form of polygamy, may be advocated, especially if a catastrophic war should chance to destroy many of the young men.

We already have policies with the effect of encouraging both marriage and procreation. Exemptions and deductions with respect to various taxes can have such an effect. There do not seem to be serious constitutional difficulties with the familiar measures that reward traditional family life.

The cases and circumstances we have been considering testify to the proposition that it is not always one's life to lead as one pleases. Thus, the limits of a cherished individualism are indicated. Indeed, without an effective social order the "degenerates" in a community would include many more than the relatively few who are likely to be condemned by their heredity.

VIII

Extensive public health programs are taken for granted among us. Both the National and the State governments are considered empowered to do much more than was anticipated by most of the Framers of the Constitution. This is in large part because "the general Welfare" can now be ministered to much more effectively because of remarkable economic and technological developments.

Massive threats to health seem to be posed by routine assaults on bodies and souls. Among these have long been the ravages of tobacco. One of the most surprising public health developments of recent decades has been the substantial "delegitimation" (not the prohibition) of tobacco in the United States, a consequence quite different from that associated with the effects of the ill-fated Prohibition Amendment of 1919.

Still to be reckoned with are the ravages of narcotics as well as of alcohol, which affect souls as well as bodies. Then there are the ravages of guns among us, a destructiveness exceeded in the Western World only, it seems, by the gun-related carnage in Brazil. In the United States, of course, our ineptitude with respect to prudent gun control is reinforced by questionable invocations of the Second Amendment.

IX

Even more serious assaults on the souls of citizens are those which affect their mental health. Important here is what has happened to serious general education. This affects not only the capacity of citizens to govern themselves properly, but also their capacity to lead and enjoy good lives.

The surrender of the mass media in recent decades to the vulgar and the salacious has been remarkable. License has been mistaken for a proper liberty, that liberty which empowers human beings to know and to pursue the good. The emphasis on self-expression, discussed in my *Reflections on Freedom of Speech and the First Amendment*, has contributed to the cheapening of the Self, leaving it subject to unpredictable passions.

It was a century ago that the United States Supreme Court ruled that reasonable measures might be taken to prevent epidemics of deadly diseases. It remains to be seen what measures might properly be taken to deal with the epidemics threatening the cultural health of the Country. But no serious cure is likely to be attempted until a sound diagnosis has been made of the condition of the souls of citizens in the United States.

10. The *Flag Salute Cases* (1940, 1943)

I

The Opinion of the United States Supreme Court in *Minersville School District* v. *Gobitis* (1940), in which seven Justices joined, opens with this sober recognition:

A grave responsibility confronts this Court whenever in course of litigation it must reconcile the conflicting elements of liberty and authority. But when the liberty involved is liberty of conscience, and the authority is authority to safeguard the nation's fellowship, judicial conscience is put to its severest test. Of such a nature is the present controversy.

Concerns about "safeguard[ing] the nation's fellowship" were very much in the air in early 1940, considering the grave perils confronting the Western democracies in Europe and elsewhere. It was widely believed that patriotism had to be shored up in anticipation of life-or-death struggles that threatened to engage the Country.

A pledge of allegiance was readily resorted to in furtherance of this effort, a pledge which did not yet have the "under God" language that has provoked challenges of its own in recent years. One difficulty with a compulsory pledge is described by the Court:

Lillian Gobitis, aged twelve, and her brother William, aged ten, were expelled from the public schools of Minersville, Pennsylvania, for refusing to salute the national flag as part of a daily school exercise. The local Board of Education required both teachers and pupils to participate in this ceremony. The ceremony [pledging allegiance to the flag, and to the Republic for which it stands] is a familiar one.

But, the Court continues,

> The Gobitis family are affiliated with "Jehovah's Witnesses," for whom the Bible as the Word of God is the supreme authority. The children had been brought up conscientiously to believe that such a gesture of respect for the flag was forbidden by command of Scripture [citing Exodus 20:3–5].

The Opinion for the United States Supreme Court continues with an account of the impasse that developed in Minersville:

> The Gobitis children were of an age for which Pennsylvania makes school attendance compulsory. Thus they were denied a free education, and their parents had to put them into private schools. To be relieved of the financial burden thereby entailed, their father, on behalf of the children and in his own behalf, brought this suit. He sought to enjoin the authorities from continuing to exact participation in the flag-salute ceremony as a condition of his children's attendance at the Minersville school.

The United States District Court judge ("on the basis of a thoughtful opinion") gave the Gobitis family the relief sought for, and this decree was affirmed by the United States Circuit Court of Appeals. The Supreme Court granted *certiorari* "[s]ince this [District Court] decision ran counter to several *per curiam* dispositions" by the Court in recent years.

II

The Opinion of the Court, reversing what had been ordered by the District Court, makes it clear that it regards as unwise and otherwise unattractive the School Board's insistence. And it is aware, as may be seen in its half-dozen references to "conscience" and "conscientious," that it is dubious about the Board's exercise of power in this manner. But, the Supreme Court can still insist, it does not want to act as "the school board for the country."

"We are dealing," the Court argued, "with an interest inferior to none in the hierarchy of legal values." The Court continues,

National unity is the basis of national security. To deny the legislature the right to select appropriate means for its attainment presents a totally different order of problems from that of the propriety of subordinating the possible ugliness of littered streets to the free expression of opinion through distribution of handbills.

National security, it seems, overrode whatever scruples schoolchildren and their parents might have had in these circumstances.

Abraham Lincoln is drawn upon by the Court for a recognition of "the profoundest problem confronting a democracy—the problem which [he] cast in memorable dilemma: 'Must a government of necessity be too *strong* for the liberties of its people, or too *weak* to maintain its own existence?'" One can suspect that Lincoln would have found it imprudent (if not simply unseemly) to insist on penalizing children in this way because of what they regarded as conforming to a divine command. He might even have seen grim humor in denying to such children the liberty of abstaining from a mandatory endorsement of "liberty and justice for all."

III

A reminder of the toleration we are inclined to show toward "religious" and other opinions that are hardly "mainstream" may be seen, by way of dubious contrast, in how one of the Justices conducted himself on this occasion, for he is recorded merely as having concurred in the result. One suspects this was because of his chronic inability to associate himself in any way with someone of the faith of the author of the Court's Opinion. He had, long before, displayed his refusal even to speak to Jewish colleagues such as Louis D. Brandeis and Benjamin N. Cardozo.

That Justice should have seen, in the Gobitis children, actors at least as "principled" as he was in responding to the demands of conscience. However that may be, it was revealing to see how the lower courts, first in *Gobitis* and thereafter in *West Virginia State Board of Education* v. *Barnette* (1943), conducted themselves when confronted by pleas on behalf of children in flag-salute cases. Those judges, it seems, were sufficiently moved by such pleas to disregard, in effect, what the Supreme Court had been saying.

It is evident in the *Gobitis* Opinion that the Court was troubled by what it "had" to do. This meant that this issue simply would not go away.

There *is* something to the proposition that a serious issue is not really
settled, at least in a decent community, until "it is settled right."

IV

The "situation" confronting the Court in the *Barnette Case* was different in several respects from what it had been in the *Gobitis Case*. First,
the Court could speak of "the fast failing efforts of our present totalitarian
enemies." Thus, even though the United States was by then at war, the
threats to "national security" did not seem as ominous as they had three
years before.

Besides, there had evidently been considerable criticism expressed in
opposition to *Gobitis*. Particularly troubling, it seems, had been the apparent efforts to coerce children to salute the flag. Besides, objections had
been made that the salute required in Pennsylvania was "too much like
Hitler's," with modifications having apparently been made "in deference
to these objections."

Then there was the tendency of the Pennsylvania legislature to require
"private, parochial and denominational schools" to provide the same kind
of promotion of patriotism, but not necessarily the flag salute, prescribed
for the public schools of the State. It seemed that *Gobitis* had, in effect, encouraged State authorities to become ever more insistent in these matters.
Overly sensitive families, it must have seemed, would have to move completely out of a State to avoid what they considered improper demands
upon their consciences.

V

By 1943, the lone dissenter in *Gobitis* had become the Chief Justice.
The Opinion in *Barnette,* with which seven Justices were substantially in
agreement, was written by a Justice who had joined the Court in 1941. He
was later to lead the prosecution for the United States during the pioneer-
ing Nuremberg Trial of 1945–1946.

The *Gobitis* Opinion had exhibited itself as uncomfortable with what
it "had" to do. Not so the *Barnette* Opinion, which could include such
memorable declarations as this: "If there is any fixed star in our constitutional constellation, it is that no official, high or petty, can prescribe what
shall be orthodox in politics, nationalism, religion, or other matters of

opinion or force citizens to confess by word or act their faith therein." The Court then ventures to add, "If there are any circumstances which permit an exception, they do not now occur to us."

There is recalled in the *Barnette* Opinion the use made in *Gobitis* of Lincoln as someone "in favor of strength" of government. "It may be doubted," the *Barnette* Opinion responds, "whether Mr. Lincoln would have thought that the strength of government to maintain itself would be impressively vindicated by confirming the power of the State to expel a handful of children from school." Earlier the Opinion had noticed developments, evidently in Pennsylvania, which must have undermined support for the *Gobitis* doctrine:

> Children from [the Jehovah's Witnesses] faith have been expelled from school and are threatened with exclusion for no other cause. Officials threaten to send them to reformatories maintained for criminally inclined juveniles. Parents of such children have been prosecuted and are threatened with prosecution for causing delinquency.

VI

The threats to dissenters that accompanied implementation of the Pennsylvania statute could have provided a gracious way out in *Barnette* for those who had been associated with *Gobitis*. Thus, two of those Justices give "a brief statement of reasons for [their] change of view," beginning with this concession to their formerly held position: "Reluctance to make the Federal Constitution a rigid bar against state regulation of conduct thought inimical to the public welfare was the controlling influence which moved us to consent to the *Gobitis* decision." But, they continued, "We believe that the [Pennsylvania] statute before us fails to accord full scope to the freedom of religion assured to the appellees by the First and Fourteenth Amendments."

These two Justices then indicate how the Pennsylvania statutory obligation had come to seem to them:

> The statute requires the appellees to participate in a ceremony aimed at inculcating respect for the flag and for this country. The

Jehovah's Witnesses, without any desire to show disrespect for either the flag or the country, interpret the Bible as commanding, at the risk of God's displeasure, that they not go through the form of a pledge of allegiance to any flag. The devoutness of their belief is evidenced by their willingness to suffer persecution and punishment, rather than make the pledge.

This kind of assessment, of a quite "human" tenor, should have appealed to the author of the Opinion for the Court in *Gobitis*. Instead, he opened his impassioned Dissenting Opinion in *Barnette* with this statement of judicial faith:

One who belongs to the most vilified and persecuted minority in history is not likely to be insensible to the freedoms guaranteed by our Constitution. Were my purely personal attitude relevant I should wholeheartedly associate myself with the general libertarian views in the Court's opinion, representing as they do the thought and action of a lifetime. But as judges we are neither Jew nor Gentile, neither Catholic nor agnostic. We owe equal attachment to the Constitution and are equally bound by our judicial obligations whether we derive our citizenship from the earliest or latest immigrants to these shores.

The Dissenting Opinion in *Barnette* then provides a statement of jurisprudential principles which begins thus:

As a member of this Court I am not justified in writing my private notions of policy into the Constitution, no matter how deeply I may cherish them or how mischievous I may deem their disregard. The duty of a judge who must decide which of two claims before the Court shall prevail, that of a State to enact and enforce laws within its general competence or that of an individual to refuse obedience because of the demands of his conscience, is not that of the ordinary person. It can never be emphasized too much that one's own opinion about the wisdom or evil of a law should be excluded altogether when one is doing one's duty on the bench.

If that which follows from the application of a law is indeed evil, then there are venerable natural right/natural law principles that should guide a judge in doing what he can to advance the cause of justice. It is a challenge to notice how and why it is that this Justice could misuse Socrates in his *Barnette* Dissenting Opinion in much the spirit that he had misused Lincoln in his Opinion for the Court in *Gobitis.*

VII

It may be partly a matter of chance who lined up where in the *Gobitis-Barnette* development. It probably did not help the equanimity of the *Barnette* Dissenter to have his *Gobitis* Opinion treated, in effect, as a brief for Pennsylvania which the Opinion for the Court in *Barnette* systematically addressed. The *Gobitis* doctrine can seem particularly odd when it is noticed that conscience-driven schoolchildren are not shown the consideration that Congress and the Supreme Court, as well as State governments, have usually shown the conscientious objectors to military conscription.

It could be instructive to consider whether the author of the *Barnette* Dissenting Opinion ever recovered thereafter his equanimity as a member of the Supreme Court. He referred in *Barnette* to personal preferences that he as a judge was duty-bound to set aside, preferences that represent "the thought and action of a lifetime." The place of natural right/natural law principles in that thought does remain something of a mystery, which can be said as well of much of modern jurisprudence, illustrated as that is by how readily scholars and judges of our day have accepted *Eric Railroad Company* v. *Tompkins* (1938) (a dubious holding discussed in my *Reflections on Constitutional Law*).

Still, it can be suggested, "the thought and action of a lifetime" did assert themselves dramatically for this Justice a decade after his unfortunate Dissenting Opinion in *Barnette.* This was in the Dissenting Opinion in which he summed up his indignation at the way that Julius Rosenberg and Ethel Rosenberg were cleared for speedy execution in June 1953. Perhaps there was momentarily revived in him on that occasion the passion and doctrines he had devoted to the *Sacco and Vanzetti Case* almost "a lifetime" before.

VIII

Something of the spirit of *Gobitis* was resurrected during the Cold War. "National security" concerns found expression in loyalty oaths and

related proceedings. It became once again difficult to invoke successfully
the old-fashioned respect for "conscientious objection."

Also old-fashioned is the suspicion of test oaths, something President
Lincoln, for one, was very much aware of. This suspicion had found expression, in 1787, in the provision in Article VI of the Constitution, that
"no religious Test shall ever be required as a Qualification to any Office or
public Trust under the United States." This did not preclude requiring an
"Oath or Affirmation" by anyone desiring to secure various posts in the
governments of the day.

Even so, the concession of allowing an "Affirmation" instead of an
"Oath" reflects deference to those with particularly sensitive consciences.
It is such deference that is likely to be sacrificed whenever "national security" concerns become particularly acute. It sometimes takes awhile to
discover—that is, to rediscover—how self-defeating it can be in a Republic for those in power to teach citizens at large that it does not "pay" to be
"conscientious."

IX

It should be apparent that some invocations of conscience, or (better
still) principles, are sounder than others. Indeed, such invocations can
sometimes be silly, if not even harmful. But that is true as well of the virtually unlimited freedom of speech upon which we depend as a self-governing,
and self-respecting, People.

The *Encyclopedia of the American Constitution* has suggested that the
Gobitis-Barnette development has been critical in our recent constitutional
history. Thus it has said,

> The Supreme Court's encounter in the early 1940s with the issue
> of compulsory flag salute exercises in the public schools was one
> of the turning points in American constitutional history. It pre-
> saged the civil libertarian activism that culminated in the Warren
> Court of the 1960s.

The emergence of the Warren Court was led, in part, by two Justices who
had been among the Majority in *Barnette.*

There remains for further consideration the traditional natural right/
natural law principles that could once be depended upon to guide judg-

ments upon both citizens and their governments. These are principles that permit proper assessments both of personal consciences and of massive international campaigns. Much depends, of course, upon an informed awareness of the facts that are relevant in the circumstances.

11. Conscientious Objectors and Military Conscription

I

There has never been any substantial doubt but that the Government of the United States can conscript citizens to serve in the military forces of this Country. The power to conscript is not expressly provided for in the Constitution, but it has long been considered available to a government authorized to "raise and support Armies." Systems of military conscription, it is noticed by the *Encyclopedia of the American Constitution,* have been employed during the American Civil War, the First World War, the Second World War, the Korean War, and the Vietnam War.

However exalted the status may be of personal liberty in the United States, it does not extend so far as to require that an American army always be made up entirely of volunteers. That the armed forces have, in recent decades, been thus constituted is the result of political, not constitutional, determinations. There does not seem to be at this time any serious effort to restore military conscription.

When conscription *is* used, it is primarily with a view to enhancing the military effectiveness of the Country. Other considerations, such as providing employment for some or contributing to the civic education of others, are properly regarded as secondary. This is not to deny, however, that social conditions and citizen morale can bear upon both the composition and the effectiveness of military forces.

II

Just as there has never been in the United States any substantial doubt about governmental power to conscript, so there has been no substantial doubt about the propriety of accommodating conscientious objection to military service. It may well be, in fact, that concessions for some conscientious objectors can make conscription more acceptable politically than it might otherwise be. Those countries that do not allow at all for conscientious objection are apt to have governments that are more authoritarian than that to which Americans are accustomed.

"The principle that society should excuse conscientious objectors from military service," the *Encyclopedia of the American Constitution* reports, "was widely recognized in the Colonies and States prior to adoption of the Constitution." This report continues thus: "James Madison's original [in 1789] for the Bill of Rights included a clause that 'no person religiously scrupulous of bearing arms shall be compelled to render military service in person,' but that clause was dropped, partly [it is said] because conscription was considered a state function." Even so, the Framers of the Bill of Rights were confident that Congress would respect conscientious objection, whether or not expressly provided for in the Constitution.

"The 1940 Selective Service Act," the eminently useful *Encyclopedia of the American Constitution* recalls,

> set the basic terms of exemption from the system of compulsory military service that operated during World War II, the Korean War, and the Vietnam War, and during the intervening periods of uneasy peace. A person was eligible "who, by reason of religious training and belief, [was] conscientiously opposed to participation in war in any form." Someone opposed even to noncombatant service could perform alternate civilian service.

Deference to religious sensibilities may also be seen in exemptions by State legislatures with respect to such matters as Sunday Closing Laws and the performance of abortions. Deference to sensibilities may be seen as well in the Constitution of 1787, where (we have seen) the alternative use of an *affirmation* is offered whenever an *oath* is required.

III

Recognition of the profound effects on citizens of "religious training and belief" may be seen in the deference shown, in the enforcement of our conscription laws, to the teachings and influence of long-recognized "peace churches." Such deference provides some assurance to the community that the young man who identifies himself as a conscientious objector has not conjured up a deference to conscience simply to avoid military service. Problems do arise, however, when the plea of conscientious objection is not grounded in a traditional pacifist association.

The United States Supreme Court assessed, in *United States* v. *Seeger* (1965), the conviction of a conscientious objector whose refusal to serve was not based upon a "belief in a relation to a Supreme Being" as required by the 1951 Universal Military Training and Service Act. This young man had "cited such personages as Plato, Aristotle and Spinoza for support of his ethical belief in intellectual and moral integrity 'without belief in God, except in the remotest sense.'" The Court, in finding for this conscientious objector, summed up thus its understanding of his stance:

> He did not disavow any belief "in a relation to a Supreme Being"; indeed he stated that "the cosmic order does, perhaps, suggest *a creative intelligence.*" He decried the tremendous "spiritual" price man must pay for his willingness to destroy human life. In light of his beliefs and the unquestioned sincerity with which he held them, we think the [Selective Service] Board, had it applied the test we propose today, would have granted him the exemption [he requested]. We think it clear that *the beliefs* which prompted his objection *occupy the same place in his life as the belief in a traditional deity holds in the lives of his friends, the Quakers.* [Emphases added.]

Five years later, in *Welch* v. *United States* (1970), the Supreme Court accepted a claim of conscientious objection by a young man who was found to have "no religious basis for [his] beliefs, opinions and convictions." But, Justice Hugo L. Black argued in an Opinion supporting the judgment of the Court in favor of the applicant, "[b]ecause his beliefs function as a religion in his life, such an individual is as much entitled to a 'religious' conscientious objection exemption . . . as is someone who derives his conscientious opposition to war from traditional religious convictions." In short, one no longer had to come to judicial view as, in effect, a fellow-traveller of the Quakers, the Amish, or the Mennonites.

IV

Justice Byron R. White opened his Dissenting Opinion in *Welch* v. *United States* with observations that do reflect widely held sentiments about what Congress had (and had not) intended when it provided for exemptions from military service:

> Whether or not *United States* v. *Seeger* . . . accurately reflected the intent of Congress in providing draft exemptions for religious conscientious objectors to war, I cannot join today's construction of [the statutory provision] extending draft exemption to those who disclaim religious objections to war and whose views about war represent a purely personal code arising not from religious training and belief as the statute requires but from readings in philosophy, history, and sociology. Our obligation in statutory construction cases is to enforce the will of Congress, not our own.

A year later, Justice Thurgood Marshall opened his Opinion of the Court in *Gillette* v. *United States* (1971) in this way:

> These cases present *the question whether conscientious objection to a particular war, rather than objection to war as such,* relieves the objector from responsibilities of military training and service. Specifically, we are called upon to decide whether conscientious scruples relating to a particular conflict are within the purview of established provisions relieving conscientious objectors to war from military service. [Emphasis added.]

The "particular conflict" objected to on this occasion was the war in Vietnam.

The *Encyclopedia of the American Constitution* summarizes in this way the Supreme Court's judgment in *Gillette* (a judgment in which Justice Black joined):

> [In a] decision covering both religious and nonreligious objectors to the Vietnam War, the Court upheld Congress's determination not to exempt those opposed to participation in particular wars. Against the claim that the distinction between "general" and "selective" objectors was impermissible, the Court responded that the distinction was supported by the public interest in a fairly administered system, given the difficulty officials would have dealing consistently with the variety of objections to particular wars.

The Court also rejected the claim that the selective objector's entitlement to free exercise of his religion created a constitutionally grounded right to avoid military service.

The Opinion of the Court in *Gillette* records the holding "that Congress intended to exempt persons who oppose participating in all war—'participation in war in any form'—and that persons who object solely to participation in a particular war are not within the purview of the exempting section, even though the latter objection may have such roots in a claimant's conscience and personality that it is 'religious' in character." The Court then provides a "further word" "to clarify [its] statutory holding":

> Apart from abstract theological reservations, two other sorts of reservations concerning the use of force have been thought by lower courts not to defeat a conscientious objection claim. Willingness to use force in self-defense, in defense of home and family, or in defense against immediate acts of aggressive violence toward other persons in the community, has not been regarded as inconsistent with a claim of conscientious objection to war as such. . . . But surely willingness to use force defensively in personal situations mentioned is quite different from willingness to fight in some wars but not in others.

To allow officially recognized exemptions for those who object to participating in particular wars would in effect convert many, if not even all, members of the armed forces into volunteers. Conscription would be limited then to the obligation to respond to what would be only a requirement that one *say* whether one supported the war one is asked to fight in. It is not surprising, then, that the Supreme Court concluded in *Gillette* "that it is supportable for Congress to have decided that the objector to all war—to all killing in war—has a claim that is distinct enough and intense enough to justify special status, while the objector to a particular war does not."

V

"Conscription" can be said to take more than one form, even without a military draft. A few object, for example, to having to pay taxes to support military expenditures. Efforts may even be made by some, in the spirit of Henry Thoreau and Milton Mayer, to deny to the General Government that proportion of their taxes regarded as destined for war.

Of course, one may have deeply felt reservations about other governmental "projects" as well. But does it make either political or constitutional sense to permit citizens to vote effectively not only with their ballots but also with their taxes? Such an arrangement can amount to recognizing a veto power for any substantial group that feels strongly about any issue.

These considerations make even more troubling than it should already be the fact that we have become accustomed to going to war without the constitutionally required declaration of war by Congress. "No taxation without representation" was once the battle cry of free men. Should a comparable insistence be heard about the proper authority for "taxing" not only our property but our youth as well?

VI

Thus, conscription or no conscription, problems remain in how we "expend" our military resources. One consequence of relying on an all-volunteer army is that it is highly unlikely, in ordinary times, to have in it many children of the privileged. The youngsters deliberately put in harm's way, in these circumstances, are likely to be strangers to those in authority.

Another questionable consequence of an all-volunteer army is that few of the civilians in authority are apt to have had military experience in their youth. This can leave them insensitive to the problems and needs of those who do serve. This can also lead to a disturbing questioning, by those who serve, of the moral authority of those who presume to make life-and-death decisions for the troops.

Questions are implicit here with respect to both duties and authority. These are questions that can challenge the contemporary tendency to make much of individualism. But even the most dedicated champion of individualism is likely to recognize (at least when pressed) that he sometimes must depend upon others for protection and sustenance.

VII

No matter how equitable a system may be for the development and use of military forces, it is likely to be a matter of chance who is put at personal risk on any occasion. Chance may be seen in the draft number one has, in what one is trained for by the military, and in where one is sent. It may be seen as well, of course, in what an enemy chooses to do, where, and how.

We can be moved to wonder, in the spirit both of fairness and of effectiveness, what the General Government is entitled, perhaps even obliged, to do in order to make it likely that youngsters all over the Country can share in its defense. This could mean, among other things, greater participation than we are accustomed to by the General Government in the supervision of the health and education policies of State governments. This would be comparable to what industrialization, the Great Depression, and economic globalization have properly done to our reading of the Commerce Clause.

Then there is the question of what may have to be done by government to promote, as well as to discipline, the spiritedness of the young. Self-centeredness has to be reckoned with, whether grounded in hedonism or in spirituality. Even the exalted term "conscience" may conceal unexpected problems, tending as it sometimes does to liberate one both from the demands of citizenship and from "a decent respect to the Opinions of Mankind."

VIII

All this is not to suggest that the traditional political, *not* constitutional, exemptions for conscientious objectors should be eliminated when conscription is resorted to. Something is to be said, however, for reminding ourselves from time to time of the reasons why such exemptions have always been available in this Country. The sincerity of the conscientious objector is thereby recognized.

Also to be recognized, at least in our circumstances, is the generosity as well as the good sense of the community that provides for such exemptions. It *is* sensible to recognize that the sincere conscientious objector is not likely to be of much use as a soldier if he is forced to wear a uniform. It is sensible to recognize as well that the damage likely to be done to the character of any community that tries to force such men to fight may be serious.

In any event, the community does have less of a problem in exempting those conscientious objectors who *are* members of the traditional peace churches, inasmuch as it can be generally believed that such men are already conscripted, so to speak, for a lifetime of what the majority considers oppressive deprivations and burdens. Still, the thoughtful conscientious objector should acknowledge that those who risk their lives in the military may well do their Country a useful service from time to time. It is a service, dehumanizing as it may appear to the conscientious objector, that the conscientious objector and his family often do depend upon, a service which ministers to the natural desire for self-preservation.

IX

Even so, it can be salutary for the community at large to be reminded in turn from time to time of the forms that principled conduct can take. After all, the conscientious objector is likely to be regarded suspiciously, if not even with contempt, while his fellow citizens confront deadly forces. In such circumstances, the despised objector can at least provide lessons in principled endurance.

And, of course, such objectors can sometimes come to seem to have been particularly prescient, as happened when the remarkable folly of the First World War had become generally apparent. Pacifism can also seem eminently sensible if the alternative should come to be uninhibited nuclear war. Even so, the pacifist does have serious problems in coming to terms with the meaning, obligations, and sacrifices of citizenship.

Questions may even be raised about Equal Protection standards when some are exempted from burdens and risks that others, of the same age and physical capacity, are conscripted to face. But then, even the most able-bodied women have, in the United States, always been exempted from compulsory military service. Perhaps the considerations, grounded in nature, that exempt women from conscription properly apply also to men of a peculiar temperament.

12. Obliteration Bombing, Civilian Casualties, and the Laws of War

I

John C. Ford, a New England Jesuit, published in the September 1944 issue of *Theological Studies* an article titled "The Morality of Obliteration Bombing." He was evidently moved to do so by the steady pounding that the by-then virtually undefended German cities were being subjected to by the American and British air forces. The civilian casualties from these air raids could not help but be substantial.

Father Ford did not, in this article, speak as a pacifist. He was willing to consider the war against Nazi Germany a just war. But he condemned as unlawful the systematic killing of noncombatants necessarily resulting from the air raids to which German cities were being subjected.

Obliteration (or area) bombing was distinguishable for him from the precision bombing consistent with the long-accepted rules of war. Precision bombing might include substantial collateral damage among its effects, but such damage (including the killing of noncombatants) is neither sought nor desired by the bombers. The relevant rules of war, grounded in nature and developed as international conventions and practices, are included in the Law of Nations recognized by the Constitution of 1787.

II

The leaders of both Great Britain and the United States affirmed, early in the Second World War (which began, officially, in September 1939), the traditional rules about how noncombatants should be treated. Thus, Winston Churchill, on January 27, 1940, "condemned Germany's policy of indiscriminate bombing as a 'new and odious form of warfare.'" He referred thus to the devastating bombing by the German air force of cities on the Continent (such as Rotterdam) and, of course, to "the Blitz" to which Great Britain was subjected.

Franklin D. Roosevelt, on September 1, 1939, "before [the United States] became engaged in the war and long before we ourselves took up the practice of obliteration bombing, . . . addressed an appeal" to the governments that seemed on the verge of going to war. President Roosevelt spoke, Father Ford reported, "as the head of a technically neutral nation, and at any rate before the arguments of military necessity were made to bear heavily on whatever consciences we have." The President said at that time:

> The ruthless bombing from the air of civilians in unfortified centres of population during the course of hostilities which have raged in various quarters of the earth in the past few years, which have resulted in the maiming and death of thousands of defenseless women and children, has profoundly shocked the conscience of humanity. If resort is had to this sort of inhuman barbarism during the period of tragic conflagration with which the world is now confronted, hundreds of thousands of innocent human beings, who have no responsibility for, and who are not even remotely participating in, the hostilities which have broken out, now will lose their lives. I am therefore addressing this urgent appeal to every Government which may be engaged in hostilities publicly to affirm its determination that its armed forces shall in no event and under no circumstances undertake bombardment from the air of civilian populations or unfortified cities, upon the understanding that the same rules of warfare will be scrupulously observed by all their opponents.

It is evident not only in the Churchill and Roosevelt statements but also in statements by many other leaders of the time (both religious and political leaders) that systematic bombardment of civilian populations had been long considered barbaric. The authorities relied upon in these assessments ranged across many centuries. And throughout the war, both sides, no matter what they themselves were doing, publicized as reprehensible any episodes of wholesale killings of noncombatants by the enemy.

III

The Germans, it can be said, "started it," at least this time around. The same can be said about the Japanese in China and the Pacific, and especially (for Americans) at Pearl Harbor. But the rules supposedly governing these matters had not permitted the systematic killing of noncombatants as a justified retaliation, no more than we permit families who have had one of their own murdered to do some retributive murdering in turn.

However all this may be, the Royal Air Force, in March 1942, "changed its policy and took up obliteration [or area] bombing," as did the United States Eighth Air Force. Thus, Father Ford reported,

> The leaders in England acknowledged the new policy. Churchill no longer condemned [as he had in January 1940] this "odious form of warfare," [but] promised the House of Commons on June 2, 1942, that Germany was to be subjected to an "ordeal the like of which has never been experienced by any country." In July, 1943, he spoke of "the systematic shattering of German cities." On September 21, 1943, he said in the House of Commons: "There are no sacrifices we will not make, no lengths in violence to which we will not go."

All this meant, in effect, that the Allies had themselves become innovators in an "odious form of warfare," once they had come to control the air over Europe.

Lawrence L. McReavy, of Ushaw College in Durham, England, in a 1945 letter in *Theological Studies,* recalled, at a time when the "principal towns [here in] England were being subjected to a 'blitz' which made little distinction between civilian and military objectives," "Our exasperated people were clamouring for reprisals as the only effective deterrent against such attacks (which, admitted, they are not), and our government had promised that reprisals would be taken." The spirit of the times is caught in an assessment by General George C. Marshall (as reported in the *New York Herald-Tribune* on February 4, 1944), an assessment by a highly respected military leader whose Country's cities had suffered no bombardment at the hands of the Germans:

> The destruction of German industrial cities is proceeding at a

constantly increasing pace. . . . Berlin is now a shambles. The destruction of other smaller targets will require much less time.

I recall, while visiting Berlin and other places in Germany at the end of the war, that those cities were indeed "a shambles," much more so than London was at that time.

IV

There *are* laws of war, rules which can be seen invoked in, say, President Abraham Lincoln's Emancipation Proclamation of 1862–1863. Consider how Lincoln, on August 26, 1863, justified what he (as Commander in Chief) had done in the Proclamation:

> I think the Constitution invests its commander-in-chief, with the law of war, in time of war. The most that can be said, if so much, is, that slaves are property. Is there—has there ever been—any question that by the law of war, property, both of enemies and friends, may be taken when needed? And is it not needed whenever taking it, helps us, or hurts the enemy? Armies, the world over, destroy enemies' property when they can not use it; and even destroy their own to keep it from the enemy. Civilized belligerents do all in their power to help themselves or hurt the enemy, except a few things regarded as barbarous or cruel. Among the exceptions are the massacre of vanquished foes, and non-combatants, male and female.

We notice here the recognition that massacres of "non-combatants, male and female," are "barbarous or cruel"—and hence not to be permitted.

Respect for the laws of war may be seen both in various chapters of Magna Carta and throughout the Declaration of Independence. The English-speaking peoples, because of centuries of experience with the common law, are familiar with how the standards of a largely unwritten set of rules may be developed and applied. Such standards were drawn on during the remarkable Trial at Nuremberg in 1945–1946 of the surviving leaders of Nazi Germany, who were found guilty of (among other deeds) promoting and carrying on wars of aggression.

But the citizens at large of a defeated country cannot be properly treated as the Nazi leaders were, no matter how much they had acquiesced in, or even supported, the crimes of their leaders. The longstanding rules against the killing of noncombatants recognized no exceptions permitting the slaughter of any acquiescent people who were the subjects of a criminal regime. Indeed, George Marshall, who supervised in 1944 the conversion of the German cities into "shambles," distinguished himself a few years later (as the American Secretary of State) by promoting that remarkable wholesale reconstruction of Europe (including Germany) that was celebrated as the Marshall Plan.

V

At the heart of the 1944 Ford "Obliteration Bombing" article is an extended illustration of "what the abandonment of the distinction between combatants and non-combatants would mean in practice, or what it would mean to say that hardly any civilians are innocent in a modern war, because all are co-operating in the aggression." This illustration consists of an enumeration of the kinds of civilians who would likely be killed when cities are subjected to saturation bombing. A score of lines (marked here by me with slashes) in the Ford article had to be devoted by him to this extraordinary enumeration (which can remind one of the sort of thing Walt Whitman could do with lists):

> Farmers, fishermen, foresters, lumberjacks, dressmakers, milliners, bakers, / printers, textile workers, millers, painters, paper hangers, piano tuners, plasterers, / shoemakers, cobblers, tailors, upholsterers, furniture makers, cigar and cigarette / makers, glove makers, hat makers, suit makers, food processors, dairymen, fish / canners, fruit and vegetable canners, slaughterers and packers, sugar refiners, / liquor and beverage workers, teamsters, garage help, telephone girls, advertising / men, bankers, brokers, clerks in stores, commercial travelers, decorators, window / dressers, deliverymen, inspectors, insurance agents, retail dealers, salesmen and / saleswomen in all trades, undertakers, wholesale dealers, meatcutters, butchers, / actors, architects, sculptors, artists, authors, editors, reporters, priests, laybrothers, / nuns, seminarians, professors, school teachers, dentists, lawyers, judges, musicians, / photographers, physicians, surgeons, trained nurses, librarians, social and welfare / workers, Red Cross workers, religious work-

ers, theatre owners, technicians, / laboratory assistants, barbers, bootblacks, charwomen, cleaners and dyers, hotelmen, / elevator tenders, housekeepers, janitors, sextons, domestic servants, cooks, maids, / nurses, handymen, laundry operatives, porters, victuallers, bookkeepers, accountants, / statisticians, cashiers, stenographers, secretaries, typists, all office help, / mothers of families, patients in hospitals, prison inmates, prison guards, / institutional inmates, old men and women, all children with the use of reason, i.e., from / seven years up. (After all, these latter buy war stamps, write letters of encouragement to their brothers in the service, and even carry the dinner pail to the father who works in the aircraft factory. They all co-operate in some degree in the aggression.)

At the least, this kind of "compulsive" listing by an author can be taken to exhibit the passion aroused in him by what he is obliged to witness and even to take some responsibility for. There is, however, a well-known saying among jugglers, which it is prudent to keep in mind in considering this remarkable Ford enumeration: "The trouble is that the balls go where you throw them." This is something that can usefully be recalled upon confronting the puzzles left in the writings of an intelligent and obviously serious author, including that often-illuminating puzzle of what the principle of order is in any work of the mind (whether it be a grocery list or Isaac Newton's *Principia Mathematica*).

That even such an outburst of apparently random enumeration may bear thinking about is suggested by the fact that there is at its core those "authors, editors, reporters" (followed immediately by "priests") who can be understood to have developed and permitted such a compilation in this article. Much more than this, providing portents of awesome potentialities, can be discovered in this symphonic census (to be discussed by me on another occasion perhaps). It suffices, at least for the moment, to recall the immediate use made by Father Ford of this shambles-like list which he several times indicates warrants "careful perusal" (and which [I have reason to believe] may hint (in certain numbering) at even worse things to come that he, as a priest, had discovered):

If, when their governments declare war, these persons are so guilty that they deserve death, or almost any violence to person and property short of death, then let us forget the law of Christian charity, the natural law, and go back to barbarism, admitting that total war has won out and we must submit to it.

VI

It should be obvious to any student of these matters that such people as those catalogued by Father Ford are for the most part probably "innocent" and yet certainly vulnerable to obliteration bombing. By the time the Ford article was published the Allies had not only invaded Europe but were well on their way to a final victory over Nazi Germany. This meant, in effect, the continued obliteration bombing of German cities had taken on even more the aspect of punishment than of military necessity.

Father Ford attempts to bring all this closer to home by suggesting how his own Boston area population might be divided between "combatants" and "non-combatants." Still, it might be agreed, *if* attacking the general population of a country led to its government's stopping what it was doing, *that* may suggest that the general population may "really" have been more in control of (if not even largely responsible for) what that government had been doing. But it should be remembered that that kind of argument had not persuaded those, across the centuries, who developed the generally recognized laws of war.

It seems, in any event, that systematic bombardment (at least short of nuclear attacks) tends to stiffen, not to undermine, the resolve of a people (whether they be the British or the Germans). An ominous harbinger of things to come was the tendency, by both Nazi and Allied spokesmen, to refer to the devastation visited upon German cities as "terror," with one German radio commentator even quoted as speaking of the "Terror . . . terror . . . terror . . . pure, naked, bloody terror" after some attacks on Hamburg. It is reported that "[t]he total weight of the bombs dropped on Hamburg in seven days equaled the tonnage dropped on London during the whole of the 1940–1941 blitz"—a report which can make our own September Eleventh terrorists seem trivial by comparison.

VII

Circumstances, varying from time to time and from country to country, may affect the measures resorted to by a people. The willingness of the

Germans to resort to massive aerial bombardment of British cities at the beginning of the Second World War may have been influenced, at least in part, by the crippling blockade to which Germany had been subjected a generation before, during the First World War. A curious reminder of that blockade is provided by Father Ford when he quotes President Roosevelt's personal envoy as saying "to the French ambassador at Ankara in the spring of 1941 [that is, even before the United States was officially at war]: 'The American people are prepared to starve every Frenchman if that's necessary to defeat Hitler.'"

The willingness of the United States to use atomic bombs in Japan in August 1945 was influenced by the profound shock in this Country of the surprise attacks at Pearl Harbor and elsewhere in December 1941. It may have been partly a matter of chance who got the atomic bomb first. Even so, the racist and other questionable policies of the Nazi regime evidently impeded its ability to develop nuclear weapons before the Allies did.

Father Ford, in his "Obliteration" article, does not explicitly anticipate the atomic bomb (whatever may be hinted at by the organization of the enumeration of victims of aerial bombardment that we have noticed). However that may be, the Ford analysis of the air campaign over Germany applied at least as much to what was being done to helpless Japanese cities well before our recourse to atomic bombs. I (as a former Air Corps flying officer) do not recall hearing, in our bomber crews preparing for the final assault against Japan in 1945, any doubts expressed among us about what we were already doing to the by-then helpless Japanese cities.

VIII

A remarkable aspect of the Ford critique of obliteration bombing is that it could be published in wartime in this Country. The obscurity of the theological journal in which it appeared may have provided some "cover," as did the fact that the author was a priest. It may also have "helped" that the Allies *were* well on the way to victory in Europe by the time the Ford article appeared in print.

It is also remarkable that there has not been any recourse anywhere to nuclear bombing since August 1945. This may be, in part, because of the obviously horrific effects of the bombs exploded over Hiroshima and Nagasaki. Indeed, the use of the Nagasaki bomb may have been due, at least in part, to our inability to recognize at once how powerful (and hence how paralyzing for the Japanese) the Hiroshima bomb had been.

The way that nuclear weapons have come to be regarded, worldwide, testifies to their now-obvious power. That power has contributed significantly to an effect upon world opinion that moral arguments such as those offered by Father Ford could not be counted on to have. The precautions that have evidently been prompted everywhere in the handling of nuclear arms, in response to the Hiroshima-Nagasaki devastation, help account for the remarkable fact that there has evidently been no accidental explosion anywhere of a nuclear weapon.

IX

It has been noticed that some large-scale bombing of cities with conventional weapons rivaled in ferocity the effects of the two atomic bombs used against Japan. The firebombing of Dresden, in particular, is singled out as particularly senseless in its devastation. But these and other Allied excesses in Europe were forgotten, at least for awhile, when the Nazi death camps were exposed to view in 1945, those camps glimpsed in Appendix I of this volume.

It was evident that too many Germans had made a principle out of killing everyone in designated groups, "innocent" and "guilty" alike. Whatever justified grievances Germany may have had (because of the First World War and the Versailles Treaty) were hard to continue to take seriously in these circumstances. The finer spirits in Germany were, of course, appalled upon learning what they may have been partly responsible for by having allowed the Nazis to come to power and, even worse, to remain there.

The finer spirits among the Allies were ministered to by Father Ford in his "Obliteration Bombing" article. The Allies did learn from their experiences not only during the Second World War, but also during the half-century preceding that war. One consequence of all this eventually was that both Germany and Japan were treated far better by their conquerors after 1945 than they as bestial conquerors had treated the peoples of Europe and Asia, with salutary long-term consequences that can be said to testify to the practicality of an informed decency.

13. Do All Somehow Aim at the Good?

I

Hypocrisy, it has been observed, is the tribute that vice pays to virtue. This is particularly evident when leaders of dubious character attempt to guide their communities with respect to life-and-death issues. It is then, when the stakes seem the highest, that public discourse tends to be the most moralistic.

Consider, as examples, how Adolf Hitler and Josef Stalin spoke during the great public crises in their careers, especially when war began between their countries. Their respective publics—the people at large in Germany and Russia—had to be appealed to by moral exhortations. Similar language was used in appealing even to their respective party loyalists, at least in what was said in public.

Certainly, it must be rare to hear anyone say openly, "We now have an opportunity to exploit others, to enslave others who have not done us any harm, and I propose that we should do so." That is, no sane human is likely to say (or, at least, to mean) what Satan says in Book Four of John Milton's *Paradise Lost*: "Evil, be thou my good." Thus, Hitler spoke instead of longstanding grievances of and dangers to the German people; thus, also, Stalin spoke instead against those who would betray the State and the People's Movement.

II

Were the moral positions taken by both Hitler and Stalin grounded enough in "reality" to elicit reliable support, for years at a time, in their diverse circumstances? No matter how ruthless, if not even cynical, rulers may seem to outsiders, the appeal to morality by those in authority can dominate the discourse of the day. It is evidently a general respect for a common morality that makes life meaningful and sacrifice acceptable.

Very little was ever said in public, by either Hitler or Stalin, that the decent people appealed to by them could not accept, if believed, however much some might have been put off either *by the tone* of what was said at times or by recollections of the evils for which these men had been responsible. Stalin's language could sometimes be particularly harsh, if not even ugly. Was Hitler's language somewhat moderated in tone because Germany was then one of the most educated societies on Earth?

We might even suspect, or at least hope, that something in men such as Hitler or Stalin could be touched by what "had" to be said publicly. Particularly to be reckoned with is whatever cannot be *said* publicly. We might also suspect (or at least hope) that the *unsayable* tends eventually to become the *unthinkable*.

III

We have seen that the longstanding grievances and vulnerability of the German people could be traced back to what was believed to have been done to them during the First World War and in the Versailles Treaty. The Germans could be repeatedly reminded thereby of both their virtues and their needs. An appeal to "one's own" can usually be counted on to have moral authority.

The peoples of the Soviet Union were accustomed to appeals based on the virtues and needs of long-exploited workers and peasants. Stalin could warn against "wreckers" and "enslavers" who would return the people at large to that economic and social bondage from which, they had long been told, they had been liberated by the Russian Revolution. Hitler could make similar appeals, warning especially against the Jews, who had long been regarded with suspicion—if not even with animosity—by many Germans.

The passions both developed and exploited by Hitler and Stalin could also be seen in the ferocity with which these leaders responded to perceived threats. Thus, Stalin's purges of Russian military leaders in the 1930s severely damaged Soviet military capacity. Thus, also, Hitler's response to the July 1944 plot against him evidently shocked the long-passive Germans when they were shown on film some of the ferocious executions resorted to by the Nazis on that occasion.

IV

Consider how Hitler talked about the Jews early and late in his career—in 1919 (in an introductory manifesto) and in 1945 (in his testament). It might even be suspected that his hatred of Jews was the principal animating principle, the very soul, of his career. This animosity, and either the fear or the envy by which it may have been nurtured, seemed at times to be more vital than Hitler's dedication to the Reich and the German people, with Germany herself exalted, at least in part, because she was (or could become) the most vigorously anti-Jewish of all the countries of Europe.

What is it about Jews that inspires such hatred, even among those who are no longer moved substantially by Christian polemics? Are Jews somehow fundamentally spiritual, however materialistic they may sometimes be taken to be? Are they, for many people, decidedly the Others, something that is reflected in their sense of Chosenness?

Jews are somehow in fundamental opposition to the death-obsessed bestiality at the core of Nazism. Judaism, it was sensed by Hitler, looked to something beyond the State, beyond the People, if not even beyond all ordinary human allegiances. Indeed, the Jews could be regarded by him as virtually Satanic, something that is reflected in Hitler's eagerness to regard them as critical both to capitalistic exploitation and to Bolshevik subversion.

V

However much Hitler hated Jews, condemning them as the unbearable essence of evil, he could still be highly selective in what he said in public even about them. That is, it could at times seem that something other (if not deeper) than his hatred of Jews could determine not only what he said about them, but even whether to speak of them at all. There was, at least, an awareness (implicit in the materials provided in Appendix I of this volume) of what people at large would tolerate in what was said publicly about the Jews, or at least in what was clearly shown to be done to them.

Critical to how Jews were thought about by the Nazis was the fact (as we have noticed) that little if anything was ever said publicly in Germany during the war about the systematic slaughter in death camps of Jewish men, women, and children by the millions. One may even wonder whether the Nazis could ever have done what they did if they themselves had truly *seen* what they were doing. Some forms of insanity may be understood as dependent upon an inability to grasp properly what obviously is—and what it means.

Jews, it can be said, stand in their very being (as developed over millennia) for life, for human life on this Earth. In this respect they can truly threaten the Nazi who may be somehow ultimately death-loving, or suicidal, in his deepest inclinations. Thus, the Nazi, in hating Jews as he does, pays them a great (however dangerous) compliment.

VI

Still, we can be challenged to discern the Good by which even the most evil of men are moved. Particularly intriguing here can be a consideration of how both Hitler and Stalin justified the German-Soviet Non-aggression Pact which dramatically cleared the way for the destruction of the Polish regime in 1939. It was a pact that deeply troubled other European governments, partly because it was between tyrants who had long professed their hatred of each other.

The justifications for this pact were most developed publicly *after* the surprise attack by Hitler against the Russians. Still, it can be suspected that that attack shocked Stalin into reality, away from the ideological posturing that he had considered it useful to be identified with. Old-fashioned patriotism had to be invoked by him, something easier to do because the German invaders had *not* offered themselves to the Russian people as liberators.

The longstanding animosity between Hitler and Stalin can make us suspect that each of them was equipped to see in the other a deadly evil, perhaps even the very evil at the core of the being of each of them. Such publicly exploited hatred of the Other can perhaps serve, that is, to conceal something dreadful in oneself. Thus, for Hitler and Stalin to condemn others as they did might have been in itself a perverse recognition by these evil men of the Good.

VII

Of course, the alliances that governments enter into can sometimes depend on chance. This suggests that something deeper than ideology or doctrine might at times move political leaders. This could be seen not only in the Nazi-Soviet Pact but also in how the Russians and the British could become allied after the German invasion of the Soviet Union.

Winston Churchill, who had been a vigorous critic for decades of the Bolsheviks, saw that invasion almost as a heaven-sent opportunity for his country. The June 1941 invasion of Russia had been such a surprise, and hence as successful as it was in its opening weeks, evidently because it simply did not make sense for the Germans to open a major second front while still at war with the British. In short, it can be suspected, the Nazis simply did not know what they were doing.

The truly self-serving actor depends, it can be argued, on rationality, which in turn depends upon and serves an awareness of the Good. The "statesmen" who had made Hitler and Stalin possible, if not even virtually inevitable, were the quite respectable European leaders who "had to have" the First World War, without regard to either the immediate costs or the long-term consequences of that massive folly. American "idealism"—a sentimental version of a proper dedication to the Good—did not contribute at that time to sensible statesmanship.

VIII

However responsible decent, if not even well-meaning, men were for the emergence of Hitler and Stalin, the remarkable evil of these two men (and of their most dedicated apostles) should be recognized. It is instructive to notice, once again, that each of these men *had* been right to recognize the other as a deadly foe. *Did* the evil in each make both of them able, instinctively, to be aware of (if not even to be repelled by) the evil in the other?

Particularly revealing was the public position taken both by the Nazis and by the Stalinists with respect to the spring 1940 Katyn Forest massacre by the Russians of thousands of Polish military officers. Each side could, when these corpses were exposed to world view in 1943, publicly condemn the other for this massacre, implicitly condemning themselves thereby for the many things like this that they had already done and that they would continue to do. Both Hitler and Stalin provided lessons in systematic slaughter on a large scale that were later used, in even grimmer ways, by Mao in China and by Pol Pot in Cambodia.

Hitler and Stalin, it can be suspected, were (despite their canniness) simply demented. The resemblances between Stalin and Hitler could even be seen in how Stalin, at the end of his career, lashed out against the Jews in Russia as newly discovered threats to his life. There is indeed a startling, however perverse, tribute paid to Jews to be seen in the deep hatred that they *can* inspire in the most evil of men.

IX

One can get then, even from monsters such as Hitler and Stalin, some sense of what the Good is. Their very distortions can reveal what it is that human beings instinctively, and properly, yearn for. Such men reveal as well what they are understandably troubled by, however "unrealistic" their perceptions and judgments may sometimes be with respect to "the current situation."

Life and death obviously have to be taken seriously, and not only in speech, by anyone who hopes to rule. This is reflected in the request made by Hitler of the Reichstag as he prepared, during a speech in the early weeks of the war, to report on the German casualties suffered in Poland— the request that the body rise to hear this part of his speech. Comparable to this may be the Stalinist invocation of old-fashioned patriotism once Russia was invaded by Germany.

It can be wondered whether anything truly useful can be said to the powerful who are determined to work their will. Something of a model is provided here by the way Nathan the Prophet went about helping King David *see* what he (in his radical self-centeredness) had done with Bathsheba and her husband. It is useful, as well as prudent in other ways, to endorse in these matters John Donne's observation:

Good we must love, and must hate ill,
For ill is ill, and good good still.

Part Two

1. Shakespeare's *Hamlet* and the Elusiveness of the Good

I

Death is very much in view throughout William Shakespeare's *Hamlet*. There is, at the outset, the Ghost of the recently deceased King Hamlet. Because he believes himself to have been murdered by his brother (his successor as King), he will not "stay" dead.

In the course of the play, Polonius, the statesman, and Ophelia, his daughter, die. So do Rosencrantz and Guildenstern, former associates of Prince Hamlet. Hamlet is responsible, directly or indirectly, for these four deaths.

Then, at the end of the play, the stage is littered with corpses. On display are King Claudius, Queen Gertrude (Hamlet's mother), Laertes, the son of Polonius, and, of course, Prince Hamlet himself. Presiding over all this carnage, at least in spirit, can be said to be the ghostly King Hamlet.

II

What *is* it that dies at one's death? The appearances of the Ghost suggest that some consciousness of oneself survives (at least for awhile) one's earthly demise. That consciousness includes, it seems, memories of what one has done (and has had done to one) while alive.

That consciousness includes as well, it also seems, a continuation of the passions one had while alive. The Ghost indicates that he is suffering torments, or at least purgation, because of the way he died. Prince Hamlet, in his celebrated "To be or not to be" soliloquy (Appendix E of this volume), indicates that he might relieve himself of his own torments by killing himself except for the strict injunction (which we associate with Christianity) against suicide, however much of an emerging modern he may be (which helps account for his popularity in our time).

99

How reliable the Ghost is may seem to be questioned in the same celebrated speech when Hamlet speaks of the realm of the dead as that "undiscovered country from whose bourn no traveler returns." Does such a supposition make the Ghost seem less reliable than he had originally seemed to Prince Hamlet? And what should be made of the early concern about the eternal dreadful consequences of killing oneself when Hamlet, in the final scene, begs the would-be suicide, Horatio, that he "absent [himself] from felicity awhile"?

III

What, then, *is* the Good? And, particularly, is there a good in living even when one is miserable? Or, at least, is there serious harm in deliberately ending even a quite miserable life?

Early on in the play, the good (for Hamlet) is simply, or at least primarily, revenge for the murder of his father. Certainly, this is what the Ghost urges, perhaps on more than one occasion. The preciousness of life seems thereby to be pointed up.

But whether life itself is the ultimate good might be questioned. After all, the Ghost (so far as we can tell) does not seem to be much concerned about the lives put at risk in the course of securing the revenge he wants. Prince Hamlet's willingness to run the risks he does may reflect his own general disillusionment with the state of affairs in Denmark, with the rapid remarriage of Gertrude being a particularly distressing development.

IV

What, in the normal course of things, is usually "the good life"? Prince Hamlet would have preferred, it seems, to be away at the university. He does not seem troubled by his uncle's possession of the throne, but only by his mother's immediate remarriage, something that had clouded Hamlet's world even before the Ghost appeared.

Both Laertes and Ophelia seem to be aspects of Prince Hamlet. She, like Hamlet, is disturbed by the state of personal relations—not by his mother's remarriage, but rather by Hamlet's seeming coolness toward her. Laertes, her brother, is also like Hamlet, perhaps even a parody of him in his determination (by any means, it seems) to secure revenge against Hamlet for the (somewhat accidental) killing of Polonius, Laertes' father.

Do we see, in Laertes' thirst for revenge, difficulties in King Hamlet's overriding insistence upon revenge? There can be in revenge, as ordinarily understood, a concern about seeing justice done. Thus, the Greek tragedies, when they portrayed Orestes seeking to avenge the murder of his father, Agamemnon the King, usually showed him as very much interested as well in reclaiming for himself the throne lost by his father.

V

What *does* our play itself (if not also the bulk of Shakespeare's work) teach, or at least presuppose, about the Good Life? Prince Hamlet, it can seem, naturally preferred a private life, subordinating himself to the rule of others. He had even courted Ophelia, which suggests an opening to domesticity on his part.

Does the Good depend ultimately on understanding? In order to be able to conclude that the Good is elusive, must not one have a reliable sense of what is truly good? May not such a sense guide one to adjust usefully one's efforts in seeking intermediate goods as circumstances change?

Whatever openness Hamlet had had toward domesticity seems to have been seriously disturbed by what has happened to what may have been his model of a good marriage. His mother need not be considered to have been aware of the murder of her first husband, but her hasty remarriage *can* arouse suspicions that Gertrude and Claudius had had some "understanding" while King Hamlet was still alive. It seems, in any event, that Hamlet was not shown the courtesy of a consultation before she married Claudius, something that may even have been done (or at least may have been announced as impending) before Hamlet could get home for his father's funeral.

VI

We can use what the play teaches about the Good in assessing how Prince Hamlet conducts himself. That conduct can be considered probably misconceived when it is seen to be responsible for eight deaths in addition to the "execution" of Claudius ordered by the Ghost. Indeed, Hamlet had an opportunity early in the play to kill King Claudius with the minimum of adverse earthly consequences.

He did not seize that golden opportunity because he had found the highly vulnerable Claudius at prayers. That is, he did not want to send an evidently contrite Claudius directly to Heaven by killing him then. Rather, he wanted to dispatch him in his sins, with the hope of assuring thereby his eternal condemnation.

Of course, the Ghost had not set any conditions for the revenge he demanded, except that Hamlet's mother should be left "to heaven." Prince Hamlet, it seems, tried to control matters too much, thereby opening the way to the series of deaths that disfigured Hamlet's career as avenger. Shakespeare suggests the dubiousness of allowing heavenly concerns to interfere with serious earthly pursuits by showing *us* (but not Hamlet) that the kneeling Claudius had *not* been able to pray on this occasion.

VII

In assessing Hamlet's desire for much more than was readily (and safely) available, one can be reminded of the answer that an early Rothschild is said to have made upon being asked how he had made his fortune in the stock market. "By selling too soon" is the kind of answer that Hamlet needed to hear. He may have needed to hear also questions and answers relating to the fierce demand that the Ghost had made upon him.

Hamlet speaks well of the way that King Hamlet had conducted himself, particularly (it seems) as a husband and father. There are, however, indications here and there (such as his "angry parle") that he may not have been the most prudent of rulers. Certainly, he was not alert enough (while still alive) to the way that his brother (if not also his wife) might act.

King Hamlet, in his ghostly form, seems to pursue "religiously" what he chances to consider his self-interest. Thus, he does not express any concern about what might happen either to his son or to his country if Claudius (like Gertrude) were simply left "to heaven." What, then, did King Hamlet really want—and should he have been satisfied with what he got?

VIII

The good for one's country should, of course, be the primary concern of a proper ruler. That this does not figure much in Prince Hamlet's calculations suggests that the instruction in royalty he had received from his father had been inadequate, if not even irresponsible. Particularly troubling for the patriotic Dane might have been the prospect at the end of the play of a competing (evidently foreign) family assuming the rule of Denmark.

One character after another in this play acts in complete confidence in the course he is pursuing. The assurance displayed by the Ghost is matched, that is, by the confidence displayed thereafter by Polonius, Claudius, and Laertes. Even Prince Hamlet, who is sometimes regarded as vacillating, pursues more or less steadily a course of action which is fatal to a half-dozen others and does seem to leave his country subjected to a foreign prince.

We can well wonder whether "anyone in charge" knew what he was doing. This is a question that was made particularly significant for us, during the past century, as we have reviewed the First World War and its horrific aftermath. We can well wonder as well whether Shakespeare suggests that spiritual guidance, or at least guidance by spirits, is of limited reliability in the conduct of the affairs of a country.

IX

We have recalled that Horatio, at the end of the play, has to be urged by Hamlet not to join him at once in death. Horatio had just announced that he was more an antique Roman than a Dane, evidently repudiating thereby the strict Christian prohibition of suicide. Hamlet, in urging Horatio to live on, invokes Horatio's aid (so that Hamlet's story may be properly told), *not* what might happen to the soul of a suicide.

The reminder here of the antique Romans can call to mind the patriotism of the Roman Republic. And this in turn could make us wonder about the status of both King Hamlet and his son as citizens. Are both of them (more modern than Roman) too much moved by their private lives and hence by supposed personal interests?

Are we given enough by Shakespeare to be able to make a reliable judgment about the way Claudius and Fortinbras conduct themselves as rulers? Claudius, like his brother, may be too much concerned about his personal interests to be a proper King who is able to identify and secure the Good. But what about Fortinbras, who, in following in the footsteps of *his* father, seems (because of the way the two Hamlets conducted themselves) to have acquired for his subjects (at least for a while) the much-troubled and -troubling country of Denmark?

2. Unconventional Religious Duties and the Good Life

I

We can see, in the career of Henry VIII, how the marital status of a ruler can affect the political fortunes of a people. This kind of effect is dramatized in William Shakespeare's *Hamlet,* where an assassination is said to have been motivated, in part, by the usurper's desire to possess his ruler's wife. That sexual relations continue to have political consequences was testified to by the ill-conceived impeachment of a recent President of the United States.

The social consequences of such relations is testified to by one of the most influential of American novels, Nathaniel Hawthorne's *The Scarlet Letter.* The universal interest in such matters is testified to, a century later, by such diverse exercises as James Joyce's *Ulysses* and Marcel Proust's *Remembrance of Things Past.* Perhaps the most critical precursors to such shenanigans in high places were seen in the careers of King David and his son, King Solomon.

The religious movement that was challenged by the Government of the United States in *Reynolds* v. *United States* (1878) found, in biblical accounts of the lives of highly esteemed patriarchs, divinely sanctioned precedents for the polygamy permitted, perhaps even required, by the directives of an American Church. This polygamy, in the Utah Territory of the United States, ran afoul of an Act of Congress that provided, "Every person having husband or wife living, who marries another, whether married or single, in a Territory, or other place over which the United States have exclusive jurisdiction, is guilty of bigamy, and shall be punished by a fine of not more than $500, and by imprisonment for a term of not more than five years." A generation before *Reynolds,* Abraham Lincoln (in a speech at Springfield, Illinois, on June 26, 1857), had linked in this fashion (as his Republican Party was doing) the case against polygamy with the case against slavery (that slavery which, he had said, was benefitted by the overly permissive doctrine of "self-government for the Territories").

> [I]n all this, it is very plain the Judge [Senator Stephen A. Douglas] evades the only question the Republicans have ever pressed upon the [Democratic Party] in regard to Utah. That question the Judge well knows to be this: "If the people of Utah shall peacefully form a State Constitution tolerating polygamy, will the [Democrats] admit them into the Union?" There is nothing in the United States Constitution or law against polygamy; and why is it not a part of the Judge's "sacred right of self-government" for that people to have it, or rather to *keep* it, if they choose? These questions, so far as I know, the Judge never answers.

II

The criminal prosecution in *Reynolds* of an alleged bigamist faced at its outset the issue of whether men "living in polygamy" could be kept from serving as jurors in this trial. The Opinion of the United States Supreme Court observed on this issue:

> From the testimony [of prospective jurors] it is apparent that all the jurors to whom the challenges related were or had been living in polygamy. It needs no argument to show that such a jury could not have gone into the box entirely free from bias and prejudice . . .

Thus, it was ruled, polygamists, or men who refused to say whether they were polygamists (one of them would admit only to being "a fornicator"), could properly be kept off a jury hearing bigamy charges.

A related question was whether the defendant could successfully challenge for cause those potential jurors who were opposed to the practice of polygamy. The *Reynolds* Court, in ruling against this kind of challenge, quoted Chief Justice John Marshall, in *Burr's Trial* (1807): "Light impressions, which may fairly be presumed to yield to the testimony that may be offered, which may leave the mind open to a fair consideration of the testimony, constitute no sufficient objection to a juror; but that those strong and deep impressions which close the mind against the testimony that may be offered in opposition to them, which will combat that testimony and resist its force, do constitute a sufficient objection to him." The *Reynolds* Court, speaking through Chief Justice Morrison R. Waite, adds,

> The theory of the law is that a juror who has formed an opinion cannot be impartial. Every opinion which he may entertain need not necessarily have that effect. In these days of newspaper enterprise and universal education, every case of public interest is almost, as a matter of necessity, brought to the attention of all the intelligent people in the vicinity, and scarcely any one can be found among those best fitted for jurors who has not read or heard of it, and who has not some impression or some opinion in respect to its merits.

It becomes, then, a question of fact, to be decided primarily by a conscientious trial judge, "whether the nature and strength of the opinion formed are such as in law necessarily to raise the presumption of partiality." However much juries have long been extolled as important elements in a system of self-government, they do depend upon proper composition and direction to be reliable. The same can be said about the social relations, including the composition of the family, upon which a solid republican community depends.

III

Vital to the *Reynolds* controversy is the issue of what a republican community is entitled, perhaps even obliged, to require in the development and maintenance of family life. It is likely, in these circumstances, that duties will be required of family members, such as with respect to the care of children. It is also likely that restraints, perhaps related to these duties, will be placed on would-be family members, among which restraints may be (at least among us) the prohibition of bigamy.

This means, to use contemporary terminology, that limits may properly be placed upon effective invocations of "choice" and "privacy." The controversy here becomes particularly acute when the alleged offender offers "the defence of religious belief or duty" to justify having done that which has been forbidden by the law of the land. This is to be distinguished, that is, from the kind of issue that was to be raised later, in the *Flag Salute Cases,* where the challenged citizen refrains, because of what he considers divine guidance, from doing something required by law.

The Supreme Court, in *Reynolds,* described thus the "defense of religious belief or duty" that was offered:

> On the trial, . . . the accused proved that at the time of his alleged second marriage he was, and for many years before had been, . . . a believer of [his church's] doctrines, [including the doctrine] "that it was the duty of male members of [his] church, circumstances permitting, to practice polygamy; . . . that this duty was enjoined by different books which the members of said church believed to be of divine origin, and among others the Holy Bible, and also that the members of the church believed that the practice of polygamy was directly enjoined upon the male members thereof by the Almighty God, in a revelation to . . . the founder and prophet of said church; that the failing or refusing to practice polygamy by such male members of said church, when circumstances would admit, would be punished, and that the penalty for such failure and refusal would be damnation in the life to come. . . ."

"Upon this [and like] proof," the Supreme Court continued, "[the accused] asked the [trial] court to instruct the jury that if they found from the evidence that he 'was married as charged—if he was married—in pursuance of and in conformity with what he believed at the time to be a religious duty, that the verdict must be *not guilty.*'" The Supreme Court endorses the trial court's response, which is recorded to have been put thus: "[The] request [by the accused] was refused and the [trial] court did charge 'that there [had to be] a criminal intent, but that if the defendant, under the influence of a religious belief that it was right,—under an inspiration, if you please, that it was right,—deliberately married a second time, having a first wife living, the want of consciousness of evil—the want of understanding on his part that he was committing a crime—did not excuse him; but the law inexorably in such case implies the criminal intent.'"

IV

Thereafter, the Supreme Court discussed how, if at all, the First Amendment affected what was done in this prosecution. The Court began with this recognition of Constitutional limitations:

Congress cannot pass a law for the governance of the Territory which shall prohibit the free exercise of religion. The First
Amendment to the Constitution expressly forbids such legislation. Religious freedom is guaranteed everywhere throughout the
United States, so far as congressional interference is concerned.
The question to be determined is, whether the [bigamy] law under consideration comes within this prohibition.

"The word 'religion' is not defined in the Constitution," the Court then
said, requiring it to "go elsewhere, therefore, to ascertain its meaning, and
nowhere, more appropriately, . . . than to the history of the times in the
midst of which the provision was adopted."

Particularly relied upon here by the *Reynolds* Court was the Virginia
Statute of Religious Freedom (1786). Thus, it is recalled by the Supreme
Court: "In the preamble of this act (12 Hening's Stat. 84) religious freedom is defined; and after a recital 'that to suffer the civil magistrate to
intrude his powers into the field of opinion, and to restrain the profession or propagation of principles on supposition of their ill tendency,
is a dangerous fallacy which at once destroys all religious liberty,' it is
declared 'that it is time enough for the rightful purposes of civil government for its officers to interfere when principles break out into overt
acts against peace and good order.'" Here, the Court adds, "is found the
true distinction between what properly belongs to the Church and what
to the State."

Thus, the Court argued, "Congress was deprived of all legislative
power over mere opinion, but was left free to reach actions which were
in violation of social duties or subversive of good order." Thereupon the
Court observed that polygamy had long been regarded, in the Anglo-
American tradition, "as an offence against society, cognizable by the civil
courts and punishable with more or less severity." The political and social
consequences of polygamy are then described:

[W]e think it may safely be said that there never has been a time
in any State of the Union when polygamy has not been an offence against society, cognizable by the civil courts and punishable with more or less severity. In the face of all this evidence, it is
impossible to believe that the constitutional guarantee of religious
freedom was intended to prohibit legislation in respect to this

most important feature of social life. Marriage, while from its very nature a sacred obligation, is nevertheless, in most civilized nations, a civil contract, and usually regulated by law. Upon it society may be said to be built, and out of its fruits spring social relations and social obligations and duties, with which government is necessarily required to deal. In fact, according as monogamous or polygamous marriages are allowed, do we find the principles on which the government of the people, to a greater or less extent, rests. Professor Lieber says, polygamy leads to the patriarchal principle, and which, when applied to large communities, fetters the people in stationary despotisms, while that principle cannot long exist in connection with monogamy. Chancellor Kent observes that this remark is equally striking and profound.

V

The sincerity of the accused, as in the *Reynolds* circumstances, should be taken into account by authorities in a position to use clemency once a conviction has been secured. Among the things to be taken into account is what is likely to happen to the "wives" and children of such a man if he is dealt with harshly. An inability to be sensible in response to misdeeds might even call into question the sound flexibility of a community grounded in monogamy.

After all, it is from their community that most people get the morality and sense of duty that are naturally relied upon. The family, which *is* the more obvious source of such inculcation, itself very much relies upon the community for its legitimation, if not even for its very being. It is usually instructed and reinforced by the community in what it undertakes with "its own."

We have seen, since the Second World War, what has happened to the cohesiveness and authority of families when the community loses its own authority. Critical to that authority has usually been the influence exercised by religious organizations, which themselves depend much more on community guidance than is generally recognized. The controversy in *Reynolds* was, in part, a struggle to determine what guidance for religious associations would be authoritative in the United States.

VI

It may well be that what proved decisive in the repudiation of polygamy in the Utah Territory was not any campaign of prosecution of alleged bigamists, but rather the conditions set by Congress for admission of Utah to the Union in 1896. Thereafter, those who persisted in the polygamy-sanctioning "revelation" (repealed, so to speak, by another "revelation") tended toward that social and moral deterioration described in a *New York Times* account of October 25, 2005. Law-abidingness does tend to promote a pervasive integrity, unless (as may be seen in Appendix I of this volume) the prevailing laws have themselves become perverted and tyrannical.

It must be wondered how much the confidence exhibited by the *Reynolds* Court depended on a recognized social order that was, or at least seemed to be, fairly sound. Can marriage be plausibly *talked about* today as it was in 1878? Is it not even likely that there have been polygamous communities, perhaps even in the Utah Territory, with a greater respect for "family values" than is evident among many of us in this Country today?

Certainly there have been some curious developments among us, dramatized not only by a devastating AIDS epidemic but also by an ever-growing insistence upon the right "to be left alone." Is *that* which is being "left alone" in these circumstances capable of truly standing alone? Does a proper character, capable of assessing things as they truly are, depend on a sturdy family (whether monogamous or polygamous) in which one is reliably grounded, however independent and self-reliant one is destined to become?

VII

Another curious development among us may be seen in the animal-sacrifice case, *Church of the Lukumi Babalu Aye, Inc.* v. *City of Hialeah* (1993). What is most curious about this case is not the ruling by the United States Supreme Court, a unanimous ruling plausibly in line with other First Amendment rulings, but rather the fact that the cult involved here (known as the Santeria religion) dared to assert itself as it did, insisting upon the right to defy City of Hialeah directives that attempted to restrain some of the practices of this cult. It may be largely a matter of

chance that some fifty thousand members of this cult should have been
in South Florida, having been persecuted out of Cuba (it is said) by the
Castro regime.

The *Reynolds* Court, more than a century before, had conceded, "Laws
are made for the government of actions, and while they cannot interfere
with mere religious belief and opinions, they may [interfere] with practices." That 1870 Court then asked,

> Suppose one believed that human sacrifices were a necessary part
> of religious worship, would it be seriously contended that the civil
> government under which he lived could not interfere to prevent a
> sacrifice? Or if a wife religiously believed it was her duty to burn
> herself upon the funeral pyre of her dead husband, would it be
> beyond the powers of the civil government to prevent her carrying
> her belief into practice?

One might usefully wonder how the *Reynolds* Court would have regarded
the cultic practices described in this fashion (in 1993, while the case was
pending in the Supreme Court) by a Seventh Day Adventist Church author friendly to the legal cause of the animal-sacrificing cult:

> Lukumi Babalu Aye is, definitely, not mainline Protestant. Its
> members, called Santeros, practice an ancient Afro-Caribbean
> faith known as Santeria. Santeros celebrate birth, death, and mar-
> riage with animal sacrifices. In their rituals they decapitate goats,
> chickens, doves, and turtles—often 20 animals at a time—usually
> in private homes. In one ceremony a priest slices the throat of a
> chicken, chops off its head, bites into the headless bird's breast,
> and rips the animal open with his teeth before stuffing the open
> chest with herbs, tobacco, and bits of dried fish—all in an attempt
> to please Babalu Aye, a Santeria god. The city of Hialeah wants
> the practice stopped.

None of the four Opinions supporting the unanimous ruling by the
Supreme Court against the Hialeah legal efforts is as graphic as the account just quoted, but we *are* told (in the Opinion of the Court) what
apparently moved the city to act as it did:

In April 1987, the Church leased land in the city of Hialeah, Florida, and announced plans to establish a house of worship as well
as a school, cultural center, and museum. [The president of the
Church] indicated that *the Church's goal was to bring the practices
of the Santeria faith, including its ritual of animal sacrifice, into the
open*. The church began the process of obtaining utility services
and receiving the necessary licensing, inspection, and zoning ap-
provals. [Emphasis added.]

Bringing theretofore concealed (perhaps instinctively concealed?) practices
"into the open" is critical to those exhibitions that are, perhaps naturally,
rejected as "obscene" by a decent community. I included in a 1994 talk to
quite sophisticated intellectuals about this case (a talk published in 2001)
the following observations:

The most troublesome feature of this entire controversy . . . is that
there is nothing (in the opinions of any of the judges involved
in this litigation or in the briefs and commentaries I have seen)
which indicates even an awareness of the interest in the morality
of its citizens that a community may have in this kind of situation.
. . . I have noticed, upon discussing this animal sacrifice matter
with people of various persuasions, that the moral issue—that is,
the corruption issue—never occurs to them as a problem. Nor are
they much moved by it when I bring it up. This suggests what has
become of the way we talk about such matters in this Country.

VIII

The key problem with the Hialeah rules invalidated by the Supreme
Court in 1993 is that they obviously applied primarily, if not even exclu-
sively, to the killing of various animals done by the Santeria cult. Other
killings, ranging from millennia-old kosher practices to the latest developments in the extermination of rodents, were ignored by the city. There
may have been a special problem because of the way that the carcasses of
the Santeria victims were disposed of, but that could have been dealt with
in a way that would probably have readily passed constitutional muster.
It has long been understood, and not only in the Anglo-American

tradition, that repressive measures that are *not* of general applicability are suspect. If they are not general, this strongly suggests that the activities proscribed are not considered intrinsically bad, but rather that they are condemned only because of who engage in them (if not even because of what they *believe* while doing so). On the other hand, measures that exempt some Believers from requirements that other citizens must obey (such as the public-school exemption recognized for the Amish in *Wisconsin* v. *Yoder* [1972]) tend to be permitted by the United States Supreme Court.

The Court might be inclined to permit limitations upon the public viewing of animal sacrifices, if similar limitations were placed by the authorities on the public viewing of other forms of killing animals, including the wholesale slaughtering upon which we depend for our meats. We can well be reminded here of the retort of J. P. Morgan to the associate who complained that Mr. Morgan was angry with him for doing in public what others did behind closed doors, "That's what doors are for!" However all this may be, it can be reasonably expected that the descendants of the first generations of the Santeria cult in this Country will become as respectable (indoors as well as outdoors) as the descendants of the polygamists discredited in *Reynolds* have obviously become.

IX

Problems with respect to the required general applicability of restrictive measures may be seen in intermittent responses to the *Flag Desecration Cases* (such as *Texas* v. *Johnson* [1989]). Efforts have been made from time to time to punish such desecration. Constitutional amendments have been proposed, such as this one: "Congress and the States shall have power to prohibit the physical desecration of the flag of the United States."

Those who believe that the First Amendment would be thereby circumvented, if not even amended, should be reminded of the observation by the Supreme Court in the *Church of the Lukumi Babalu Aye Case*, "The challenged [Hialeah] laws . . . [violated] . . . the principle of general applicability because the secular ends asserted in defense of the laws were pursued only with respect to conduct motivated by religious beliefs." Once a valid flag desecration statute is enacted, by Congress or by a State, what will be the significance of its serious applications only against those who desecrate the flag in pursuit of unpopular political or social positions?

That is, it will then be even more obvious than it should be now that most flag desecrations (which are resorted to for commercial purposes, for costumes and exhibitions [including bikinis], and even for some patriotic manifestations) are apt to be ignored by the authorities, which means, in effect, that only those few instances of general flag-related misconduct *are* prosecuted which offend our political or religious sensibilities.

However that may be, one likely consequence of the successful prosecution of flag desecration would be an increased number of such provocative episodes. That is, would-be flag desecrators are far less likely to "expose themselves" thus when they are apt to be immediately thrashed by onlookers and to be completely ignored by the authorities. Would polygamists and animal sacrificers, too, tend to be discouraged if they came to be more pitied than either prosecuted or envied by their immediate associates, associates who thereby manifest in still another way the power as well as the duty and the desire of the community to "legislate morality"?

3. *Griswold* v. *Connecticut* (1965) and the Prevention of Conception

I

"Seen in the perspective of the development of constitutional doctrine," it is suggested in the *Encyclopedia of the American Constitution,* "*Griswold* v. *Connecticut* (1965) stands among the most influential [United States] Supreme Court decisions of the latter part of the twentieth century." Under attack on that occasion was a Connecticut law forbidding the use of contraceptive devices to prevent pregnancies. In *Griswold,* the Supreme Court, by a vote of 7–2, held the law invalid after "operators of a birth control clinic had been prosecuted for aiding married couples to violate the law, furnishing them advice on contraceptive devices."

This was an obviously contrived case involving, among others, local university personnel who made themselves available for arrest and prosecution. "The appellants were found guilty as accessories and fined $100 each . . ." That those were much tamer times than ours today is suggested by the understanding that the illegally serviced clients of this birth control clinic *were* identified as married persons.

The term "married persons" is italicized at the outset of the Court's opinion in this case. Justice William O. Douglas, as his Opinion for the Court draws to its close, warns against allowing "the police to search the sacred precincts of marital bedrooms for telltale signs of the use of contraceptives." This Opinion, by a much-married Justice, concludes with an often-quoted paean to marriage:

> We deal with a right of privacy older than the Bill of Rights—older than our political parties, older than our school system. Marriage is a coming together for better or for worse, hopefully enduring, and intimate to the degree of being sacred. It is an association that promotes a way of life, not causes; a harmony in living, not politi-

cal faiths; a bilateral loyalty, not commercial or social projects. Yet it is an association for as noble a purpose as any involved in our prior decisions.

II

The Connecticut prohibition invalidated on this occasion did not seem to have been seriously enforced for some time. Prosecutors had probably been reluctant to work up cases. Judges and juries probably could not be counted on to cooperate.

This particular case seems to have relied upon the cooperation of defendants who apparently volunteered evidence of their violations of the statute. It is unlikely, that is, that anyone who preferred not to be prosecuted would have been at risk. Besides, the prohibited information and services were legally available nearby across State lines.

Thus, the everyday situation with respect to birth control services in Connecticut was probably pretty much that to be found at the time in the Country at large. It was already notorious, for instance, that Roman Catholic couples, despite the supposed strictures of their Church, conducted themselves in these matters much as did their non-Catholic neighbors (something noticed in my 1975 volume, *Human Being and Citizen*). And yet it can plausibly be said that *Griswold* "stands among the most influential Supreme Court decisions" in recent decades.

III

The use of the judicial system to clear away obsolete legislative provisions that few would defend is familiar. There are everywhere such provisions "on the books" which are not politically convenient to repeal, even when they are rarely enforced. Something more than a concern about a quaint prohibition, however, seems to have been involved in *Griswold*.

It can be suspected that the participants in this case recognized that bigger game was in view than that provided by the particular Connecticut statute that was being challenged. After all, even one of the two dissenting Justices in this case could disparage the prohibition as "an uncommonly silly law." They worried, even so, about having the Court exercise the power of a "superlegislature."

"Superlegislating" by judges had been seen, most notoriously earlier in the century, in the case of *Lochner* v. *New York* (1905). It had taken the Supreme Court a half-century to purge the *Lochner* influence from constitutional doctrine. Critical to that purgation had been the insistence that it was not the duty of courts to assess the wisdom of legislatures.

IV

It is far from certain what the ruling by the Court in *Griswold* rested on. The Syllabus provided with the Opinion of the Court says only, "The Connecticut statute forbidding use of contraceptives violates the right of marital privacy which is within the penumbra of specific guarantees of the Bill of Rights." Critics have been intrigued by the use here of "penumbra," a term which assumes that emanations from various rights may sometimes be more significant than the rights upon which such emanations are said to depend.

The *Griswold* approach, as described in the *Encyclopedia of the American Constitution,* includes this observation: "[T]he Opinion of the Court recognized that the Connecticut birth control law violated no specific guarantee of the Bill of Rights." But the encyclopedist observed (quoting from the Opinion of the Court), "The *Griswold* case concerned 'a relationship lying within the zone of privacy created by several fundamental constitutional guarantees.'" And so, it is further observed,

> Enforcement of Connecticut law would involve intolerable State intrusion into the marital bedroom. The law was invalid in application to married couples, and the birth control clinic operators could not be punished for aiding its violation.

Nothing is said by the Court about whether such a law would be considered applicable to *unmarried* couples seeking birth control counseling. Nor is anything said by the Court about the uses to which the ruling in this case might be put, including that far-reaching use described in the *Encyclopedia* article:

> *Griswold* served as an important precedent eight years later when the Court held in *Roe* v. *Wade* (1973), that the new constitutional right of privacy included a woman's right to have an abortion. . . .

The *Roe* opinion, abandoning the shadows of *Griswold's* penumbras, located the right of privacy in the "liberty" protected by Fourteenth Amendment due process. *Griswold* thus provided a bridge . . . to the Court's modern revival of substantive due process.

Of course, even more shadowy, or at least more obscure, than penumbras is reliance by courts upon that linguistic oddity, "substantive due process," a reliance that appears particularly contrived when it is recalled that there *are* Privileges and Immunities Clauses available for use.

V

The most intriguing feature of the *Griswold* speculations may be the Concurring Opinion by Justice Arthur J. Goldberg. His extended suggestions about the Ninth Amendment are perhaps his principal contribution to the development of American constitutional law, a contribution not noticed, however, in the biographical entry devoted to him in the *Encyclopedia of the American Constitution.* Among the implications of the Ninth Amendment ("The enumeration in the Constitution, of certain rights, shall not be construed to deny or disparage others retained by the people.") is the understanding that important rights, in addition to those explicitly reaffirmed in the Bill of Rights, had been generated and would continue to be generated in the ways that the enumerated rights had been.

Particularly significant in the development of *Griswold* and its progeny can be said to be the Dissenting Opinion of Justice Louis D. Brandeis in *Olmstead* v. *United States* (1928), an Opinion that includes these sentiments (quoted by Justice Goldberg in *Griswold*):

> The makers of our Constitution undertook to secure conditions favorable to the pursuit of happiness. They recognized the significance of man's spiritual nature, of his feelings and of his intellect. . . . They sought to protect Americans in their beliefs, their thoughts, their emotions and their sensations. They conferred, against the Government, the right to be let alone—the most comprehensive of rights and the right most valued by civilized men.

Even so, it should be noticed that the *civilizing* of human beings very much depends upon constant attention by responsible communities. That is, someone who is completely "let alone" is likely (no matter what Jean-Jacques Rousseau sometimes seems to say) to turn out barbaric.

Thus, the Privileges and Immunities respected by the Constitution depend on a well-ordered community not only for their protection but also for their identification and enthronement. The good order required here depends, in turn, on governments that know what they are doing. This means, among other things, that judges and legislators should do only, but do well, what they are expected and equipped to do.

VI

Concerns about judges "legislating" are voiced in a *Griswold* Dissenting Opinion: there, as elsewhere, Justice Hugo L. Black protested against judicial usurpation. One can imagine what he, as a former Member of Congress, would have said about the exercise by the Supreme Court of vital legislative prerogatives in *Bush* v. *Gore* (2000) (discussed in my *Reflections on Constitutional Law*). Questions can also be raised here about the assumption by the Court of the power of a comprehensive judicial review of Acts of Congress for their constitutionality (also discussed in my *Reflections on Constitutional Law*).

Justice Black, in his *Griswold* Dissenting Opinion, condemns several times the dependence by judges upon any "natural law due process philosophy." In such suspicion he is very much a New Deal–era judge sensitive to the abuses of the *Lochner* era. Assurances should have been provided for him here by recollections of how common law judges had contributed to the identification and development of vital rights singled out for protection in the Bill of Rights and elsewhere.

The Supreme Court abdicated, in *Erie Railroad Company* v. *Tompkins* (1938), its common law duties and prerogatives. This has made it difficult for judges and lawyers to recognize the reasoning, and not just the exercise of will, which contributed to the development of the system of justice and liberty enshrined in the common law (still another matter discussed in my *Reflections on Constitutional Law*). Of course, judges in such a system recognize the sovereign authority of the People and their Legislatures to regulate what is done by officers of government for the common good.

VII

Measures appropriate for realization and maintenance of the common good vary from time to time and from place to place. Standards grounded in nature have to be identified and respected if an enduring constitutional system is to be established. A sound system generates an awareness of the Privileges and Immunities appropriate for a People's circumstances.

Privileges and Immunities, appropriate for thirteenth-century circumstances in England, were collected in the Magna Carta of 1215. Some of them, in the forms appropriate for American conditions, may be found in the Bill of Rights of 1791. Among these guarantees, both in 1215 and in 1791, is a respect for what we know as due process of law.

It may be partly a matter of chance which rights were singled out for Amendments I–VIII in 1791. This is recognized, in effect, by the caveat provided in the Ninth Amendment. It is also partly a matter of chance, going back to mistakes made by the United States Supreme Court after the Civil War, that the Privileges and Immunities Clause of the Fourteenth Amendment was so weakened that the Due Process Clause of that Amendment has had to be used to provide for the development and protection of the rights naturally called for in a healthy constitutional system.

VIII

When the natural processes of a system cannot, for one reason or another, be relied upon, contrivances are likely to be resorted to. This may be seen, for example, in the bizarre use of the Treaty Power in *Missouri* v. *Holland* (1920) to do what the use of a properly interpreted Commerce Clause would have done. It may be seen as well in what the Supreme Court "had" to do to correct the grossly malapportioned State legislatures two generations ago, something that Congress (using, say, the powers provided it by the Republican Form of Government Guarantee) should have done, and done less mechanically than the Court has been obliged to do it.

The contrivance of the case conjured up in *Griswold* is obvious enough. It is exposed for all to see in the concluding note of a Dissenting Opinion in this case, where it is recorded:

The Connecticut House of Representatives recently passed a bill . . . repealing the birth control law [being litigated in *Griswold*].

The State Senate has apparently not yet acted on the measure, and today is relieved of that responsibility.

It seems that the public and hence the legislature became aware of the birth control law as a "problem" only because of the *Griswold* litigation.

But, it bears repeating, it is hardly likely that that law was what the fuss was really all about. The way *was* opened, in effect, for the development of litigation with respect to the abortion laws of the Country. Did the judges involved recognize where they were heading?

IX

It can be tempting to rely upon judges rather than legislators to guide, or at least to stimulate (to "jump-start"), far-ranging changes in the governance of a community. This is especially so when legislatures are, for one reason or another, stymied. But are courts, with the best will in the world, likely to be equipped to do adequately what legislatures *could* do better?

Certainly, it is a limited view of things that considers courts substantially responsible for massive changes in social policies. We should be reminded that the changes in this Country that we very much associate with courts during the past half-century were happening worldwide as well. In other countries those changes (encouraged by public opinion) were obviously brought about largely because of technological developments and legislative initatives, not because of judicial interventions.

Prominent among these changes in the Western World have been not only the considerable recourse to abortion but also the general promotion of racial equality. What, we may well wonder, inclines Americans to believe (as they evidently did already in Alexis de Tocqueville's day) that judicial pronouncements are more critical to social developments here than they appear to be elsewhere? Do Americans testify thereby to their faith in argument and hence to the power of reason in the direction of "human Events"?

4. *Roe* v. *Wade* (1973) and the Law of Abortion

I

Two abortion-related cases, one from Texas and the other from Georgia, were decided on January 22, 1973, by the United States Supreme Court. The fateful Opinion of the Court, in the Texas case, *Roe* v. *Wade*, opens with a description of the two cases:

> This Texas federal appeal and its Georgia companion, *Doe* v. *Bolton* [1973] . . . present constitutional challenges to State criminal abortion legislation. The Texas statutes under attack here are typical of those that have been in effect in many States for approximately a century. The Georgia statutes, in contrast, have a modern cast and are a legislative product that, to an extent at least, obviously reflects the influences of recent attitudinal changes, of advancing medical knowledge and techniques, and of new thinking about an old issue.

The rulings of the Court that day seemed to mean, in effect, that no State could ever again prohibit most of the abortions that women in this Country were likely to consider having.

The Opinion of the Court in the Georgia case, *Doe* v. *Bolton,* recognized that the State statute under consideration permitted more abortions than did the Texas statute (which permitted only "an abortion procured or attempted by medical advice for the purpose of saving the life of the mother"). Although the Georgia statute was curbed by the Court in the ways that the Texas statute was, it was recognized by the Court that the Georgia statute *was* based on modern models, permitting an abortion "performed by a physician duly licensed" in a State when, "based upon his best clinical judgment, [he believed that] an abortion [was] necessary because

(1) A continuation of the pregnancy would endanger the life of the pregnant woman or would seriously and permanently injure her health; or
(2) The fetus would very likely be born with a grave, permanent, and irremediable mental or physical defect; or
(3) The pregnancy resulted from forcible or statutory rape.

It was evidently considered by the Georgia authorities that the reference to "rape" was intended to include incest.

No matter what the Supreme Court or others might say, the most vigorous opponents of abortions will continue to regard a deliberate abortion as tantamount to murder. That is, they insist that the fetus is a human being entitled to protection from very early in its existence if not even from the moment of its conception. They are reinforced in their insistence by that progress in medical techniques which permits premature infants to survive outside the womb at ever-earlier stages in their development.

II

The purest anti-abortion position is compromised by the concessions that most of the current opponents of abortions are willing to make. These concessions may be found in the Georgia statute considered in *Doe* v. *Bolton*, which (as we have seen) authorized abortions in several circumstances. They may be seen as well in the Dissenting Opinion by Justice William H. Rehnquist in *Roe* v. *Wade*, where it is said,

The Due Process Clause of the Fourteenth Amendment undoubtedly does place a limit, albeit a broad one, on legislative power to enact laws such as this. If the Texas statute were to prohibit an abortion even where the mother's life is in jeopardy, I have little doubt that such a statute would lack a rational relation to a valid state objective.

Such concessions probably have to be made if the anti-abortion position is to secure much support, not only among judges but also among legislators. At the very least, it seems, public opinion at large would permit (if not even require) the sacrifice of the fetus (however innocent it might be) if the life of the expectant mother is endangered by carrying it to term. It might also be said by some (in the tradition of Oedipus?) that any dutiful being would want to have his or her life sacrificed for the sake of a parent.

It can be answered: sacrificing one's life for another is one thing; being deliberately killed for the sake of another (even for one's prospective parent) is something quite different. However high-minded such removal of another may be, it can still look like murder to at least a few. But, to repeat, these anti-abortion purists cannot routinely insist upon such an assessment if they are to have any substantial success today among legislators and judges or with the public at large anywhere in the Western World.

III

No matter what State legislatures or others may say, the most vigorous advocates of the right to an abortion will continue to regard it as critical to a woman's "right to choose." They do not—or, at least, they will not—recognize the fetus as truly a human being. Fetuses, they insist, are not persons, an insistence which is recognized by the fact that fetuses have never been counted, say, in the decennial census of persons in this Country prescribed by the Constitution.

Even so, some of the more vigorous opponents of abortions regard themselves as the spiritual heirs of the nineteenth-century abolitionists who considered slavery an obvious abomination. Proponents of abortions, on the other hand, would remind everyone that slaves could be counted as three-fifths of a person in a census (with Southerners, however, often arguing that they should be counted fully). Also, abortion proponents insist, to deny women all access to abortions is in effect to enslave them, trapping them in their unwanted pregnancies.

The pro-abortion movement is for many, of course, part of the feminist revolution. An aspect of that "revolution" is the notorious sexual freedom in our time, a freedom that would be considered by some to be improperly abridged if women should continue to be trapped by unwanted pregnancies that cannot be terminated. Thus, these pro-abortion people, too, are "abolitionists," directing *their* efforts against those laws that are said to re-enslave women through the procreation process.

IV

The purest pro-abortion position among us is compromised, in turn, by the personal conduct that leads to *most* of the decisions to seek an abortion. The liberation sought, from the fetters of an unwanted pregnancy, *usually* follows upon a choice that was not truly sensible. It can once again be wondered whether one is free if one does not act as one should.

That is, many, perhaps most, of the abortions sought for in this Country do seem to follow upon conduct that should not have been chosen. The misconduct here is usually by males and females together. This is not to deny, of course, that there is much to be said on behalf of the mutual attraction that leads to these productive (though sometimes unfortunate) liaisons.

Thus, it is realistic to recognize that most abortions would not be "needed" if people simply behaved themselves—if they acted as they know they are supposed to act. Particularly troubling is what seems to be the tendency among some to treat abortion as a form of contraception (or birth control). Thus, it can appear particularly unseemly to have had a decades-long epidemic of assaults on fetuses, fetuses that should not (and need not) have been generated at all.

V

The difficulties encountered by the embattled contenders in the abortion controversy are reflected in the names that they assign themselves. On one side are the *pro-choice* advocates, who prefer *not* to identify themselves as advocates of abortion or of the destruction of fetuses. On the other side are the *pro-life* advocates, who prefer *not* to identify themselves as advocates of the suppression of abortions or of the control of women.

The labels chosen for themselves reflect judgments as to what the public wants or, at least, what it will tolerate. The rhetoric resorted to on both sides may reflect, that is, an awareness of fundamental standards that are widely intuited. It may be wondered to what extent each side in this controversy conceals even from itself what it is seeking and doing.

Neither side, in any event, seems to be willing to recognize the ultimate sovereignty of the community in determining how many children there should be and who should have them. But each side, at least in our current controversy, would like to use governmental power (exercised either by a legislature or by a court) to advance its position—that is, either to restrict abortions severely or to remove most if not all legal restrictions on abortions. Still, neither side, in this Country, wants government either to set a limit upon or to require pregnancies.

VI

Every United States Supreme Court vacancy these days prompts intense speculation about how prospective nominees would vote on efforts to reverse *Roe* v. *Wade*. It is not appreciated, however, that *Roe* v. *Wade* may be, for practical purposes, now irreversible. This is not because of any doctrine of *stare decisis* (which probably should not apply, anyway, to constitutional adjudications), but rather because of the enduring effects of the ready recourse to abortions in this Country since the 1970s.

What seems to be irreversible, that is, is what has happened to public opinion, especially among women, because of the unprecedented access to abortion there has been in this Country during the past quarter-century. This access has not been due as much as has been believed to *Roe* v. *Wade*, however, but rather (as I have indicated) to profound changes, at least in the Western World, in public opinion. These changes, including with respect to how sexuality is regarded, have been influenced in part by remarkable technological developments both in medicine and in communications.

Changes with respect to the availability of abortions, comparable to those changes witnessed in the United States, have been seen since the Second World War in much of Europe. But in those countries there were no courts, but rather public opinion, nullifying inherited legislative or other restrictions on abortions. In a sense, then, *Roe* v. *Wade* has kept us from *seeing* what was happening "everywhere"—and what would probably have happened here, as well, sooner or later, no matter how the Supreme Court ruled in *Roe* v. *Wade*.

VII

This is not to suggest that *Roe* v. *Wade* has not mattered. It has mattered very much that it was widely believed to matter much more than it really did. The political life of the Country was affected, even distorted, by the electoral allegiances of "pro-life" and "pro-choice" factions in recent decades.

The dubious effects on our politics of the abortion controversy were due in part to chance. The Supreme Court accelerated, or perhaps only dramatized, the remarkable developments that could already be seen elsewhere in the Western World. If the abortion-inducing medication now readily available in Europe had been available here in 1970, would it have mattered much what any American court said about abortion laws?

If it should become generally known that fairly safe abortion-inducing medication exists, the abortion-control issue would become primarily a drug-control issue. It would then become virtually impossible, no matter what our Federal Drug Administration says or does, to prevent women from securing such medication if they believe it is proper for them to have and to use it. Both the availability of such medication *and* the opinion that it is proper to use it would be enhanced by any general recognition that this kind of medication is deemed acceptable and is lawfully used in the countries from which we have gotten, for two centuries now, most of our notions of right and wrong, of the good and the bad.

VIII

However limited the effect of *Roe* v. *Wade* may eventually become, the constitutional inquiries of the Justices relating thereto invite investigation. We can see among the Justices a continued, or at least a revived, interest in "substantive due process." We still do not see among the Justices, however, a proper assessment of that term.

Of course, critics of the use of "substantive due process" warn that it is reviving the supposedly discredited doctrines of *Lochner* v. *New York* (1905). But such critics do not seem to recognize (I have indicated) that "substantive due process" represents an attempt to provide a plausible substitute for the "privileges or immunities" language of the Fourteenth Amendment, language that had been severely restricted by the Supreme Court during the decades after the Civil War. The deeply rooted public opinion that evidently called forth the somewhat revolutionary Fourteenth Amendment language was eventually going to find renewed expression, one way or another, even if by way of something as semantically curious as "substantive due process."

The *Abortion Cases* can also prompt some to take the Ninth Amendment more seriously than constitutional scholars tend to take it. The Ninth Amendment recognizes, in effect, that there are rights that are of a stature comparable to the stature of those rights enumerated in Amendments One through Eight. Why should it not be understood, furthermore, that such rights can continue to be developed by and on behalf of the People (but not only by judges), just as the rights already enumerated in the Constitution and the Bill of Rights had originally been developed and recognized?

IX

It remains to be seen, of course, how firmly the supposed Right to Privacy, among others, is developed and established in our constitutional system. It also remains to be seen whether access to an abortion may be eligible for permanent recognition pursuant either to the Ninth Amendment or to the Privileges or Immunities Clause of the Fourteenth Amendment. It remains to be seen, as well, whether the desperate humanitarian sympathy for millions of vulnerable fetuses can itself eventually come to be recognized, in turn, as having a substantial constitutional stature.

Our pro-choice people, in thinking about the persistent abortion problem in this Country, can find some support in Classical authors such as Plato and Aristotle, who seemed to defend, if not even to require, abortions in some circumstances. But such arguments in antiquity also seemed to look primarily to the community, not to "private" citizens, to make this kind of determination. Thus, however receptive such authors were to the usefulness and propriety of abortions, they do not seem to have intended to license any individual to have the principal say in such matters.

Our pro-life people, in thinking about the abortion problem, can also find some support in the same Classical authors, for such authors assumed that the community has the duty and hence the power to encourage and even to require the moral virtues that citizens should practice. But such an assumption presupposed that the community would also be entitled, and perhaps obliged, to regulate, if not even to determine, the opinions about the Divine that citizens need if they are to be reliable in how they conduct themselves. This would be, however, a "faith-based" approach to public life with which neither typical American conservatives today nor their liberal counterparts would likely be comfortable.

5. *Planned Parenthood* v. *Casey* (1992) and the Persistence of the Abortion Issue

I

The number of United States Supreme Court Justices permitting most abortions in this Country was reduced from seven in 1973 to five in 1992. This reduction reflects the steady efforts of pro-life people to organize themselves. Their efforts have contributed to the shaping of the Supreme Court for more than a quarter-century.

This shaping followed upon that mobilization of voters which contributed to recent Republican Presidencies. This development contributed in turn to the nomination of Justices with a view to curtailing *Roe* v. *Wade* (1973). It contributed as well to Congressional initiatives to curtail financial and other support for abortions by the United States government not only in this Country but also abroad.

The pro-choice people, on the other hand, tended to be less concerned about political action to support their cause. They tended, that is, to consider the "right to abortion" reliably protected by the Supreme Court. They could, therefore, "afford" to devote themselves much more to other causes.

II

Many women, during the decade after *Roe* v. *Wade,* got used to the notion that substantial access to abortions was a right they could count on. They were reinforced in this expectation, we have noticed, by what was happening worldwide with respect to this and related matters. And politicians in some of our States became reluctant to arouse the more "liberated" women among their constituents by declaring themselves to be "pro-life," no matter what their national party said it supported.

Each side to this controversy has had a plausible position. The pro-choice cause was that of personal liberty, a cause that can be regarded as sacred. The pro-life cause was that of respect for human life, a cause that can see the typical abortion as a callous destruction of an innocent human being.

The passions aroused by *Roe* v. *Wade* reminded citizens of the passions aroused by *Brown* v. *Board of Education* (1954). But *Brown* could depend, immediately and for decades thereafter, not only upon a unanimous Supreme Court but also, eventually, upon substantial Congressional support. On the other hand, Congress has repeatedly attempted to develop measures that would limit the application, or extension, of *Roe* v. *Wade*.

III

Another way of making these distinctions is to notice that *Brown* v. *Board of Education* could come to be identified, after the fierce initial resistance to it in some quarters, as fundamentally in accordance with a critical principle of the American regime, that "all Men are created equal." This recognition may be found in the South as well as in the North. It remains much more difficult, despite an emphasis upon the liberation of women, to identify *Roe* v. *Wade* with a principle that had been generally accepted as somehow longstanding and authoritative.

The vulnerability of the pro-choice position, at least among the Justices of the Supreme Court today, is suggested by the apparent unwillingness of some judicial defenders of *Roe* v. *Wade* during the past decade to say much, if anything, about the nobility of abortion (as distinguished, say, from what is said about the nobility of desegregation). Rather, such defenders are much more inclined to speak of the importance of *stare decisis*. Related to this is a concern that they not be seen as bowing to organized protests, especially since they sense that women (especially younger women) do tend to expect abortions to be legally available.

Of course, the reluctance of the Justices to repudiate *Roe* v. *Wade* may be due in part to their sense that what the Court might do to permit the curtailment of the typical abortion would be condemned by many women and their male allies as "reactionary" and "political." That is, Justices may sense that the repudiation by them of *Roe* v. *Wade* would provoke a firestorm in response. And, perhaps even more sobering for them, the medical developments I have referred to may soon (if they do not already) make such a provocative repudiation of little enduring practical consequence except perhaps for the reputation of the Court.

IV

All this is to suggest that a fifth vote in favor of repudiating *Roe* v. *Wade* may be difficult to secure, no matter who nominates Justices for the Supreme Court. Whatever the assurances and expectations associated with a new Justice, the temptation to accommodate oneself to the "reality" of modern expectations will be hard to resist for long, whatever may be ventured from time to time. This is aside from the difficulties that legislators would face in many States if they should once again be authorized to make State laws curtailing significantly the access to abortions, especially if "safe" abortion-inducing medication should truly come to be generally available.

Indeed, it seems, many women now believe that they are entitled to have abortions just as many men still believe that they are entitled to own guns. Some governmental regulation may be conceded in both cases. But the presumption for many is against any proposed regulation, whether of guns or of abortions.

Concern is expressed by the Court in *Planned Parenthood* v. *Casey* (1992) about the likely consequences of a repudiation of *Roe* v. *Wade*. Thus it can be said by the Justices,

> A decision to overrule *Roe's* essential holding under the circumstances would address error, if error there was, at the cost of both profound and unnecessary damage to the Court's legitimacy, and to the Nation's commitment to the rule of law. It is therefore imperative to adhere to the essence of *Roe's* original decision, and we do so today.

Such Justices almost seem to concede that *Roe* v. *Wade* might have been, in 1973, a mistake which it would now be an even more serious mistake to repudiate altogether.

V

It is left open, of course, what "*Roe's* essential holding" includes. Justice Antonin E. Scalia, in his vigorous Dissenting Opinion in *Planned Parenthood* v. *Casey*, recognizes how politically charged the status of *Roe* v. *Wade* is. Thus, he argues,

The States may, if they wish, permit abortion on demand, but the Constitution does not *require* them to do so. The permissibility of abortion, and the limitations upon it, are to be resolved like most important questions in our democracy: by citizens trying to persuade one another and then voting. As the Court acknowledges [in *Casey*], "where reasonable people disagree the government can adopt one position or the other." . . . [T]he issue in these [abortion] cases [is] not whether the power of a woman to abort her unborn child is a "liberty" in the absolute sense; or even whether it is a liberty of great importance to many women. Of course it is both. The issue is whether it is a liberty protected by the Constitution of the United States. I am sure it is not.

The passions that continue to be aroused by the abortion controversy are indicated by Justice Scalia when he is moved to say,

> . . . I will not swell the *United States Reports* with repetition of what I have said before . . . I must, however, respond to a few of the more outrageous arguments in today's opinion, which it is beyond human nature to leave unanswered.

However deeply a judge may feel about the issues of the day, should he not at least pretend to be considering them dispassionately? Such judicial passion as is exhibited here by a Justice legitimates, in effect, the passions exhibited in opposition to him and to those of like mind by the most vehement advocates of *Roe* v. *Wade*.

This is not to suggest that there is not any merit to Justice Scalia's observations in *Casey*, as when he says,

> Not only did *Roe* not . . . *resolve* the deeply divisive issue of abortion; it did more than anything else to nourish it, by elevating it to the national level where it is infinitely more difficult to resolve. National politics were not plagued by abortion protests, national abortion lobbying, or abortion marches on Congress before *Roe* v. *Wade* was decided. Profound disagreement existed among our citizens over the issue—as it does over other issues, such as the death penalty—but that disagreement was being worked out at the State level. As with many other issues, the division of sentiment within

each State was not as closely balanced as it was among the population of the Nation as a whole, meaning not only that more people
would be satisfied with the results of State-by-State resolution,
but also that those results would be more stable. Pre-*Roe*, moreover, political compromise was possible.

Indeed, there is much to be said for Justice Scalia's interpretation of events
here, as there is for what he says in the passage immediately following:

Roe's mandate for abortion on demand destroyed the compromises
of the past, rendered compromise impossible for the future, and
required the entire issue to be resolved uniformly at the national
level. At the same time, *Roe* created a vast new class of abortion
consumers and abortion proponents by eliminating the moral
opprobrium that had attached to the act. ("If the Constitution
guarantees abortion, how can it be bad?"—not an accurate line
of thought, but a natural one.) Many favor all those developments, and it is not for me to say that they are wrong. But to
portray *Roe* as the statesmanlike "settlement" of a divisive issue
. . . is nothing less than Orwellian. *Roe* fanned into life an issue that has inflamed our national politics in general, and has
obscured with its smoke the selection of Justices to this Court in
particular ever since.

Still, it can be wondered whether Justice Scalia truly believed ("it is not for
me to say that they are wrong") that he had not made it clear, in this and
other Opinions, what he personally believed about abortions.

VI

The reduction of the pro-*Roe* contingent on the Supreme Court from
seven to five has been mostly in response to what may be considered
"fringe issues." That is, the more effective opponents of *Roe* v. *Wade* have
dramatized such issues as "partial-birth abortions," parental notification
when teenage girls seek abortions, and requirements for waiting periods
and counseling before abortions are performed. That these issues can be
regarded as ways of reconsidering *Roe* itself is suggested by the abundance
of *amicus* briefs stimulated by such litigation.

This litigation does seem to keep alive the moral issues associated with recourse to abortions. These do not seem to be issues that are as vigorously argued, in public, in those Western countries where abortions are performed on a scale comparable to that in the United States, but without much if any significant participation historically by judges in the overall development. It may well be, then, that we would not continue to have the debate we do have about abortions if there had not been the emergence of *Roe* v. *Wade* as the *apparent* authorization, if not even the cause, of most abortions among us.

The continuing prevalence of abortions does reflect the general relaxation in recent decades of long-established rules (in this Country as well as abroad) for the governance of sexual relations. Thus, it is said (in the *Chicago Sun-Times,* of October 13, 2005), "About 30 percent of new mothers in Illinois are unmarried, mirroring the national average, the U.S. Census reports . . ." Without the abortions we have, this percentage might be substantially higher, unless (it might also be argued) the availability of abortions itself contributes to that relaxation of standards evident in the disturbing prevalence of unwed motherhood among us.

VII

These and like developments follow upon that series of social traumas which was very much "advanced" by the follies of the First World War. The language of intellectuals both reflects and contributes to these changes. This may be seen, for example, even in the language of so ardent an advocate of the old way as Justice Scalia.

Thus, he, in his *Planned Parenthood* v. *Casey* Dissenting Opinion, can speak several times of profound differences in moral opinion as being dependent on "value judgments." And, it seems, such "judgments" are not based primarily on reasoning, however much rhetoric (or the appearance of reasoning) may be employed by partisans. That is, nature does not seem to be considered authoritative in the determination of the standards we do and should have.

Instead, nature is assumed to be a source more of our passions than of our standards. This is implied in the uses of "human nature" and "natural" in passages that have been quoted in this Essay from the Scalia Dissenting Opinion in *Casey.* But to rule out nature as a substantial guide is, in effect, either to depend on chance (such as where one has been reared, by whom, and when) or to depend on that more exalted form of chance known by some as Divine Providence.

VIII

Ready access to abortions *has* shaped a generation of youngsters. One can still be startled to discover how much passion can be aroused by any suggestion that the community should be able to regulate recourse to abortions. Law students have been outraged by the suggestion, when I have ventured to invent it as a "hypothetical" in class, that the State take over and bring to viability any fetus that is aborted, even if this could be done without either any additional discomfort for the aborting woman or any future responsibility for the resulting child by its natural originators.

It is not persuasive for such students that this suggested compromise, dependent of course on medical technology not yet available, would go far in appeasing those sensitive citizens among us desperately opposed to abortions. Rather, *these* proponents of the right to an abortion want to see destroyed any fetus ejected from the place where it is not wanted. This passion, which *is* startling, bears thinking about, as does of course the passion exhibited by some of the partisans on the other side.

After all, passions may have an instructive (albeit not-fully-conscious or disciplined) hold upon reasons and reasoning, as may be seen in this passage from the Scalia Dissenting Opinion in *Planned Parenthood* v. *Casey*:

> The Court's reliance upon *stare decisis* can best be described as contrived. It insists upon the necessity of adhering not to all of *Roe*, but only to what it calls the "central holding." It seems to me that *stare decisis* ought to be applied even to the doctrine of *stare decisis*, and I confess never to have heard of this new, keep-what-you-want-and-throw-away-the-rest version. I wonder whether, as applied to *Marbury* v. *Madison*, 1 Cranch 137 (1803), for example, the new version of *stare decisis* would be satisfied if we allowed courts to review the constitutionality of only those statutes that (like the one in *Marbury*) pertain to the jurisdiction of the courts.

There may be something providential in the Justice's use here of *Marbury*, for it *can* be argued, with some support in the principles and sources of the Constitution of 1787, that judicial review of Acts of Congress for their constitutionality could properly be limited (I indicate in my *Reflections of Constitutional Law* volume) primarily to review of legislation that purports to deal with the jurisdiction and operations of the Courts of the United States. Of course, *Marbury* was never needed to authorize those Courts (as well as Congress and perhaps the Executive) to review the constitutionality of *State* legislation and other actions by *State* governments.

IX

It is not only Justice Scalia who reveals, in his *Casey* language (with such things as "value judgments"), an inadvertent reliance upon relativism. Something similar may be seen as well in the Opinion of the Court in the same case. Consider, for example, these sentiments:

> Our law affords constitutional protection to personal decisions relating to marriage, procreation, contraception, family relationships, child rearing and education. . . . Our cases recognize "the right of the *individual,* married or single, to be free from unwarranted governmental intrusion into matters so fundamentally affecting a person as the decision whether to bear or beget a child."
> . . . Our precedents "have respected the private realm of family life which the State cannot enter." . . . These matters involving the most intimate and personal choices a person may make in a lifetime, choices central to personal dignity and autonomy, are central to the liberty protected by the Fourteenth Amendment. At the heart of liberty is the right to define one's own concept of existence, of meaning, of the universe, and of the mystery of human life. Beliefs about these matters could not define the attributes of personhood were they formed under compulsion of the State.

Various of the terms relied upon here by the *Casey* Court exhibit the influence of that modern relativism evident in Justice Scalia's language as well. Such terms include "individual," "private," "intimate," "autonomy," and "personhood." All this is reinforced by "the right to define one's own concept of existence, of meaning, of the universe, and of the mystery of life."

It can be revealing that the sovereign activity here is that of "defin[ing] [that is, ordaining?] one's own concept[s]," not that of *discovering* the truth about these and like matters. We are all moderns and hence relativists here, the Supreme Court reveals, with the Self very much in the forefront of our constitutional ruminations. Emblematic of these self-centered developments has been the transformation (discussed in my *Reflections on Freedom of Speech and the First Amendment*) of the traditional "freedom of speech [and] of the press" into "freedom of expression," an aspect of which can be said to be the sometimes desperate efforts to rid oneself of inconvenient pregnancies and even of one's most intimate sexual associates, to say nothing of ridding oneself as well of the traditional demands of citizenship.

6. Capital Punishment and the United States Supreme Court

I

The opening paragraph of the Essay "On Capital Punishment" in my *American Moralist* collection recognizes the enduring issues that can be confronted here:

> The arguments *against* capital punishment in the United States today are in many respects rather dubious. But perhaps even more dubious has always been the case *for* capital punishment. Why is that so? There does seem to be something about this issue which makes it difficult for advocates to be completely persuasive one way or another. One consequence of this is that the issue is never really settled. Even in the days when the issue was hardly one for judicial consideration on constitutional grounds, there was considerable agitation of the issue, if only in the form of pleas for executive clemency in cases where the death sentence had been imposed.

That 1984 introduction to the subject continues thus:

> The question about what should be done about capital punishment is one that simply will not remain answered in this Country today. It is complicated by the fact that those who argue for capital punishment as a public safety measure are inclined to be somewhat open to military adventures and even to the prospects of nuclear war, and by the fact that those who demand an end to capital punishment in the name of the sanctity of life are inclined to be somewhat open to abortion on demand and perhaps even to euthanasia.

The conscientious opponent of capital punishment today does not readily confront the problem implicit in the fact that thoughtful men and women had, for millennia, regarded it as not only permissible but even necessary.

Of course, there have always been protests against particular death sentences that were believed to be unjust. In those instances the challenge might have been as to the guilt of the person condemned. Or questions might have been raised as to whether a death sentence was at all appropriate for the particular action thus punished.

But during the past century the challenge has been more than formerly to the death sentence itself. Perhaps even more of a break with the past has been the attempt, at least in this Country, to abolish capital punishment by recourse to judges rather than to legislators. This approach conceded, in effect, that public opinion in most of our States was not inclined to rule out death sentences altogether.

II

The campaign against capital punishment in this Country led to the 1972 rulings by the United States Supreme Court in *Furman* v. *Georgia* (1972) and related cases. One immediate result of these rulings was the suspension of all executions in the United States for several years. During those years State legislatures and Congress developed laws designed to pass muster with the Supreme Court.

The Opinions in *Furman* ranged across more than two hundred pages in the *United States Reports.* A majority of the Court on that occasion could agree only on a Per Curiam Opinion occupying less than one page in the *Reports.* That Opinion (omitting only its citations to State statutes and to State judicial rulings) reads as follows:

Petitioner in No. 69-5003 was convicted of murder in Georgia and was sentenced to death pursuant to [the Georgia Code] . . . Petitioner in No. 69-5030 was convicted of rape in Georgia and was sentenced to death pursuant to [the Georgia Code] . . . Petitioner in No. 69-5031 was convicted of rape in Texas and was sentenced to death pursuant to [the Texas Penal Code] . . . Certiorari was granted limited to the following question: "Does the imposition and carrying out of the death penalty in [these cases] constitute cruel and unusual punishment in violation of the Eighth and Fourteenth Amendments?" 403 U.S. 952 (1971). The Court holds that the imposition and carrying out of the death penalty in these cases constitutes cruel and unusual punishment in violation of the Eighth and Fourteenth Amendments. The judgment in each case is therefore reversed insofar as it leaves undisturbed the death sentences imposed, and the cases are remanded for further proceedings.

One hundred and thirty pages later is the first of the four Dissenting Opinions in the case, the one by Chief Justice Warren E. Burger, who opens with a useful description of what the Majority had (and had not) done:

> At the outset it is important to note that only two members of the Court, MR. JUSTICE BRENNAN and MR. JUSTICE MARSHALL, have concluded that the Eighth Amendment [which forbids "cruel and unusual punishments"] prohibits capital punishment under all circumstances. MR. JUSTICE DOUGLAS has also determined that the death penalty contravenes the Eighth Amendment, although I do not read his opinion as necessarily requiring the final abolition of the penalty. For the reasons set forth in Parts I–IV of [my] opinion, I conclude that the constitutional prohibition against "cruel and unusual punishments" cannot be construed to ban the imposition of the punishment of death. [Two other Justices] have concluded that petitioners' death sentences must be set aside because the prevailing sentencing practices do not comply with the Eighth Amendment. For the reasons set forth in Part V of [my] opinion, I believe this approach fundamentally misconceives the nature of the Eighth Amendment guarantee and flies directly in the face of controlling authority of extremely recent vintage.

The Chief Justice adds, "If we were possessed of legislative power, I would either join with MR. JUSTICE BRENNAN and MR. JUSTICE MARSHALL, or at the very least, restrict the use of capital punishment to a small category of the most heinous crimes." Then, he goes on to say,

> Our constitutional inquiry, however, must be divorced from personal feelings as to the morality and efficacy of the death penalty,

and be confined to the meaning and applicability of the uncertain language of the Eighth Amendment. There is no novelty in being called upon to interpret a constitutional provision that is less than self-defining, but, of all our fundamental guarantees, the ban on "cruel and unusual punishments" is one of the most difficult to translate into judicially manageable terms. The widely divergent views of the [Eighth] Amendment expressed in today's opinions reveal the haze that surrounds this constitutional command. Yet it is essential to our role as a Court that we not seize upon the enigmatic character of the guarantee as an invitation to enact our personal predilections into law.

III

Chief Justice Burger distinguished, as we have seen, between legislative and judicial judgments as to "the use of capital punishment." Thus, he observed, he as legislator would, like Justices William J. Brennan and Thurgood Marshall, "restrict the use of capital punishment to a small category of the most heinous crimes." What did he rely upon in making such an assessment about what offenses called for capital punishment?

That is, did the Chief Justice not draw here upon considerations that might bear on what should be regarded as "cruel and unusual punishments"? This approach is reflected in what he says immediately after the passages just quoted: "Although the Eighth Amendment literally reads as prohibiting only those punishments that are both 'cruel' and 'unusual,' history compels the conclusion that the Constitution prohibits all punishments of extreme and barbarous cruelty, regardless of how frequently or infrequently imposed." He obviously did not see *himself* "legislating" when he read and applied "cruel and unusual" as he did here.

There is, in what the Chief Justice says here (in an Opinion that is joined by the other three Dissenting Justices), a significant answer to the objection sometimes heard, that the Eighth Amendment cannot be read as permitting the questioning of capital punishment itself since there may be found elsewhere in the Constitution (as in the Fifth Amendment) an acceptance of such punishment. It should be obvious, that is, that most uses of capital punishment in 1791 were not being permanently validated, so to speak, by the Eighth Amendment, no matter how opinions (whether legislative or judicial or that of the people at large) have subsequently changed. Nor, of course, can it be expected that those punishments have to be considered still proper today which were in use in 1689, when there was promulgated the English Bill of Rights from which the "cruel and unusual punishments" language seems to have been taken.

IV

Thus, it was noticed in my 1984 Essay on capital punishment quoted at the outset of this particular discussion,

> [T]he advocates of capital punishment today defend only a very small part of the executions that were once believed necessary and proper, whether as retribution, or as requirement for the defense of society, or as affirmation of the worth of human life. The typical argument for capital punishment today is, in effect, a powerful argument *against* capital punishment both as it has long been practiced and as it is still being practiced in much of the modern world.

The more responsible advocates of capital punishment today emphatically repudiate, as simply unacceptable, many of the practices defended by the greatest thinkers of the past with respect to these matters. They obviously do not look back to 1791 for authoritative guidance as to what offenses should now be punished and how.

Similarly, scholars caution against taking at face value all of the capital offenses catalogued in the Hebrew Bible. We are told that by the time of Jesus very few executions were carried out among the Jews. It seems that "sensibilities" had changed enough to moderate substantially the historic reliance by the Israelites upon capital punishment.

We would not tolerate today the prompt hanging of apprehended horse thieves—or contemporary counterparts. Nor would we tolerate various others forms of corporal punishment (such as flogging or cutting off ears or hands), no matter how prevalent and accepted they might have been somewhere in 1791. That is, we simply would not tolerate in this Country today most of the measures that are now considered intolerable in much of the Western World.

V

It can be instructive to notice, if only in passing, how opinions have changed among us with respect to other deeply controverted issues. Consider, for example, how opinions have changed, in the United States as well as worldwide, with respect to chattel slavery, an institution also recognized (however reluctantly) by the Constitution of 1787. The constitutions and laws of various States in the Union provided for slavery for some four score years.

Not only was slavery provided for in this Country, but it was vigorously defended by citizens as able and as conscientious as the defenders among us today of capital punishment. So distinguished a political thinker as John C. Calhoun could even be moved to speak of slavery as "a positive good." And yet it is rare to find in the Western World today anyone who can be taken seriously as an advocate of chattel slavery.

Adam Smith argued, in his *Wealth of Nations,* that neither the slavery nor the colonies of his day made economic sense for those nominally in control of those institutions. But, he indicated, the desire to enjoy *dominion* over others can induce some people to perpetuate institutions that are clearly not otherwise in their interest. It can be wondered whether something of the passion that Smith discovered with respect to both slaves and colonies may also be found in the conscientious insistence among us today upon capital punishment, no matter what is thought about it elsewhere among peoples apparently as civilized and resolute as we are.

VI

Some among us, including occasional Justices of the United States Supreme Court, argue that *we* should not be bound, in our constitutional adjudications, by what is thought, said, or done elsewhere in the world today. We are counseled, for example, that it should not matter to us (in interpreting and applying the Eighth Amendment) how capital punishment has come to be regarded in other countries. Among the practices of others is the insistence, as a condition for membership in the European Union, upon the abolition of all, or almost all, capital offenses in civil courts.

We can be reminded, by the dismissal of foreign influences, of that deliberate repudiation in *Erie Railroad Company* v. *Tompkins* (1938) of the guidance with respect to how the common law should be developed and applied—the guidance provided by other courts in the English-speaking world. Yet the Declaration of Independence *could* speak of a "decent Respect for the Opinions of Mankind." And the Constitution of 1787 exhibits considerable respect both for the prevailing Anglo-American common law and for the "Law of Nations."

The guidance with respect to "cruel and unusual" provided by the practices of the rest of the world cannot be determined, however, simply by counting. There are still more countries that permit the death penalty than forbid it. But we should consider the troubling implications about the company we keep inherent in such statistics as these found in *The Time Almanac 2000*: "There were 1,625 executions in 1988: of these, 80% were in China (1,067), Congo (100), the United States (68), and Iran (66)."

VII

Of course, the United States is far less efficient than China in carrying out death sentences, as may be seen in the thousands we keep on death row for decades at a time. In addition, American juries (unlike, apparently, the curiously grim Chinese authorities) have evidently become less and less willing to impose death sentences. In this we do seem to be influenced somewhat by what is being said and done in those countries with which we are most sympathetic, especially those in the Western World.

Of course, the decline in reliance upon capital punishment in the Western World has been accompanied by ever greater efficiency in killing people (combatants and noncombatants) in military campaigns. But such killing tends (even in the age of the Internet) to be kept out of sight, while executions receive considerable local publicity, making it more likely that they will be assessed by the public. When someone *is* about to be executed among us, his awful offenses are naturally recalled for that assessment.

There *are*, from time to time, chance candidates for execution, such as Ted Bundy, Larry Eyler, and John Wayne Gacy, whom it is hard even to want to feel sorry for. The abolitionists have to argue, when confronting such monsters, that it is not for *their* sake but, rather, for ours that reliance on capital punishment should be resisted—and that, in fact, such men should be forced to live on because they may simply be better off dead. And especially is all this so when questions are raised with respect to Equal Protection criteria and to adequate representation by counsel in the trials out of which death sentences come (both of which issues will be discussed further on in these *Reflections*).

VIII

The capital punishment abolitionists who have generally prevailed in Europe, evidently against the preferences there of "public opinion," may have been influenced by the carnage of two world wars. Then there were the revelations about the appalling abuses of death sentences seen in the Nazi death camps and in the Stalinist "liquidation" programs (followed up by the ferocious campaigns in China and Cambodia). On the other hand, it is (it can be said) only natural to want to see the monstrous eliminated.

In most such instances, the worst cases, there usually can be no serious questions about the possible innocence of the accused. But is the desire to kill the killer somewhat primitive in its passion? Is it somehow related to the primitiveness of the substantial assurance provided to some among us by owning one's own gun?

It should not be denied, however, that most of those among us who do advocate retaining capital punishment, as well as the right to possess firearms, are decent people. Even so, it should be remembered that the man who was long recognized as the first murderer—and the murderer, indeed, of his innocent, pious brother—had (we are told) his life spared on the highest authority. How should we understand such a dramatic manifestation of divine mercy?

IX

However all this may be, there *was* a moratorium placed on all executions in the United States by the *Furman* Court in 1972. Legislatures did go to work in order to deal with the deficiencies in their laws and practices pointed out by the Supreme Court. The range of capital offenses had to be narrowed, the power of the jury had to be broadened, and the deliberateness and fairness of the relevant processes had to become more evident (even as it has also become ever more evident that it now costs far more to execute a man than to imprison him for life).

The American public, it seems, has remained somewhat in favor of having the capital punishment option available for use in extreme cases.

Even so, there did develop among juries, not without some guidance from the Supreme Court, a greater reluctance to order executions. European opinion continued to disparage American passions with respect to these matters, something reflected even in the occasionally publicized European refusal to extradite an accused to the United States without an official assurance from us that he (upon conviction) will not be at risk of execution.

Executions resumed in the United States in 1977. By late 2005, one thousand executions had been carried out in this Country, almost all of them in the South. It was somehow appropriate, considering the perhaps instinctive character of the urge to kill the killer, that the first execution after the *Furman* respite (it was *not* in the South) was by a method so old-fashioned as a firing squad.

7. Capital Punishment Reconsidered

I

Once American executions resumed in 1977, the principal efforts of abolitionists were devoted to piecemeal critiques of the uses of capital punishment rather than to its complete elimination. It was not likely, after the United States Supreme Court's 7–2 ruling in *Gregg* v. *Georgia* (1976), that capital punishment could soon be stopped altogether, not even temporarily. "The three statutes upheld in 1976 (those from Georgia, Texas, and Florida)," it is recalled in the *Encyclopedia of the American Constitution* (second edition),

> permitted jury sentencing discretion but attempted to reduce the likelihood of abuse to a tolerable minimum. All three statutes . . . embodied procedures intended to impress on judge and jury the gravity of the judgment they are asked to make in capital cases. For example, all three required the sentencing decision to be separated from the decision as to guilt or innocence. In one way or another, all three implied that a sentence of death must be regarded as an extraordinary punishment not to be imposed in an ordinary case, even an ordinary case of first-degree murder.

The *Encyclopedia* observes, "The Court's [1976] decisions were a bitter disappointment not only to the hundreds of persons on death row who now seemingly faced the real prospect of being executed but also to the equally large number of persons who had devoted their time, talent, and in some cases their professional careers to the cause of abolishing the death penalty." It is then said that these abolitionists

> had been making progress toward that end. In other Western countries, including Britain, Canada, and France, the death pen-

147

alty had either been abolished by statute or been allowed to pass
into desuetude; in the United States almost a decade had passed
since the last legal execution. In this context it was easy for the opponents of capital punishment to see the Supreme Court's 1972
[*Furman* v. *Georgia*] decision as a step along the path leading inevitably to complete and final abolition of the death penalty [in
the United States]. This hope was dashed, at least temporarily, in
1976 [with the rulings in *Gregg* v. *Georgia*].

The *Encyclopedia* continues: "Not only did the Court for the first time
squarely hold that 'the punishment of death does not invariably violate
the Constitution' but it also gave explicit support to the popular principle
that punishment must fit the crime and that in making this calculation,
the community may pay back the worst of its criminals with death."

Further on we are told, "This sanctioning of the retributive principle
especially disturbed [Justice Thurgood] Marshall, one of the two dissenters." It is then reported by the author of this *Encyclopedia* entry, "Along
with many opponents of the death penalty, [Justice Marshall] would be
willing to allow executions if they could be shown to serve some useful
purpose—for example, deterring others from committing capital crimes—
but to execute a criminal simply because society 'demands' its pound of
flesh is, he said, to deny him his 'dignity and worth.'" Abolitionists of
capital punishment seem to be left, therefore, in the same position that
abolitionists of abortion are left by other rulings by the Supreme Court:
that is, both abortions and capital punishments are permitted, with abolitionists in each realm having to rely primarily on efforts to narrow the
range of the applications of the Court's rulings.

II

Thus, abortion abolitionists can make much of, say, "partial-birth
abortions." Thus, also, capital punishment abolitionists can make much
of dubious uses of executions. Particularly telling here in both camps of
abolitionists, of course, is the concern about killing the innocent.

The use of DNA testing has led in recent years to the exoneration of
an occasional convict on death row. A series of such reevaluations contributed in Illinois, in 2003, to an exercise of executive clemency that
commuted the sentences of all those (more than one hundred and fifty)

sentenced to death in that State. Death sentences are still recommended by Illinois juries, but the moratorium on executions continued into the term of the next Governors.

No one, it can be generally agreed, would want to execute the innocent. But there can be serious controversies as to how often, and in what circumstances, claims of innocence can be renewed and examined. Of particular concern is how often such reconsiderations can be brought before the Courts of the United States (the Federal Courts) by means of *habeas corpus* petitions.

III

Capital punishment abolitionists, when obliged to narrow the scope of their efforts, have worked to reduce the number of crimes for which death sentences are considered appropriate. The "cruel and unusual punishments" standard can be brought to bear here. Contemporary standards are generally regarded as relevant.

Thus, hardly anyone—certainly no one on the United States Supreme Court—would countenance death sentences for many of the crimes that were considered capital offenses in 1791. Justice Lewis F. Powell, in his Opinion for the Court in *McCleskey* v. *Kemp* (1987), recognized that "where the objective indicia of community values have demonstrated a consensus that the death penalty is disproportionate as to a certain class of cases, we have established substantive limitations on its application." This was said by a Justice who never questioned the constitutionality of death sentences in *some* cases.

Justice Powell, in his *McCleskey* Opinion, noticed three classes of cases for which the Court had ruled that "the death penalty is disproportionate":

In *Coker* v. *Georgia* . . . (1977), the Court held that a State may not constitutionally sentence an individual to death for the rape of an adult woman. In *Enmund* v. *Florida* . . . (1982), the Court prohibited imposition of the death penalty on a defendant convicted of felony murder absent a showing that [he] possessed a sufficiently culpable mental state. Most recently, in *Ford* v. *Wainwright* . . . (1986), we prohibited execution of prisoners who are insane.

Serious doubts have developed, in recent years, about the execution of youngsters, no matter how intelligent they may be. Still other exemptions can be expected in the years ahead, even as the principle of capital punishment is reaffirmed by the Supreme Court.

IV

There has been, in short, a steady narrowing of the range of offenses for which death sentences may properly be sought. But there are still serious problems with the convictions of some, perhaps of most, of those faced with death sentences. Particularly acute are questions about the adequacy of counsel for these defendants.

The large majority of those on death row are represented by usually overworked public defenders. Such services have been hard both to secure and to assess. Consider how a law school classmate of mine, Ramsey Clark, chronicled developments here (in a 1984 Loyola University of Chicago lecture, "The Lawyer's Duty of Loyalty"),

> It is fascinating to read the Scottsboro Boys case, *Powell* v. *Alabama* [1932], and think of Justice [George] Sutherland with his starched collar. He is writing about young men [charged with rape] who were threatened with execution. And he pronounces an extreme and [then] widely condemned principle that in cases like this, where we are dealing with the illiterate, the ignorant, the mentally incompetent and the like, perhaps we should have court-appointed counsel. That Opinion referred only to capital cases. But it did recognize the principle that a lawyer should be able to do better in a court than someone who is ignorant, illiterate, mentally incompetent or the like. By that time we had gone through generations of people standing before the bar in fear without any effective right to counsel.

A general right to counsel in criminal cases, and not only in capital cases, was recognized by the United States Supreme Court in *Gideon* v. *Wainwright* (1963). But serious questions about the adequacy of counsel persist, especially in capital cases. The problems here are suggested by a number of observations by Mr. Clark in his 1984 law school lecture, of which the following is illustrative:

We create public defender offices. We have a major one in New York City. It's called the Legal Aid Society. It was created over a hundred years ago. It has by contract taken on the criminal work in New York City. It does ninety percent of all the criminal work in Brooklyn, which has a lot of criminal work. In all of the years until 1983, no attorney working for the Society had ever filed a workload grievance. . . . In the fall of last year, a lawyer was fired immediately after having represented to courts and to his employer (the Legal Aid Society) that the volume of cases assigned to him was so great that it was impossible for him to provide effective assistance of counsel. He said that the Sixth Amendment to the United States Constitution and Disciplinary Rule Number 2 of the New York Canons of Ethics for attorneys required him to seek relief.

V

It is prudent to remember that most of the people convicted of murder in this Country are rather unattractive people. Some of them *are* moral monsters. Proper representation of such people usually consists of efforts to spare them, and the community, their execution.

But no matter how heinous the crime, the perpetrator, unless he is suicidal in his inclinations, will rarely be executed if his family has the money to finance full representation both at the trial court level and on appeal. Thus, Justice William O. Douglas is quoted (in the *Encyclopedia of the American Constitution*) as saying,

> One searches our chronicles in vain for the execution of any members of the affluent strata in this society. The Leopolds and Loebs are given prison terms, not sentenced to death.

Still, it should be recognized, it must be rare for the wealthy in this Country to commit capital offenses.

However that may be, the obstacles confronting the typical death-case lawyers can be formidable. Consider this recollection by Ramsey Clark (in his 1984 lecture):

I had a death case in Texas. The fellow had been on death row nine years, two hundred and forty-seven days. One of the points on appeal was that the Texas statute provided only $250 for investigation in both the guilt-or-innocent phase and the penalty phase of his trial. The case was tried in an out-of-the-way place. You couldn't get an investigator or anybody else even to go down there for $250, much less to investigate what he was supposed to go down there to learn about. . . . In a notorious murder trial in Houston, Texas, a defendant spent four million dollars in attorneys' fees.

Consider, also, the aspiration set in stone on the facade of the United States Supreme Court building, "Equal Justice Under Law."

VI

Emphasis is placed in these matters, properly enough, upon the rights, interests, and disabilities of those at risk of execution. Questions can be raised about how the relevant evidence was acquired by authorities, what use was made of accomplice testimony (and on what terms), and how it is determined who (among the many available villains) is selected for potential execution. Particularly troubling can be questions about how confessions are secured and what should be made of them, especially when torture is alleged by a defendant.

Legislators, if not also judges, have a duty to consider what the effects are on the community at large of repeated recourse to executions. They have a duty to consider as well what the effects may be on citizen morale of a denial of what is often regarded as healthy retribution. These considerations bear on what may be properly done to "legislate morality."

It can be wondered, of course, how the occasional execution compares in its effects on citizens at large with the multitudes of "killings" witnessed on television screens and the Internet in this Country. Are youngsters made callous by such routine exhibitions, reinforced now (it seems) by gripping video games? Both abortion abolitionists and capital punishment abolitionists can decry "the culture of death" by which we sometimes seem to be mesmerized.

VII

We return, however briefly, to the "cruel and unusual punishments" standard reaffirmed in the Eighth Amendment. How *does* it look when we permit ourselves, because of the thousands we have on death row, to appear to be the most bloodthirsty country in the Western World? Or is it that we should be pitied for appearing ineffectual in our ability to kill as many people as we set out to execute?

Is it a matter of chance, then, not only as to which of our murderers are condemned to death, but also as to who of the condemned are eventually executed? The chance factors here include the State one happens to be in when one's crime is committed. These factors may include as well the ambitions and experience of the prosecutor entrusted with a case.

Is a community less likely to be trapped by the experiences and passions it happens to have if it is indeed sensitive to, if not even guided by, "the Opinions of Mankind"? Is nature more likely to be noticed if worldwide practices are studied and respected? We have no problem appreciating such a question when we learn about social aberrations, such as with respect to the oppressive treatment of girls and women in other countries.

VIII

Perhaps the most dramatic form that questions take in death penalty cases these days is with respect to the discrepancies in the treatment of the races among us. The capital punishment issue in the United States is largely an issue colored by race relations. That is, do we have here a serious Equal Protection problem as well as an Eighth Amendment problem?

This question is addressed in *McCleskey* v. *Kemp* (1987). The Syllabus provided with the Justices' Opinions includes this description of the development of the controversy under review:

> After unsuccessfully seeking post-conviction relief in State Courts, petitioner sought habeas corpus relief in Federal District Court. His petition included a claim that the Georgia capital sentencing process was administered in a racially discriminatory manner in violation of the Eighth and Fourteenth Amendments. In support

of the claim, petitioner proffered a statistical study (the [David C.] Baldus study) that purports to show a disparity in the imposition of the death sentence in Georgia based on the murder victim's race and, to a lesser extent, the defendant's race. The study is based on over 2,000 murder cases that occurred in Georgia during the 1970's, and involves data relating to the victim's race, the defendant's race, and the various combinations of such persons' races.

Although the *McCleskey* Court found the proffered statistical study to be inconclusive, it is likely that the issue of racial discrimination in death penalty proceedings will be developed even further in the coming decades.

Indications of how this issue will be developed are provided by the Dissenting Opinion of Justice Thurgood Marshall in *Furman* v. *Georgia* (1972), which is reinforced by the Dissenting Opinion of Justice William J. Brennan in *McCleskey* (a Dissenting Opinion recognized by the Majority of the Court on that occasion as "eloquent"). It can be sobering to notice that the State of Georgia, with a population of fewer than 7 million people, should have had "over 2,000 murder cases . . . during the 1970's." Perhaps the most reliable relief for African Americans from the racial discrimination that they *may* be subjected to in the criminal justice system will come from their informed use of the voting power inherent in the fact that they make up a quarter of the population of Georgia, which should eventually permit them to influence significantly the selection of legislators, prosecutors, judges, and juries.

IX

Thus, much is to be said for raising in State legislatures and in State courts the issues that litigants try to get the often-overworked United States Supreme Court to resolve. Governors, too, should be encouraged to rely, more than they have in recent decades (except in Illinois), on their clemency powers in death cases. At the State level, that is, there are not the jurisdictional and other hurdles that litigants in the Courts of the United States (that is, the Federal Courts) must face.

Among these obstacles are the efforts made from time to time to restrict *habeas corpus* access to the Courts of the United States, including the United States Supreme Court. State courts and State legislatures do need to be obliged to face up to the critical social problems inherent both in our murder rates and in how alleged murderers are treated in our criminal justice systems. Related to these problems, evidently worsened by an often-misguided "War on Drugs," is that so many African American young men should be enmeshed in the criminal justice system.

We can bring this discussion to a close, for the time being, by drawing again upon the Essay "On Capital Punishment" (in my *American Moralist* collection), from which I have taken (earlier in these *Reflections*) the introductory paragraphs. Here my concluding paragraphs can be drawn on, beginning with this:

> It may well be, then, that the opponents of capital punishment will have the better case in the years immediately ahead, while the advocates of capital punishment will have the better arguments. The opponents may have the better case as reflected in the fact that even the advocates of capital punishment have conceded during the past two centuries that very few of the many offenses once regarded as capital should continue to be treated as such. The advocates of capital punishment may have the better arguments, as perhaps they always have had, in that they do continue to defend an old-fashioned morality, however mistaken they may be in the application of enduring moral principles to the present matter. The advocates of capital punishment tend to be more serious than the opponents of capital punishment about the very same moral principles that have been put to such good use during the past two centuries in staying [at least domestically] the bloody hand of government.

Then there are these suggestions in the closing lines of that 1984 "Capital Punishment" Essay: "Thus, the contest *among us* today is between the ninety percent abolitionists and the one hundred percent abolitionists. That is, the most effective case *against* capital punishment among us today comes from considering carefully the arguments *for* capital punishment, especially when those arguments are compared with the arguments made to that end a century or two ago. In short, there is not such an abolitionist in the nation today as the more thoughtful advocate of capital punishment, after all."

8. Nancy Cruzan and "The Right to Die"

I

An Opinion of the United States Supreme Court, of June 25, 1990, recalls that Nancy Cruzan had been severely injured in an automobile accident on January 11, 1983. She "was discovered lying face down in a ditch without detectable respiratory or cardiac function." "Paramedics," it is further recalled, "were able to restore her breathing and heartbeat at the accident site, and she was transported to a hospital in an unconscious state."

She "remained in a coma for approximately three weeks and then progressed to an unconscious state in which she was able to orally ingest some nutrition." Then, it seems, a critical step was taken: "In order to ease feeding and further the recovery, surgeons implanted a gastronomy feeding and hydration tube in Cruzan with the consent of her then husband." The Supreme Court Opinion continues thus:

> Subsequent rehabilitative efforts proved unavailing. She now lies in a Missouri state hospital in what is commonly referred to as a persistent vegetative state: generally, a condition in which a person exhibits motor reflexes but evinces no indications of significant cognitive function. The State of Missouri is bearing the cost of her care.

The litigation reviewed by the United States Supreme Court in 1989–1990 had developed in this fashion:

> After it had become apparent that Nancy Cruzan had virtually no chance of regaining her mental faculties, her parents asked hospital employees to terminate the artificial nutrition and hydration procedures. All agree that such a removal would cause her death. The employees refused to honor the request without court ap-

proval. The parents then sought and received authorization from the state trial court for termination. The court found that a person in Nancy's condition had a fundamental right under the State and Federal Constitutions to refuse or direct the withdrawl of "death prolonging procedures."

But that was not the end of the matter:

> The Supreme Court of Missouri reversed by a divided vote. The court recognized a right to refuse treatment embodied in the common-law doctrine of informed consent, but expressed skepticism about the application of that doctrine in the circumstances of this case. . . . The [Missouri Supreme Court] also declined to read a broad right of privacy into the State Constitution which would "support the right of a person to refuse medical treatment in every circumstance," and expressed doubt as to whether such a right existed under the United States Constitution. . . . It then decided that the Missouri Living Will statute . . . embodies a state policy favoring the preservation of life. . . . The court found that Cruzan's statements to her roommate regarding her desire to live or die under certain conditions were "unreliable for the purpose of determining her intent," . . . "and [were] thus insufficient to support the co-guardians' claim to exercise substituted judgment on Nancy's behalf."

The United States Supreme Court, by a 5–4 vote (with Chief Justice William H. Rehnquist writing the Opinion of the Court), upheld the ruling by the Missouri Supreme Court.

II

The considerable interest nationwide in the *Cruzan Case* is testified to by a score of briefs filed in the United States Supreme Court by *amici curiae* urging reversal, and a like number urging affirmance, of the Missouri Supreme Court ruling. Also urging affirmance was the Solicitor General of the United States, Kenneth Starr. Longstanding "party lines," not unrelated to the enduring abortion controversy, were evident on both sides during this litigation.

Those urging affirmance generally supported the Missouri Supreme
Court ruling that "no person can assume [the termination-of-medical-
treatment] choice for an incompetent in the absence of the formali-
ties required under Missouri's Living Will statutes or the clear and con-
vincing, inherently reliable evidence absent here." The Opinion of the
United States Supreme Court noticed, with evident approval, that the
Missouri Supreme Court had expressed the view that "[b]road policy
questions bearing on life and death are more properly addressed by representative assemblies" than by judicial bodies. Some Court watchers
came to regret that the United States Supreme Court Majority did not
stand by this anti-activist Court approach a decade later when it was
confronted by that *Bush* v. *Gore* litigation which can be said to have
usurped in 2000 the constitutional duty of Congress to settle contested
Presidential elections.

On the other hand, some Court watchers might well have thought
that the Court could have exhibited in the *Cruzan Case* some of the speed
evident in *Bush* v. *Gore.* Instead the Court waited more than six months,
after hearing oral Argument, before it ruled in *Cruzan,* prolonging thereby the agony of Nancy Cruzan's relatives. The delay probably reflected the
deep division of the Members of the United States Supreme Court on this
occasion.

III

The *Cruzan* Majority in the United States Supreme Court endorsed
the Missouri Supreme Court's presumption in favor of human life. This
approach is identified as deeply grounded in the common law tradition.
There is no reason to believe that the Cruzan family and their advocates
ever questioned this presumption.

But it can be wondered what a truly human life presupposes. It cannot be thought of simply as an indefinite prolongation of mere biological functions. Such prolongation includes, to use the Supreme Court's
formulation, "what is commonly referred to as a persistent vegetative
state."

Questions were raised by the Missouri Supreme Court as to whether
there had been sufficient indication, by the pre-accident Nancy Cruzan, as
to how she would have wanted her body treated. Suppose, however, nothing at all had been available as to her wishes—what should be inferred,

from the circumstances, as to what a rational human being would very likely prefer? Should there not even be, in our circumstances, a presumption, unless someone had explicitly indicated otherwise, that "a persistent vegetative state" should not be permitted to continue for years, no matter who is paying for it?

IV

The odd "player" on this occasion may have been the Missouri Supreme Court, that divided Court whose ruling the United States Supreme Court felt obliged to affirm. It can seem almost perverse that the ruling by a Missouri trial court had not been allowed to stand by the Missouri Supreme Court. It is suspected by some that influential, and ambitious, politicians in the Missouri government had insisted on the appeal to the State Supreme Court.

It seems, in any event, that the case for terminating the Cruzan life-support procedures had been widely regarded as so obvious that no exhaustive effort had been made in the trial court to establish what Nancy Cruzan's pre-accident "preferences" had been. Once the United States Supreme Court had ruled, the disappointed Cruzan counsel decided to exploit this passage in the Chief Justice's Opinion for the Court:

> An erroneous decision not to terminate [life-sustaining treatment] results in a maintenance of the status quo: the possibility of subsequent developments such as advancements in medical science, the discovery of new evidence regarding the patient's intent, changes in the law, or simply the unexpected death of the patient despite the administration of life-sustaining treatment at least create the potential that a wrong decision will be corrected or its impact mitigated. An erroneous decision to withdraw life-sustaining treatment, however, is not susceptible of correction.

Counsel looked particularly to what came to be regarded as an invitation implicit in the reference to "the discovery of new evidence regarding the patient's intent."

This led to still another Missouri trial court hearing, with much more evidence presented as to how the pre-accident Nancy Cruzan had expressed herself about any extended dependence on life-support systems.

And this led in turn to another trial court ruling (by the same judge) permitting Nancy Cruzan's parents to have the treatment of their daughter terminated. The Missouri Supreme Court, perhaps partly because of a growing public sentiment in support of the parents, allowed the substantially reinforced trial court ruling to stand.

V

The United States Supreme Court had suggested that the "maintenance of the status quo" could do no serious harm, aside perhaps from the expense incurred by the State of Missouri. This suggestion ignored, however, such consequences as the agony of parents who could not see their daughter properly buried for almost a decade. This agony, which can remind us of Sophocles' *Antigone,* evidently contributed to the angry despair exhibited in the suicide of Nancy Cruzan's father shortly after his daughter was allowed to finish dying on December 26, 1990.

The responsibility of the United States Supreme Court in such controversies can properly be debated. Perhaps we can see here, however, still another unfortunate consequence of the Supreme Court's abdication, in *Erie Railroad Company* v. *Tompkins* (1938), of its traditional power as the most significant judicial exponent of the common law in the United States. It is that common law, as well as constitutional precepts, that American courts look to in assessing, as the Supreme Court said in *Union Pacific Railroad Company* v. *Botsford* (1891), "the [sacred] right of every individual to the possession and control of his own person, free from all restraint or interference of others, unless by clear and unquestionable authority of law."

Furthermore, it can seem, the United States Supreme Court is empowered to review what may be said by State Supreme Courts (such as that in Missouri) about American constitutional principles. In any event, the United States Supreme Court, when confronted by such issues as those presented to it in the *Cruzan Case,* might even attempt to draw upon the prudence and justice implicit in the common law in order to clarify what it means to be the kind of *person* that the law is obliged to protect. The United States Supreme Court could well have said, in 1990, that it could not be unreasonable for decent people to believe (and to attempt to act on the belief) that Nancy Cruzan had "really" died in early 1983.

VI

Compromised as the response of the United States Supreme Court was in *Cruzan,* even more questionable was Justice Antonin E. Scalia in his Concurring Opinion. He opens with a humane concession, "The various opinions in this case portray quite clearly the difficult, indeed agonizing, questions that are presented by the constantly increasing power of science to keep the human body alive for longer than any reasonable person would want to inhabit it." Does Justice Scalia seem to begin here with the suggestion that a "reasonable person" is to be considered still "inhabit[ing]" in 1990 such a body as Nancy Cruzan had used before January 1983?

Much is made by the Justice, plausibly enough, of the proposition that the United States Supreme Court should leave much of the governance of the Country to legislatures and to State courts. But he nevertheless takes advantage of the opportunity to provide guidance as to how State judges and legislators, among others, should think about what Nancy Cruzan's parents and doctors were trying to do. Thus, he believes it instructive to remind everyone (at some length) that American law, both statutes and the common law, has "criminalized assisted-suicide."

The Scalia sermon against both those who would commit suicide and those who would assist others in doing so can seem rather callous at times, as when he draws on Blackstone to recall, "Suicide was not excused even when committed 'to avoid those ills which [persons] had not the fortitude to endure.'" Still, he does concede, as he prepares to conclude his Concurring Opinion,

What I have said above is not meant to suggest that I would think it desirable, if we were sure that Nancy Cruzan wanted to die, to keep her alive by the means at issue here. I assert only that the Constitution has nothing to say about the subject.

We can suspect, however, that even Justice Scalia, if he had truly recognized that no sensible person would want to have her body kept "alive by the means at issue here," might have found something in the Constitution to use in order to call a halt to the atrocity systematically visited by ideologues for almost a decade upon the Cruzan family.

VII

It was unfortunate for the Nancy Cruzan family in Missouri, as later perhaps for those caught up in the Terri Schiavo family controversy in Florida, that the most influential local political actors chanced to have been who they were. Had Nancy Cruzan chanced to have been afflicted as she was in another State, less than a year would probably have sufficed to "prove" that "her" condition was irreversible. There was even talk in the Cruzan family circle, therefore, about trying to take "her" to another State, where the relevant authorities could be expected to be more sensible.

Of course, a generation earlier there was not available the technology to keep human bodies such as hers on life-support systems for years at a time. Now, we are told, there are in the United States "coma wards" in hospitals and hospices where ten thousand "people" are kept "alive" for extended periods. Such technology can be expected to "improve" in the future.

No doubt, comprehensive legislation will eventually have to be considered, perhaps even by Congress (which funds a substantial part of our medical establishment), to regulate what may and may not be done here. In the process, thoughtful judges should provide guidance, for legislators and other citizens, as to how the law should think about the truly human. Some help may be found in, among other places, the Preamble to the Constitution of 1787 and its Ninth Amendment.

VIII

There may be found expressed, in the Preamble, as in Section 8 of Article I of the Constitution, a concern for the General Welfare. Such a concern could properly encourage assessments of how our vast (and yet often inadequate) expenditures for medical treatment are spent. Similar assessments (not necessarily by judges, of course) could well be made of our ever-growing expenditures for Homeland Security.

It is suggested in Justice William J. Brennan's Dissenting Opinion in *Cruzan* that *this* patient could "remain a passive prisoner of medical technology . . . perhaps for the next 30 years." The Brennan Dissenting Opinion draws on the brief for the American Medical Association as *amici curiae* when it reports,

Out of the 100,000 patients, who like Nancy [Cruzan], have fallen into persistent vegetative states in the past 20 years due to loss of oxygen to the brain, there have been only three even partial recoveries documented in the medical literature.

It is then added by Justice Brennan, evidently drawing on another source, "The longest any person has ever been in a persistent vegetative state and recovered was 22 months."

The community is obliged, as well as entitled, to consider what the best uses of its resources may be with a view to saving lives and enhancing public health. Justice John P. Stevens, in his own Dissenting Opinion in *Cruzan*, quotes from a dissenting opinion in the Missouri Supreme Court: "If [Nancy Cruzan] has any awareness of her surroundings, her life must be a living hell." That Missouri judge also observed, "Nor am I impressed with the crypto-philosophers cited in the principal [Missouri Supreme Court opinion in *Cruzan*], who declaim about the sanctity of any life without regard to its quality."

IX

It is not surprising, therefore, that the position that had originally been taken by the Missouri Supreme Court in *Cruzan* was unusual, if not even unique, among the State courts in this Country. Most judges probably share the national public opinion noticed in the Brennan Dissenting Opinion: "A 1988 poll conducted by the American Medical Association found that 80% of those surveyed favored withdrawal of life-support systems from hopelessly ill or irreversibly comatose patients if they or their families requested it." Whether the authoritative governmental decisions in such matters are made by legislators or by judges, citizens at large can properly invoke constitutional, as well as ethical and political, principles in assessing what is said and done in their name.

It is noticed, by Justice Stevens in his Dissenting Opinion in *Cruzan*, "One learned observer [a medical doctor] suggests, in the course of discussing persistent vegetative states, that 'few of us would accept the preservation of such a reduced level of function as a proper goal for medicine, even though we sadly accept it as an unfortunate and unforseen result of treatment that had higher aspirations, *and even if we refuse actively to cause such vegetative life to cease*'" (emphasis added). One consequence of our general approach to these matters is that the comatose patient, by being taken off life-support systems, is left to starve to death, a "remedy" that many find profoundly disturbing. Whatever may *not* properly be done by medical doctors to hasten death, it needs to be considered by us what *others* may properly do, recognizing as we do so that humane doctors here and there have always done more to hasten death than it is prudent for them or anyone else to publicize.

Of course, the patient in a persistent vegetative condition, if already spiritually "gone," may not "feel" anything—but relatives and friends in attendance may suffer unnecessarily when the "dying" is prolonged. If, however, such "dying" can be deliberately hastened, what about the "situation" of the conscious patient who "has" to endure an excruciatingly painful (and deeply unseemly) death for an extended period? How, in short, should the community regard recourse to and assistance for the hastening of death in such dreadful circumstances?

9. *Washington* v. *Glucksberg* (1997)
and Assisted Suicide

I

It seems to be generally agreed among medical doctors, at least in this Country, that the deliberate withholding or withdrawing of life-sustaining treatments from a terminally ill patient may be neither euthanasia nor assisted suicide. Our State laws regulating medical practice among us generally distinguish between "killing" (which is forbidden) and "letting go" (which is permitted). Furthermore, the American Medical Association guidelines with respect to these matters also seem to permit the use by doctors of "terminal sedation," the administration of an amount of sedation for intense pain which is likely (but which is not *said* to be primarily intended) to shorten the patient's life.

It is recognized that ethical and legal issues here have been complicated by the development of unprecedented means for ministering to the bodies of severely afflicted patients. This could be seen, for example, in the facts provided by the *Cruzan Case* (1990), which dealt (we recall) with a comatose "person" who had been in a "persistent vegetative state" for almost a decade. Particularly troubling for some was the prospect of allowing this "person" to starve to death once life-support systems were disconnected.

Whether the patient in such circumstances is likely to "feel pain" can be debated, but not whether observers do so. Hastening death can be argued for by some not only here but also when a dying patient is conscious of great and unrelenting pain. What may or should a doctor do then, aside from having recourse to the somewhat limited relief and perhaps a hastened death that may be provided by terminal sedation?

II

The Washington State doctors who brought the suit dealt with in the *Glucksberg Case* sought to be authorized to help terminally ill patients who wanted to kill themselves. State law prohibited them (as it did all other persons) from providing such assistance. These were doctors obviously deeply troubled by the pain that their dying patients "had" to endure.

Whatever the distress of these particular doctors, most of their medical colleagues still seem to be opposed to having doctors provide obvious assistance in any suicide attempt. Even more doctors, it seems, are opposed to euthanasia (or mercy killings), something that was *not* directly an issue in the *Glucksberg Case*. The question, answered in the negative in this case, was as to whether the United States Constitution keeps a State from forbidding a doctor (or anyone else) from assisting in the suicide of a desperately ill patient.

There were in this case, as in the *Cruzan Case,* many *amicus* briefs filed, which means that the controversy dealt with here is apt to continue to divide citizens for years to come. To *some* terminally ill patients and to *some* of their champions, so much unrelenting pain can appear to be like torture, especially when it is obvious that someone *could* do something to stop that pain. Indeed, some attending physicians may sometimes feel like torturers when they could readily stop the pain if only they would intervene.

III

The resistance faced by the *Glucksberg* doctors testifies to the settled opinion against suicide in the Western World. The longstanding abhorrence of suicide among us is in marked contrast to what has been thought and done elsewhere. In Japan, for example (as we have seen, in an affair of honor), it can sometimes seem that suicide is called for as the only proper course of action.

Even in the West the repudiation of all suicides was questioned, both in word and in deed, by the Ancient Romans. The examples of Brutus, Cassius, Cato, and Marc Antony come to mind, as does that of Lucretia. But, however much Lucretia could be extolled by the ancients for her heroic self-sacrifice, which is said to have contributed to the overthrow of the Roman Kings and thus to the establishment of the Roman Republic, her conduct could, much later, be condemned by Saint Augustine as woefully misconceived.

Suicide, in the English-speaking tradition, could even come to be condemned as "self-murder" (not simply, as the term itself suggests, "self-killing"). That tradition could (as we have also seen) even lead Blackstone to condemn "the pretended heroism, but real cowardice, of the Stoic philosophers, who destroyed themselves to avoid those ills which they had not the fortitude to endure." It is likely that such condemnations of suicide in Christendom depended, at least in part, on a lively expectation of an unending life to come after death, for which all that we endure now is but a temporary trial.

IV

One is obliged to wonder about the case now made for assisted suicide and for euthanasia when one encounters the deeply felt reservations of some learned scholars. Thus, it can be pointed out by such observers that the suicidally inclined are often depressed people who may not really understand either their prospects or what they ask for. Besides, it is argued, it has always been understood that doctors simply should neither kill nor help others kill human beings.

For doctors to proceed otherwise, it is argued, would weaken the faith that people need to have in their doctors. Physician-assisted suicide, it is argued in the Opinion of the Court in *Glucksberg,* could undermine the trust that is essential to the doctor-patient relationship by blurring the time-honored line between healing and harming. The Court then seems to endorse a thoughtful scholar's observation, "The patient's trust in the doctor's wholehearted devotion to his best interest will be hard to sustain."

But, it might further be wondered, what happens to a patient's trust, and (sometimes even more important) the trust of his family, if the attending physician will not help to stop excruciating (and permanent) pain in what seems to be the only available way? Even so, the serious reservations—indeed deep repugnance—by decent, well-informed observers at the prospect of physician-assisted suicide has to be taken seriously, especially when that repugnance is backed up by centuries of authority and is reinforced by plausible arguments about the risks and abuses to be expected whenever physician-assisted suicides are permitted. Among the risks to be expected, it is argued by the tradition-minded doctor, is that the most vulnerable (but yet not terminally ill) may be manipulated by selfish relatives or others into agreeing to be killed.

V

It is significant that there were no Dissenting Opinions filed by Supreme Court Justices in the *Glucksberg Case.* That the lower court opinion in this and a companion case from New York (*Vacco* v. *Quill* [1997]) were more receptive to the challenges against prohibitions of physician-assisted suicides may reflect a kind of experimentation by "inferior Courts" (who may be somewhat closer to a developing public opinion)—by the judges who count upon the Supreme Court to set matters straight, if need be. The prevailing public opinion of our day still seems to be reflected, however, in the Federal Assisted Suicide Funding Restriction Act of 1997.

Furthermore, it seems to be believed by many observers that physician-assisted suicide would eventually become, if it would not be so from the outset, mercy killing by doctors. And such "mercy killing" still tends to be associated, at least in the Western World, with Nazi Germany (an insane regime recalled in Appendix I of this volume). Thus, the memory of the notorious Dr. Mengele is readily conjured up, however merciless he himself was.

All this is not to deny (we gave noticed) that doctors have "always"— here and there, but most discreetly—done what they could to speed the departure of intensely suffering patients. The use of discretion here (which can mean that it is "cleaner" for the doctor to kill directly than to assist in a suicide) pays deference to the sensibilities and limitations of the community. It may also help restrain those who might not be as prudent as they should be in exercising the great powers with which the medical profession has to be entrusted.

VI

The ambivalence of the public with respect to euthanasia is reflected in a story first published by a London tabloid, in September 2005, about the *agony* of an unnamed New Orleans doctor who was *said* to have given fatal injections to her incapacitated terminally ill patients who "had" to be left behind when the city was evacuated because of Hurricane Katrina.

The details needed to corroborate such a story were not provided at that time. Although this episode probably did not happen as originally reported, it does dramatize the dilemmas that conscientious doctors have always faced in extreme situations.

Guidance in these matters is usually provided by the culture (including the religion) of a people and by the laws that result. Is there also, it can be wondered, a basis in nature for dealing with such matters? Should even the received religion of a people be subjected to the tests that nature suggests?

What do the teachings of natural right/natural law say about these and like matters? This bears on the intended meaning of the Privilege and/or Immunity Clauses of the Constitution and of the Fourteenth Amendment. It also bears on the intended meaning of the Ninth Amendment to the Constitution, a matter to which we shall return.

VII

Is there, in short, a Constitutional issue properly raised when any State or the United States forbids assistance to anyone contemplating suicide, no matter how permanently desperate that patient's circumstances may seem to be? Is one's liberty to manage sensibly one's affairs thereby unreasonably interfered with by those in authority? What, if anything, does the community gain by such a restriction which compensates for the unrelenting torment that dying patients and their families are forced to endure?

It may not be prudent to try to develop and apply general rules in such matters, especially since chance can very much affect the circumstances of patients, their families, and their doctors. The issues here can become difficult to deal with sensibly when either ignorance or demagoguery is permitted to dominate public discourse about such matters. Doctors may have to be depended upon, therefore, to do "the right thing" with a minimum of publicity.

But this dependence presupposes that doctors are properly educated, which means that they can safely be entrusted with powers that can never be fully supervised by the community at large. The same may be said about the lawyers involved in these controversies. Here, as elsewhere, our dependence upon self-governing and reliable professions should be evident.

VIII

It remains to be seen how the 1997 Oregon assisted suicide law will be assessed not only in the courts but also in the Country at large (including in Congress). Concerns about possible abuses helped shape various features of the Oregon law, which has survived (in *Gonzales* v. *Oregon* [2006]) its preliminary (but far from final) assessment by the United States Supreme Court. Thus, the patient who may legally be helped to kill himself in Oregon not only must be a resident in that State but also must be someone who is not expected to live more than six months.

Even more significant is the Oregon provision that the suicide must be by medication provided by the doctor to the patient, who will then have to take it on his own. Concerns have been expressed on behalf of those patients who, though aware of their circumstances, are so far gone that they cannot *do* anything on their own. It seems evident, however, that Oregonians do not yet want doctors (or anyone else?) to do anything that could be seen as directly killing their patients.

A quite different approach may be seen in the Netherlands, where doctors are authorized to kill patients in carefully delineated circumstances. The Dutch experiment remains to be reliably assessed elsewhere. It is an experiment which has aroused considerable concern among European medical people for what it permits doctors to do and which has been repeatedly charged with abuses in its implementation.

IX

The Dutch experiment is not likely to be resorted to in this Country anytime soon, whatever doctors here have "always" quietly done in extraordinary circumstances. Nor is even assisted suicide, as distinguished from euthanasia (or mercy killing), likely to be generally authorized among us. The community at large remains profoundly suspicious, if not even resentful, of anyone who makes use of suicide—and that is not likely to change soon.

Still, the desperation generated by the avoidable "torture" of terminally ill patients must be reckoned with. Desperate patients do sometimes resort to crude forms of suicide, demoralizing everyone around them, if they are not helped to die, and to die soon, "with dignity." Thus, the choice may sometimes be not between "suicide" and "no suicide," but rather between less and more troubling forms of this awesome action, matters touched upon in a *New York Times Magazine* article (of December 2, 2007) reporting on efforts to extend the Oregon practice to Washington State.

The Opinion of the United States Supreme Court in *Vacco* v. *Quill,* argues, "By permitting everyone to refuse unwanted medical treatment while prohibiting anyone from assisting a suicide, New York Law follows a longstanding rational distinction." It is then said by the Court that New York's reasons for recognizing and acting on this distinction are discussed in greater detail in the Court's Opinion in *Glucksberg*. These reasons, which it is probably prudent for legislatures and their constituents (rather than courts and their litigants) to reconsider and revise as circumstances (including public opinion) change, are said to include those of "prohibiting intentional killing and preserving life; preventing suicide; maintaining physicians' role as their patients' healers; protecting vulnerable people from indifference, prejudice, and psychological and financial pressure to end their lives; and avoiding a possible slide towards euthanasia."

10. The Legislation of Morality and the Problem of Pain

I

What can the General Government of the United States properly do to regulate health- and safety-related matters? In what ways may governmental measures take moral issues into account? What, in the development and assessment of such measures, is the status of life-and-death issues?

The concerns here can extend over a wide range of matters, as illustrated by concerns about food safety, the use and abuse of narcotics, medical procedures, firearms possession, and transportation safety. It seems to be generally accepted today that the General Government can substantially regulate activities relating to these and like matters. It is debated, however, whether and how State governments may develop measures on their own, with respect to such matters, measures that somehow seem to conflict with policies pursued by the General Government.

Illustrative of the problems here is the case of *Gonzales* v. *Raich* (2005), which assesses the power of the State of California to authorize, in its Compassionate Use Act of 1996, private access to marijuana for medical purposes, especially in order to relieve persistent excruciating pain. California, which had been (in 1913) one of the first States to restrict the use of marijuana, is now one of at least nine States that have attempted to authorize its use pursuant to the supervision of doctors. The Attorney General of the United States challenged the authority of California to disregard what, it was argued by the Attorney General, was the intent and reach of an Act of Congress prohibiting the private possession and use of marijuana in this Country.

II

The "classic" experiment with the regulation of substance abuse in this Country culminated in the provision, in the Eighteenth Amendment, which prohibited "the manufacture, sale, or transportation of intoxicating liquors within, the importation thereof into, or the exportation thereof from, the United States . . . for beverage purposes . . ." This 1919 amendment was repealed in 1933 by the Twenty-first Amendment, which includes the provision, "The transportation or importation into any State, Territory, or possession of the United States for delivery or use therein of intoxicating liquors, in violation of the laws thereof, is hereby prohibited." State authority to regulate the consumption of intoxicating liquors was thereby recognized and reinforced by the General Government.

It is generally believed that the Eighteenth Amendment, as a national policy, proved unenforceable. It is even said to have been responsible for the development and establishment of Organized Crime in this Country. Furthermore, Prohibition did seem to give attempts to legislate morality a bad name among us.

A concern about the organized resistance by the more vigorous guardians of public morality to repeal the Eighteenth Amendment may be reflected in the directive issued by Congress that the proposal that became the Twenty-first Amendment (unlike all the other amendments proposed before and since) would be submitted for ratification *not* to the State legislatures but rather to "conventions in the several States." It was evidently believed that the organizations seeking to perpetuate Prohibition would have much more influence on State legislatures than on the people at large in the several States. Does *Gonzales* v. *Raich* suggest, on the other hand, that morality-minded organizations may have more influence these days with the General Government than with some State governments?

III

It is generally regarded as understandable, if not even as laudable, that the California legislature tried to do what it did with its Compassionate Use Act. It is obvious that there are many who believe that drugs such as marijuana can sometimes have beneficial effects. It is debated, however, whether a State may authorize the use for medicinal purposes of any substance controlled by Acts of Congress.

The recourse to such permissive legislation in California and elsewhere suggests that this use of marijuana *is* coming to be more or less tolerated, if not generally accepted. Also tolerated, even if not deeply supported, are the efforts of the General Government to control the use of narcotics in this Country. A critical question raised in the *Gonzales* v. *Raich* litigation, therefore, is whether the California legislation improperly interfered with what Congress had done.

Thus, it was argued by the Department of Justice that for a policy to be effective in these matters it must be national in its scope. An extensive reach of the Commerce Clause is very much relied upon here by the General Government. The unilateral effort by California was successfully likened by its critics to that of the independent wheat farmer who was disciplined by the governmental directive upheld in *Wickard* v. *Filburn* (1942).

IV

The *Filburn Case* (which is discussed in my *Reflections on Constitutional Law*) testifies to the extensive powers now widely recognized to have been vested in Congress by the Commerce Clause, especially when reinforced by the Necessary and Proper Clause (also in Article I, Section 8 of the Constitution). The Great Depression can be understood to have taught the lesson that an economic policy, to be effective, has to be national. Thereafter the Cold War and then economic globalization have reinforced that lesson, which seems now to have been reinforced even further by the demands of the "War on Terror," demands which are assessed in the closing Essay of this volume.

Justice Clarence Thomas was very much distressed by these Commerce Clause developments. He opened his Dissenting Opinion in *Gonzales* v. *Raich*:

> Respondents Diane Monson and Angel Raich use marijuana that has never been bought or sold, that has never crossed state lines, and that has had no demonstrable effect on the national market for marijuana. If Congress can regulate this under the Commerce Clause, then it can regulate virtually anything—and the Federal Government is no longer one of limited and enumerated powers.

Of course, whether "the Federal Government" was indeed intended to be "one of limited and enumerated powers" can itself be questioned.

However that may be, it did seem bizarre to Justice Thomas that the

Attorney General of the United States could be concerned about the effect of the California actions on "the national market for marijuana." He observed, further on in his Dissenting Opinion,

> But even assuming that States' controls allow some seepage of medical marijuana into the illicit drug market, there is a multibillion-dollar interstate market for marijuana. . . . It is difficult to see how this vast market could be affected by diverted medical cannabis, let alone in a way that makes regulating intrastate medical marijuana obviously essential to controlling the interstate drug market.

The Justice insisted, again and again, that there may be seen in this controversy improper "assertions [by Congress] of power," with the Congressional aim being "really to exercise police power of the sort reserved to the States . . ."

V

Are there life-and-death issues that need to be addressed nationwide in order to be dealt with effectively? People generally believe this to be so whenever "national security" efforts have to be developed. The same is generally believed about efforts to control life-threatening epidemics, especially when the ease of worldwide traveling contributes to the spread of diseases.

What about "epidemics" that undermine the moral health of a people? It has yet to be generally recognized, for example, how insidious television—first broadcast television, and now cable television—has been in this Country, if not worldwide. The Internet, for all of its achievements in making a tremendous amount of information readily available, threatens to reinforce the questionable effects on us of television.

It seems, in these matters, that local options are apt to have quite limited effects. China and, even more, North Korea provide dubious "models" of the repressive efforts that have to be resorted to in order to keep worldwide "corrupting influences" at bay. It remains to be seen whether our own governments, State and General, can reliably identify and effectively deal with the corrupting influences that ultimately threaten our capacity for effective self-government.

VI

The Dissenting Justices in *Gonzales* v. *Raich* resisted what they considered unacceptable inroads upon Federalism and State Sovereignty. The *Federalist* is drawn on, without a recognition, however, of the vigorously political purpose (in the State of New York) of those newspaper articles of 1787–1788. Indicative of this failure is the insistence upon identifying the authors of those celebrated articles as Alexander Hamilton and James Madison, instead of as that "Publius," who could offer, as needed, sometimes sophistic assurances for New York readers about the limited powers of the General Government provided for in the proposed Constitution.

The unreliability of judicial scholarship is revealed in the unwarranted identification of James Madison, by one of the Dissenting Justices, as "the father of the Constitution." It is such scholarship, for which the Academy is largely responsible, that insists upon seeing the General Government provided by the Constitution of 1787 as a government of quite limited, enumerated powers. And it is such talk that makes invocation of "the original intent" of Constitutional provisions quite unpersuasive these days.

What the Justices generally fail to recognize is that the branch of the General Government that is the most limited in its scope, with its powers distinctly enumerated, is the Judiciary. It probably does not make much sense for the Congress to insist upon comprehensive regulatory control of the distribution and use of narcotics in this Country, to the exclusion of virtually all State control. But it is hardly part of the mandate of the United States Supreme Court to accede to the request of States' Rights advocates that the Court moderate here such an insistence by the General Government.

VII

It can be a matter of chance what the General Government, from time to time, believes itself empowered and obliged to try to control. Consider, for example, the overwhelming response nationwide to the September Eleventh atrocities. And yet, there has long been, year in and year out, far more serious, avoidable damage inflicted upon the American people than that of September Eleventh.

The uses made, and blatantly encouraged to be made, of tobacco and alcohol kill annually tens of thousands among us. The same can be said about highway traffic. And, then, of course, there is the rather immature fascination with firearms among us, so much so that the Mayor of Toronto can lament that life in Canada is seriously threatened because "the United States does not have commonsensical gun laws."

Indeed, the responses made to the September Eleventh attacks have been far more costly for us than the attacks themselves. In such matters, which Courts are hardly in a position to do much (if anything) about, a sense of proportion is needed. Suggestions to that effect may be seen both in the concluding Essay in this volume and in my Letter to the Editor of December 20, 2005, a letter which was provided against the grim background of the multitudes known to have been slaughtered over decades by the Saddam Hussein regime in Iraq:

> What has happened to that Sense of Proportion essential for the development of just and sound policies by this Country? Our President said, on December 12, that about 30,000 Iraqis have died because of our Intervention there in March 2003. This number is equivalent to some 400,000 dead in the United States, a country which is about fifteen times larger in population than Iraq. How would we regard even well-meaning "liberators" who seemed somewhat responsible for a third of a million deaths among us in less than three years? After all, this would be more than the total American combat deaths because of the Second World War.

VIII

The long-term resolution of the medical marijuana standoff is yet to be developed. It was obvious from the outset of this California litigation that the people who found themselves critically in need of relief from permanent pain would usually be able, if driven to it by misguided law-enforcement efforts, to secure marijuana readily from a long-flourishing illegal market. If tormented patients should be arrested for thus relieving unrelenting pain, it will be interesting to see how much deference will be paid by courts and juries to old-fashioned pleas of "necessity."

It can be wondered, of course, whether the Department of Justice should ever have insisted on any national exclusivity with respect to the control of narcotics. Did this make it more likely, in the short-term, that the demands for illegal drugs would grow if the Department succeeded in court? Such demands would have compelling moral claims supporting them, helping to undermine thereby the already troubled "War on Drugs."

Conservatives of Justice Thomas's persuasion might well have wondered why an obviously conservative national administration took the position it did. It was almost as if it had "a death wish" that it could not resist. One result of the Attorney General's initiative was to oblige the Supreme Court, speaking through one of its more liberal members, to recognize once again the extensive power provided Congress by the Commerce Clause, going back in effect to cases such as *Wickard* v. *Filburn* (1942), if not even further back to *Gibbons* v. *Ogden* (1824).

IX

Justice Sandra Day O'Connor recalled, in her apprehensive Dissenting Opinion in *Gonzales* v. *Raich,*

> In [*United States* v.] *Lopez* [1995], we considered the constitutionality of the Gun-Free School Zones Act of 1990, which made it a federal offense "for any individual knowingly to possess a firearm . . . at a place the individual knows, or has reasonable cause to believe, is a school zone." . . . We explained that "Congress' commerce authority includes the power to regulate those activities having a substantial relation to interstate commerce . . . , *i.e.,* those activities that substantially affect interstate commerce."

She further recalled, "The Constitution, we said [in *Lopez*], does not tolerate reasoning that would 'convert Congressional authority under the Commerce Clause to a general police power of the sort retained by the States.'" She was, therefore, moved to protest,

> If the Court is right [in *Gonzales* v. *Raich*], then *Lopez* stands for nothing more than a drafting guide. Congress should have described the relevant crime as "transfer or possession of a firearm anywhere in the nation"—thus including commercial and noncommercial activity, and clearly encompassing some activity with assuredly substantial effect on interstate commerce. Had it done

so, the majority hints, we would have sustained its authority to regulate possession of firearms in school zones. . . . If the Court always defers to Congress as it does today, little may be left to the notion of enumerated powers.

Justice Thomas was even more troubled than was Justice O'Connor by the implications of this marijuana-use ruling. It seems, from the following passage in his Dissenting Opinion in *Gonzales* v. *Raich,* that he believed that the Supreme Court had, in *Lopez,* permanently returned, in effect, almost to a pre–New Deal reading of the Commerce Clause:

> As I explained at length in *United States* v. *Lopez* . . . , the Commerce Clause empowers Congress to regulate the buying and selling of goods and services trafficked across State lines. . . . The Clause's text, structure, and history all indicate that, at the time of the founding, the term "commerce" consisted of "selling, buying, and bartering, as well as transporting for these purposes." . . . Commerce, or trade, stood in contrast to productive activities like manufacturing and agriculture.

It had long been apparent to some students of Supreme Court adjudication, however, that it was not likely (whatever the merits of the gun-control law considered there) that the *Lopez* retrenchment would stand if it really meant that the United States would have the only national government in the world unable to deal comprehensively with the advanced economy of its Country.

It can seem somewhat odd that a concern about the immoral use of narcotics, even to alleviate intense physical pain, should have led a "conservative" national administration to promote litigation which restored the reach of the Commerce Clause to what "liberals" have long insisted upon. Even so, there does remain here a remedy that "conservatives" *can* endorse, the remedy of an insistence by the People (if so inclined) that Congress permit the States to provide for supervised use of marijuana by the certifiably desperate. Thus, the Opinion of the Court, in its concluding paragraph, reminds everyone that there is still available, in such situations as the one in California, "the democratic process, in which the voices of voters allied with these respondents may one day be heard in the halls of Congress."

11. Evolution and the Law

I

The evolution controversy, which finds its way into our courts from time to time, is in large part about how to understand and deal with life, death, and the prospects of human beings generally. Such inquiries are at the heart of this constantly recurring controversy, which bears upon intriguing questions about the meaning of life, questions noticed in my 2007 Essay (appended to my *Bible* book) "Yearnings for the Divine and the Natural Animation of Matter." What, if anything, can be done to settle this issue, or at least to "contain" it, perhaps even putting it thereby to good use?

Virtually all "working" biologists worldwide, we are told, accept the current forms of the Darwinian evolutionary account. There seems to be, despite sometimes sharp differences among them, substantial agreement about how the development of life-forms on Earth, over millions of years, probably took place. Evolutionary biologists generally agree, it also seems, that human beings and other species of animals are descended from bacterialike ancestors.

There are of course, among those who do appear knowledgeable about the biological sciences, some who question the presuppositions and implications of evolutionary biology, particularly with respect to the ultimate origins of the human soul. On the other hand, prominent biologists insist that such critics have not identified any significant problems in evolutionary theory. It is said, that is, there is nothing in their criticisms that can be taken seriously, nor do they offer any alternative suggestions that can be tested or otherwise usefully investigated.

II

An early legal controversy in this Country with respect to evolution was the 1925 Scopes Trial, "the Monkey Trial," in Dayton, Tennessee. The

State legislature had prohibited public school instructors from teaching "any theory that denies the story of the Divine Creation of man as taught in the Bible, and to teach instead that man has descended from a lower order of animals." The trial shortly thereafter of a Dayton high school teacher became something of a carnival, drawing considerable national attention.

The constitutionality of the Tennessee statute was upheld by the Supreme Court of the State in 1927, after the accused was convicted and fined $100. That Court, however, reversed the conviction on the ground that the jury and not the judge should have assessed the fine. Since, by that time, the accused was no longer in the State's employ, the Tennessee Supreme Court, seeing "nothing to be gained by prolonging the life of this bizarre case," directed that a *nolle prosequi* be entered, in the interests of "the peace and dignity of the State."

This case did not do the faithful much good in the eyes of intellectuals; nor did it do intellectuals much good in the eyes of the faithful. Of all the prominent players on that occasion, the Tennessee Supreme Court may have come off best. Evidently nothing more was ever done, in Tennessee, with the statute relied upon in the Scopes Trial, a statute which was repealed in 1967.

III

But Arkansas picked up where Tennessee left off. And *its* statute, unlike Tennessee's 1925 *Scopes Trial* statute, was eventually assessed by the United States Supreme Court in *Epperson v. Arkansas* (1968). The Opinion of the Court on that occasion, delivered by Justice Abe Fortas, opens with this description of the controversy:

> This appeal challenges the constitutionality of the "anti-evolution" statute which the State of Arkansas adopted in 1928 to prohibit the teaching in its public schools and universities of the theory that man evolved from other species of life. The statute was a product of the upsurge of "fundamentalist" religious fervor of the twenties. The Arkansas statute was an adaptation of the famous Tennessee "monkey law" which that State adopted in 1925. . . . The Arkansas law makes it unlawful for a teacher in any state-supported school or university "to teach the theory or doctrine

that mankind ascended or descended from a lower order of animals," or "to adopt or use in any such institution a textbook that
teaches" this theory. Violation is a misdemeanor and subjects the
violator to dismissal from his position. The present case concerns
the teaching of biology in a high school in Little Rock.

"In the present case," the Opinion by Justice Fortas for the Court in
Epperson went on to explain,

> there can be no doubt that Arkansas has sought to prevent its
> teachers from discussing the theory of evolution because it is con-
> trary to the belief of some that the Book of Genesis must be the
> exclusive source of doctrine as to the origin of man. No sugges-
> tion has been made that Arkansas law may be justified by consid-
> erations of State policy other than the religious views of some of
> its citizens. It is clear that fundamentalist sectarian conviction was
> and is the law's reason for existence.

The Justice quotes at this point from an advertisement that, he says, was
"typical of the public appeal which [had been] used in the campaign to
secure (by public initiative) the adoption of the [Arkansas] statute" forty
years before:

> All atheists favor evolution. If you agree with atheism vote against
> Act No. 1. If you agree with the Bible vote for Act No. 1. . . .
> Shall conscientious church members be forced to pay taxes to sup-
> port teachers to teach evolution which will undermine the faith
> of their children? The [*Arkansas*] *Gazette* said Russian Bolsheviks
> laughed at Tennessee [because of the Scopes Trial]. True, and that
> sort will laugh at Arkansas. Who cares?

The United States Supreme Court, speaking through Justice Fortas, explained its disposition of this case thus:

> [We] do not rest our decision upon the asserted vagueness of the
> statute. On either interpretation of its language, Arkansas' stat-
> ute cannot stand. It is of no moment whether the law is deemed
> to prohibit mention of Darwin's theory, or to forbid any or all

of the infinite varieties of communication embraced within the term "teaching." Under either interpretation, the law must be stricken because of its conflict with the constitutional prohibition of state laws respecting an establishment of religion or prohibiting the free exercise thereof. The overriding fact is that Arkansas' law selects from the body of knowledge a particular segment which it proscribes for the sole reason that it is deemed to conflict with a particular religious doctrine; that is, with a particular interpretation of the Book of Genesis by a particular religious group.

On the other hand, the overriding fact here for Justice Hugo L. Black was that there did not seem to be a genuine controversy before the Court. He therefore opened his Concurring Opinion thus (there were no dissents on this occasion):

I am by no means sure that this case presents a genuinely justiciable case or controversy. Although Arkansas Initiated Act No. 1, the statute alleged to be constitutional, was *passed by the voters of Arkansas* in 1928, we are informed that there has never been even a single attempt by the State to enforce it. And the pallid, unenthusiastic, even apologetic defense of the Act presented by the State in this Court indicates that the State would make no attempt to enforce the law should it remain on the books for the next century. Now, nearly 40 years after the law has slumbered on the books as though dead, a teacher alleging fear that the State might arouse from its lethargy and try to punish her has asked for a declaratory judgment holding the law unconstitutional. . . . But whether this Arkansas teacher is still a teacher, fearful of punishment under the Act, we do not know. It may be, as has been published in the daily press, that she has long since given up her job as a teacher and moved to a distant city, thereby escaping the dangers she had imagined might befall her under this lifeless Arkansas Act. [Emphasis added.]

Justice Black has provided in the passage just quoted the comic touch that the *Evolution Cases* can inspire, at least in this Country, concluding his Concurring Opinion in this fashion:

Certainly the Darwinian theory, precisely like the Genesis story of the creation of man, is not above challenge. In fact, the Darwinian theory has not merely been criticized by religionists but by scientists, and perhaps no scientist would be willing to take an oath and swear that everything announced in the Darwinian theory is unquestionably true. The Court, it seems to me, makes a serious mistake in bypassing the plain, unconstitutional vagueness of this statute in order to reach out and decide this troublesome, to me, First Amendment question. However wise this Court may be or may become hereafter, it is doubtful that, sitting in Washington, it can successfully supervise and censor the curriculum of every public school in every hamlet and city in the United States. I doubt that our wisdom is so nearly infallible.

IV

After *Epperson* v. *Arkansas,* the anti-evolution people could no longer remain on the offensive, forbidding the teaching of Darwinism in the public schools. Nor, it seems, could they adapt to their own cause the advice given by Justice Black in *Epperson,* that the issue simply be let alone. What they did, instead, was to seem to go on the defensive.

Their defense, in its most provocative form, was to demand "equal time" in schools for non-evolutionary accounts in biology (not, say, in literature) courses. But what was it "equal time" to do, besides simply (and somewhat naively) discounting evolution as "only a theory"? One current approach is to emphasize the problems that evolutionary biology has not adequately solved, shortcomings that seem to depend substantially, however, on what professional biologists have discovered and hence are themselves aware of.

Another approach is to offer a radically different account of the origins of life, and especially of human life. One such alternative account was offered as "Creation Science," which was defined (in a Louisiana statute) as "the scientific evidences for creation and inferences from those scientific evidences." Still another account, also offered in opposition to contemporary evolutionary biology, is "Intelligent Design," which builds on the argument that various attributes of living organisms, especially human beings, are of such a complexity as to be incapable of explanation unless contributions by an Intelligent Being are recognized.

V

The consequences of much-dramatized litigation can sometimes be far less than the engaged opponents might believe. This may even be true, for example, of the sometimes fierce abortion controversy in our courts. We have noticed that the abortion rates in various European countries, including "Roman Catholic" countries such as Italy and Poland, are quite high—but this is not because judges *there* have invalidated anti-abortion legislation.

Is it not likely that worldwide developments in the study of biology will continue as they have, regardless of what an American legislature or court here and there might say or attempt to do? One can be reminded here of the folly of the attempt centuries ago to repudiate Galileo, an attempt that the Roman Catholic Church eventually apologized for. It is perhaps significant that the charge this time is *not* being led, or (it seems) even supported, by the Vatican, but rather by "Fundamentalist" Protestants who consider themselves conservatives.

A debate ("Conservatives, Darwin and Design") in the November 2000 issue of *First Things* concluded with these comments by an evidently Christian conservative scholar (a fellow-traveler of contemporary biologists):

> To infer that the laws of nature point to God as the First Cause of these laws is a reasonable position. Such thinking is implied in the traditional appeal in American political thought to "the laws of nature and of nature's God." It is also compatible with Darwinism. Indeed, theistic evolutionists . . . see no necessary conflict between theistic religion and Darwinian science. But [some proponents of "Intelligent Design theory"] are not satisfied with this. Do they believe that the "intelligent designer" must miraculously intervene to separately create every species of life and every "irreducibly complex" mechanism in the living world? If so, exactly when and how does that happen? By what observable causal mechanisms does the "intelligent designer" execute these miraculous acts? How would one formulate falsifiable tests for such a theory? Proponents of "intelligent design theory" refuse to answer such questions, because it is rhetorically advantageous for them to take a purely negative position in which they criticize Darwinian

theory without defending a positive theory of their own. That is why they are not taken seriously in the scientific community. And that is why it would be a big mistake for conservatives to think that "intelligent design theory" offers a serious scientific alternative to Darwinism.

The "theistic evolutionists" questioned here are sometimes reminded that the marvels of modern medicine, upon which we all depend, are said by medical researchers to be very much grounded in "Darwinism." What, indeed, should be made of various remarkable claims by contemporary biology researchers, such as that 92 percent of our genes are also those of the giraffes, and that 98 percent are also those of the chimpanzees?

VI

Twenty years after *Epperson* v. *Arkansas* the anti-evolutionists do seem to have contented themselves, in the laws they develop, with defensive measures. First, there were the efforts made on behalf of Creation Science described in the Syllabus provided in the *United States Reports* for *Edwards* v. *Aguillard* (1987):

> Louisiana's "Creation Act" forbids the teaching of the theory of evolution in public elementary and secondary schools unless accompanied by instruction in the theory of "creation science." The Act does not require the teaching of either theory unless the other is taught. It defines the theories as "the scientific evidences for [creation and evolution] and inferences from those scientific evidences."

Justice William J. Brennan, in the Opinion of the Court in this case, observed,

> It is clear from the legislative history [here] that the purpose of the legislative sponsor . . . was to narrow the science curriculum. During the legislative hearings, [he] stated: "My preference would be that neither [creationism nor evolution] be taught." . . . Such a ban on teaching does not promote—indeed, it undermines—the provision of a comprehensive scientific education.

Justice Brennan explained, "We do not imply that a legislature could never require that scientific critiques of prevailing theories be taught." "But," he went on to say, "because the primary purpose of the [Louisiana] Creationism Act is to endorse a particular religious doctrine, the Act furthers religion in violation of the Establishment Clause." Justice Antonin E. Scalia's Dissenting Opinion on that occasion included these useful reminders:

> [P]olitical activism by the religiously motivated is part of our heritage. Notwithstanding the majority's implication to the contrary, . . . we do not presume that the sole purpose of a law is to advance religion merely because it was supported strongly by organized religions or by adherents of particular faiths. . . . To do so would deprive religious men and women of their right to participate in the political process. Today's religious activism may give us the [Louisiana] Balanced Treatment Act, but yesterday's resulted in the abolition of slavery, and tomorrow's may bring relief for famine victims.

Since "Creation Science" was dealt with as it was in *Edwards,* the efforts of anti-evolutionists have been diverted (we have noticed) to the promotion of "equal time" for "Intelligent Design," which however seems to its critics essentially "Creation Science" with a change of nomenclature resorted to with a view to passing Constitutional muster—and as such is not likely to fare better in the courts. Besides, the proponents of these alternatives to standard evolutionism cannot yet offer much scientific material of their own which would occupy the "equal time" that is asked for. It does not suffice, that is, simply to remind students of the difficulties in contemporary biology, difficulties that (as we have also noticed) competent biologists have often first exposed to public view and that they are best equipped (as well as usually motivated) to examine and explain.

VII

This is not to deny that there *are* difficulties with biology, as with much of modern science, that scientists often neglect (difficulties glanced at in Appendix H of this volume). It would probably be healthy for scientists to be challenged, more than they are, to examine, and to explain from time to time, their First Principles and Methods. It could be instructive, for example, for them to notice, and to consider the implications of having, the apparent sanctification of the principle of self-preservation at the heart of modern evolutionism.

Chance may determine what particular science threatens (or seems to threaten) deeply held beliefs of a religious character. In different circumstances, demands might be made for "equal time" for other alternatives—such as equal time for astrology whenever astronomy is taught, or equal time for faith-healing whenever medicine is taught—and here, too, various things taught about astronomy and medicine can be disparaged as merely "theories." Even so, we live and risk dying, every day, acting on fairly well-established and obviously useful "theories."

It may be, in fact, that much more threatening to traditional religious beliefs, at least in the Western World, are not the reported discoveries of biology but rather those of astrophysics. Thus, the implications of a "theory" that insists upon at least a fourteen-billion-year time span for the universe and a census of hundreds of billions of galaxies—the implications of all this can be staggering for those of us (that is, many, if not even most, of us) raised with the assurance that what is all-important (perhaps even to some Superintending Intelligence) is what happens to one animal species on one planet. Against the awesome cosmic background that is now offered us, the possibility that a Creator made use of evolutionary biology to develop the human species is far less threatening than it might have once seemed as a challenge to conventional piety.

VIII

However all this may be, Intelligent Design is likely to go the way of Creation Science in the Courts of the United States, a development anticipated by a United States District Court in the Pennsylvania case *Kitzmiller* v. *Dover Area School District* (2005). Whatever the merits of these particular disciplines insofar as they *are* sciences, religious conservatives, or fundamentalists, should not permit themselves to appear to be identified with sham sciences, or with intellectual contrivances designed to serve other than the scientific interests they are identified with. Certainly they should take care not to be regarded as incompetents (or as Know-Nothings).

Nor should fundamentalists permit themselves to be identified with repressive, or illiberal, politics. It is possible that they, in the long run, will find themselves a distinct minority even in this Country. As such they will want to enjoy the privileges of freedom of speech, not only protecting themselves thereby but also continuing to instruct others about the Good in ways that perhaps only they can do on a substantial scale.

Even more important for them, again in the long run, may be the assurance that Church and State continue to be usefully separated in this Country. Thus, they should not have to risk suffering someday from efforts by others to impose unwelcome sectarian dogmas on the community at large in some plausible guise. In such circumstances our present-day fundamentalists could find themselves grateful for such cases as *West Virginia State Board of Education* v. *Barnette* (1943), *Epperson* v. *Arkansas* (1968), and even *Edwards* v. *Aguillard* (1987).

IX

It is only prudent to recognize as well the proper uses to be made of fundamentalists and fundamentalism at this time. Of use here may be a talk I made in 1981, "The Moral Majority: The New Abolitionists?" (included in my *American Moralist* collection). The Moral Majority was a vigorous fundamentalist movement of that day, decisively conservative in its inclinations.

My 1981 talk, to the liberal Elijah Lovejoy Society in St. Louis, Missouri, included these remarks:

> The abolitionists of Abraham Lincoln's day and the Moral Majority of our day share various attributes that I should like to examine with you. For one thing, each group has been dubious about various orthodox constitutional interpretations of its day and about the political "establishment." I need not dwell, before this society, upon the obvious merits of the old abolitionists. They were deeply troubled by the evil of African slavery in this Country. They did not see slavery withering away. It seemed to them rather to be growing, and the repeal of the Missouri Compromise, the resort to "Popular Sovereignty," and the *Dred Scott* decision all seemed to confirm their fears of an ever more vigorous expansion of the slave power on the North American continent. The abolitionists invoked something deep in the human soul and in the American regime, a regime with roots in the "created equal" language of

the Declaration of Independence. They struck out against slavery and even against the Constitution, laws and compromises or deals which, it seemed to them, made slavery possible if not even permanent. Yet the abolitionist position could be seen by a Lincoln as in some ways making matters worse. For one thing, it threatened to abandon the Southern States to slavery and to a revived slave trade, unimpeded by the Government of the United States.

Further on, in that 1981 talk, I made these suggestions about how fundamentalists should be regarded:

> The question remains, then, of how it is best for liberals to deal with these people and their inevitable successors over the years, to deal with them even if these people may be in principle against "deals." Their moral concerns and calls for "moral sanity" should be respected and made use of; their naivete and errors should be anticipated and guarded against. There is, I repeat, something healthy in their old-fashioned appeal, however self-righteous and hence self-defeating it may all too often seem. Certainly they should not be responded to in such a way as to make the cause of morality even more fragile than it is today. The more enlightened among us should not permit moral concerns to be left to the unenlightened, just as patriotism and the flag were left not too many years ago. It would also be salutary for the enlightened to remind the community that morality can be considerably more complicated than the Moral Majority makes it out to be. For one thing, morality should include a lively concern for social justice and for peace, about which too the Bible, as well as sound politics, has a good deal more to say than one would gather from the pronouncements of the curiously self-centered Moral Majority.

That 1981 talk concluded with an endorsement of temperance:

> Temperance in discourse reflects the recognition that this is bound to be an imperfect world and that we must often choose between unattractive alternatives. We as citizens really have to trust our fellow Americans to be sensible most of the time, and to be patient

as we wait for the pendulum to swing our way, when the time seems out of joint, as it no doubt does seem to be on occasion.

I have already noticed, in passing, a problem with the virtual sanctification by modern evolutionism of the principle of self-preservation (which was anticipated by thinkers such as Thomas Hobbes). This is a problem that was delved into during the course of the following exchange I had, during a 1969 symposium at the National Institutes of Health in Bethesda, Maryland—an exchange (endorsed, Leon Kass tells us, by an astute observer, Hans Jonas) about survival and the Good with B. F. Skinner, who was something of an evolutionist:

> **GA:** . . . You used, on at least two occasions [in comparing us moderns with the ancients], the notion of progress, that "we" are better than "they." I find that heartening because any serious notion of progress has some place, if only dimly, an awareness of what *the best* is. Are you prepared to say there *is* a best? **BFS:** I thought I was addressing that question in my talk this afternoon. There are ways in which we act to make things, as we call them, "better," and we do say that this is good and that is not good, and so on, and I suppose that if you have good and better, you have a best, but the notion of the evolution of a species or of culture never gives you the opportunity of foreseeing the final state. If it's a question of eschatology, I pass. **GA:** May I comment on that? Look, you can't talk about the better or the good without a notion of the best. I think you do have a notion of the best. I think you have a notion of the best by which you guide your life and on which your own comments just now are based. Your notion of the best, I think, whether you recognize it or not, is a full development of the human reason, primarily with a view to understanding man and the world around him. I think that's your secret best. If that is so, then we can begin to talk seriously about which societies, which cultures, are more apt to contribute to that, and which ones are less apt to contribute to that. We don't talk about survival as [the basis for] judgment. For instance, you observed that survival is the only value by which we will be judged. That simply is not true. That is not a fact. We know—we look back over ancient "cultures" (as we call them) and we see

some that we judge and judge very highly, and by any ordinary notion of survival, they have failed, compared to the trivial or bestial, barbaric culture that overwhelmed them. And yet I think *you* would say that they were better than the ones that conquered them. If you don't say it, I think that you would have serious problems talking about progress. If you *do* say it, then, as I say, we can begin talking seriously about what makes for the best man, what the proper questions are and how one goes about discovering what [the answers to] those questions are. **BFS:** I take survival to be a value only in a survival framework, and if you like to call that begging the question, you can. . . . You can't judge a culture simply by choosing those particular features that you admire, and say that Greek culture was great because of its law and its scripture and so on. It was extremely weak in many respects and it happened to be weak because it overlooked the fact that it made itself extraordinarily attractive to barbarians, and that was a weakness. . . . In the long run, I think the culture which abandons its interest in surviving is not going to survive and in that sense it is a weak culture, and not a good culture.

All this, too, bears upon ever-intriguing questions about the meaning of life, an inquiry that can well take into account such glorious non-"survival"-minded proclamations as, "Give me liberty, or give me death!"

12. Life and Death in Abraham Lincoln's Gettysburg Address

I

Abraham Lincoln's speech upon the dedication in 1863 of the cemetery at Gettysburg, Pennsylvania, can remind us of the funeral speech that was said by Thucydides to have been given, for those who had died in battle, by Pericles in Athens at the end of the first year of the Peloponnesian War. Pericles' speech, we have seen in Part One of these *Reflections*, keeps death out of sight. He, in a speech several pages in length, refers explicitly to death only once, and even then (we have also seen) to no more than an "unfelt death."

Lincoln, in a speech of fewer than three hundred words, begins by speaking of providing "a final resting place for those who gave their lives." Thereafter he speaks of the "living and dead," of "those honored dead," and of the resolve "that these dead shall not have died in vain." The dead that Pericles must deal with are Athenians, while Lincoln's dead (so far as can be gathered from his overall policy) includes Southerners (buried elsewhere) as well as the Northerners buried here.

The fact of human mortality poses a challenge not only for human beings personally but also for the institutions they depend upon to sustain themselves. One senses that Pericles' reticence about death reveals something troubling about his understanding of "the human condition." This reticence may have something to do with the general opinion among Athenians that their *polis* had always been, that it was somehow rooted in the soil of Attica, unlike the other *poleis* of Greece, which were believed to have been founded centuries before by immigrants.

II

Lincoln's "funeral" speech recognizes from its outset that his community had a known historical beginning. It recognizes as well that the very existence, or perpetuation, of this community has been threatened. That is, its mortality and hence its vulnerability are implicit in that it *was* born.

This community is referred to, at the outset of the speech, as *a nation* which had been "brought forth on this continent" by "our fathers." The use by Lincoln of "nation" has him tacitly reaffirming thereby the insistence of Unionists that the United States was more than the "compact," or "contract," or "federation" that the Secessionists were insisting upon. This is confirmed by the use, in effect, of 1776 (rather than, say, of 1787 or 1789) as the date of birth for this Nation.

The Union, Lincoln had said many times before, is older than the States. Robert E. Lee, on the other hand, could speak of Virginia as his *country,* but such nomenclature must have been difficult to use with respect to States known to have been fashioned and authorized (after 1789) by the General Government. The transformation over which Lincoln presided may be suggested by the fact that *Nation* is never used in the Constitution and *Union* (which *is* used there several times) is never used in the Gettysburg Address.

III

The Secessionists were dubious not only about terms such as *nation,* but also about the suggestion that one's sovereign community rested upon anything but blood ties. They seemed to resist any notion that one's country depended at all upon an idea or doctrine. Particularly threatening wherever slavery was found, it could seem, was the notion that "all men are created equal."

Lincoln's invocation of that language presents the Nation as rooted in the Declaration of Independence. But there the "created equal" assertion had been confidently identified as a "self-evident" truth. By Lincoln's time it had become no more than a "proposition," something to be tested, which "a great civil war" had had to do.

Decades of efforts by many in defense of slavery—an institution that was no longer generally recognized in the United States (as Lincoln insisted it had once been recognized) as "in the course of ultimate extinction"—made it difficult to continue to regard the "created equal" assertion as a self-evident truth. This is partly why it had become, for practical purposes, no better than a proposition to be demonstrated. Such testing was to be done not only by the use of arguments but also by the use of arms.

IV

Propositions very much depend upon words. But this is a time for those deeds which will resurrect a vital truth of 1776 that had come to be questioned. This means, among other things, "The world will little note, nor long remember what we say here, but it can never forget what they did here."

We know, of course, that the Lincoln speech at Gettysburg in November 1863 is remembered much better than the three-day battle there the previous July. Deeds without words tend to be (or to become) senseless, however important they may appear to be at the time. The words of Lincoln, especially the Gettysburg Address and his Second Inaugural Address, have done much "to make sense" of that grand deed we know as the Civil War.

If the right kind of deed is properly explained, the self-evidentness, or inherent truth, of the "created equal" language can be once again recognized. Does Nature itself support such a truth? Is it nevertheless a truth that is more readily recognized at some times than it is at others?

V

Pericles, although a leader of the more popular party in Athens, was aristocratic in his origins, while Lincoln was obviously plebeian in *his* origins. The appeal to the common man may be seen in Lincoln's characterization of the requisite deeds as "work" and "task." Such work can be said to have been "*nobly* advanced" by the warriors at Gettysburg, which expression provides an aristocratic veneer for their deeds.

The common touch—the humanity of this enterprise—is further suggested by the absence in this speech of all proper names. The universality of what this Nation is understood to mean is thereby reinforced. This elevation of the plebeian tacitly supports the assertion in 1776 that "all Men are created equal."

The central words of the Gettysburg speech are found in the sentence, "The brave men, living and dead, who struggled here, have consecrated [this ground], far above our poor power to add or detract." Even so, the "power to add or detract" can identify what is truly praiseworthy not only in the sacrifices that may be made, but also in the cause eliciting such sacrifices. We have seen how the even greater sacrifices in Europe of the First

World War, for which the military tactics of the American Civil War can be said to have prepared the way, came to be corrosive for decades thereafter because that war could not be talked about, in an enduring fashion, the way that the American Civil War could be, no matter how lofty the Wilsonian vision had once seemed to be.

VI

Properly directed and explained work leads to the decisive confirmation and rededication of a regime. This naturally culminates in "government of the people, by the people, for the people," a formulation evidently adapted by Lincoln from something said a generation earlier by Daniel Webster. This can even be understood as an explication of that "Republican Form of Government" affirmed in Article IV of the Constitution of 1787.

A government, to be "of the people," has to be drawn from the people—that is, it somehow or other has to be authorized by them. To be "by the people," it has to be a government conducted by them, directly or indirectly. And to be "for the people," it has to be conducted primarily for their benefit.

Lincoln had many times said that the regime for which they were struggling was one that provided opportunities for all to develop fully their capacities. His own career testified to what could be done, consistent with the limits placed by one's mortality. Such testimony could be provided by him in responses to regiments that serenaded him at the White House, suggesting to common soldiers that their own sons could accomplish what his father's son had done.

VII

Slavery was to be restricted and eventually eliminated as a denial of a principle vital to the American regime, that "all men are created equal." It was in part a matter of chance, worldwide, who was enslaved and where. Slavery, because of its presuppositions and influence, could be seen to enslave both masters and servants.

Nothing is said explicitly about slavery in the Gettysburg Address. The vindication of the principle that "all men are created equal" and the reaffirmation of "government of the people, by the people, for the people" left no place for slavery in the system that would survive the war. The Emancipation Proclamation, of January 1, 1863, had significantly advanced that complete abolishment of slavery that was to be furthered by the Thirteenth Amendment of 1865.

The constitutional system for which Lincoln and his allies stood had been anticipated by generations of Americans. Thus, almost four score years before, it had been said by Publius in the opening paragraph of *Federalist,* No. 1:

> It has been frequently remarked that it seems to have been reserved to the people of this country, by their conduct and example, to decide the important question, whether societies of men are really capable or not of establishing good government from reflection and choice, or whether they are forever destined to depend for their political constitutions on accident and force.

We should notice here, even before the Constitution of 1787 was ratified, the use of "country" to identify the United States.

VIII

We should notice as well the recognition by Publius, here as elsewhere in the *Federalist,* of the unpredictable elements that *are* to be reckoned with in human affairs. This is inevitable for mortal beings. Even so, salutary use can be made of "reflection and choice" not only in establishing but also in conducting "good government."

This nation, Lincoln asserts, was "conceived in Liberty." Without *some* liberty, reflection and choice would be quite limited, sometimes leaving one only with the option of death as something that can be chosen. An exercise of liberty may be seen in how "the brave men, living and dead," had conducted themselves on this and other battlefields of the war, contributing thereby to "a new birth of freedom."

The use first of "conceived" and then of "new birth" may invite Lincoln's audience to compare "Liberty" and "freedom." A communal-minded *freedom* may connote more of reflection and restraint than does a more individualistic *liberty.* Popular government may be seen thereby to be properly disciplined.

IX

Both Pericles and Lincoln see their respective "cities" as models for the world. Thus, Athens is "the school of Greece" and the United States (or, at least, what it stands for) "shall not perish from the earth." Cultural and political durability can serve thereby as a check on mortality.

Lincoln argues that a purgation of the crippling compromise with slavery opens up an indefinite future for the Nation. This development is reflected in how the speech as a whole is organized. I have had occasion to describe it in this fashion (in my *Abraham Lincoln* book):

> The structure of the sentences Lincoln employed in sketching this development reflects and reinforces the content. The sentences get generally shorter and shorter, down to, "It is altogether fitting and proper that we should do this." We reach the dedication for which they had gathered, having moved "down" from the continent to a nation on that continent to a battlefield in that nation to a portion of that field. Then the movement is reversed; from here to the end, there is an expansion in sentence lengths, heralded by, "But, in a larger sense." The sentences get longer and longer—as does the dedication of the Country, which had theretofore contracted—and the scope of vision becomes larger: he moves from a "portion of that field" to "the earth." The time with which he deals also expands, moving from "four score and seven years" and the contest over whether this government "can long endure" to the recitation of deeds that will never be forgotten and to the expression of the determination that this government "not perish from the earth." This sense of expansion is reinforced by the final sentence, the last of ten, which contains almost one-third of the entire address. This sentence, which marches steadily along to the drumbeat of a high proportion of one- and two-syllable words, runs on and on, as if forever.

The qualification "as if forever" suggests the salutary illusions upon which a healthy political order may depend. The audience is reminded of "the unfinished work" left by "the brave men, living and dead," who had fought not only here but everywhere in the war. It is perhaps salutary as well that such work be described as "unfinished," *not* as that "unfinishable" state of things which may indeed be the prospect of mortal beings.

13. The Unseemly Fearfulness of Our Time

I

A proper caution, particularly in the form of defensive measures, is to be encouraged in our affairs. We do tend to be enough aware of our mortality to take precautions. Recklessness is certainly to be avoided.

There is provided in my 1971 treatise, *The Constitutionalist,* a detailed examination of principles vital to the American regime. The sources and applications of these principles are examined. Those principles, especially with respect to the First Amendment guarantee of "freedom of speech [and] of the press," seemed to be undermined then because of desperate Cold War concerns in recent decades.

The apprehensiveness exhibited at times was hardly edifying. This is not to deny the ferociousness of Stalinist regimes, in Russia and elsewhere, but there were better and worse ways of responding to such threats. Particularly troubling were those responses in this Country that tended to make sensible measures on our part less likely.

II

Our sometimes crippling Cold War responses went back, for important doctrinal justification, to Justice Oliver W. Holmes's ill-conceived Opinion for the United States Supreme Court in *Schenck* v. *United States* (1919). His talk in *Schenck* about such things as a "clear and present danger" was brought to bear on efforts to justify the suppression during the Cold War of "conspiracy" and "subversion." Since September 11, 2001, the campaign against "terrorism" and "Islamic fascism" has sometimes looked for inspiration and authority to Cold War measures.

However misconceived some of our Cold War measures were, they did have in the Soviet Union a formidable adversary, or at least a potential adversary, to contend with. An anticipation of our current misconceptions is indicated in my first prepared remarks in response to the monstrous attacks of September Eleventh. Those remarks, of September 12th, addressed to a law school audience, were entitled, "A Second Pearl Harbor? Let's Be Serious."

It was already evident that day, it seemed to me, that the worst damage we would suffer in the months and years ahead would be self-inflicted. That has certainly been true of the economic reverses endured by us. Even more serious has been our moral, or spiritual, damage, illustrated by the campaign led in 2005 by the Vice President of the United States to block Congressional efforts to forbid American use (directly or by proxies) of torture, restraining efforts led by a Senator who had himself been tortured for several years by the North Vietnamese.

III

It was obvious in September 2001 that any regime that had permitted the development of the September Eleventh plot would have to go. It probably would have been prudent to regard the resulting campaign in Afghanistan as primarily a police action. This would have served as a sufficient warning to any regime anywhere that might harbor criminal activities aimed at the United States.

Our antidrug campaigns in South America should remind us of the limits of "nation-building" even by a great power. The obstacles in Afghanistan are even more formidable, something that can be testified to by both the British and the Russians after their experiences in that land during the past two centuries. Even so, American casualties in Afghanistan have been far less than those in Iraq.

The longer we stay and suffer in Iraq, the harder it is to justify our 2003 Intervention. The best that can be said for this adventure is that it began as a sincere invocation of Wilsonian idealism against a bloodthirsty tyrant. But as a defensive measure on behalf of the United States, it has been a dubious undertaking, not least because Iraq now seems to have been turned (with our help) into a remarkably productive breeding ground of suicidal terrorists.

IV

Of course, if Iraq had truly been as powerful as we sometimes made it out to be, we would never have invaded it. Our different responses to

Iraq and to North Korea (which is sometimes believed to possess usable nuclear weapons) instructs vulnerable regimes worldwide as to the safety that may come with any publicized acquisition by them of nuclear weapons. This is a lesson that the Iranians seem to have taken to heart, along with what they see as an opportunity, because of the American Intervention in Iraq, to ally themselves as Shiites with the prospective Shiite regime in that country.

For the United States, the price of the Iraqi Intervention continues to mount. It soon cost far more in lives, resources, and worldwide respect than was anticipated. Nor has it been edifying to see the domestic apprehensiveness displayed by citizens of the most powerful nation in the history of the world.

Such assessments do not excuse those, sick of soul, who planned and executed the September Eleventh attacks, no matter what grievances they believed themselves to have had against the United States and the West. However crafty these attackers may have been, they did not seem to recognize how much they would undermine the standing of their cause among civilized peoples everywhere. Also, there may even be survivors of the Taliban government in Afghanistan who recall warnings that must have been given by some among them against allowing preparations on their soil of an insanely provocative sneak attack on the United States.

V

Our primary concern in these matters should be with what has happened among citizens of the United States. It has been far from edifying to have the remarkably costly silliness we have seen in the measures devoted to domestic security, measures that have sometimes been developed with the use of a strategy that seems to include the deliberate manipulation of scare tactics. Comfortable Americans have been encouraged to recognize their mortality in a particularly corrosive manner.

We can be reminded, upon surveying these matters, of the limits of any political regime, no matter how well-ordered it may be. Thus it is argued, in the concluding chapter of *The Constitutionalist,* that the dismal Cave depicted in Book VII of Plato's *Republic* could be taken to represent even "the best regime" (ruled by philosophers) described by Socrates in that dialogue. That is, critical to the limits of any regime is the awareness that people generally have of their mortality, something which can make them apprehensive about anything that seems to threaten their comfort, to say nothing of their very existence.

Even so, there *are* better and worse ways of responding to the dangers that we are likely to encounter. Certainly, it is unbecoming to be as intimidated as we sometimes appear to be (and as we are all too often stimulated to be) by the plots of the evil-minded. Clear thinking is the key to being able to recover from our mistakes and to keep to a minimum our inevitable vulnerability as human beings.

VI

The analysis provided in *The Constitutionalist* of Cold War delusions can help us assess what is being said and done these days. It is curious to see that some of the people who were deceived by our Vietnamese delusions have lived long enough to be taken in as well by rhetoric conjured up for the current Iraqi Intervention. Unless one is a pacifist, a position that is difficult to maintain in all circumstances, one must be discriminating in how one responds to calls for armed intervention by the United States.

Even when such intervention seems justified, or at least justifiable, there can be, as in Korea in 1950, better and worse ways to conduct the necessary operations. On the other hand, passivity in the face of extreme provocation can be demoralizing, as happened when American diplomatic personnel were held for months by "revolutionaries" in Teheran. It would probably have been more prudent, for the long run, if an ultimatum backed up by the prospects of discriminating aerial bombardment had been issued by the United States government, even if that had put at greater risk the lives of the hostages themselves (as well as the lives of innocent Iranians).

Miscalculations of risks can make a people less equipped than they could be to deal with the serious challenges they do face. For example, it should have been apparent, to any visitor to Russia in the 1950s and 1960s, how weak it was, something that should have encouraged us to be more sensible in preparing properly for how to deal with that country (with its vast store of nuclear bombs and other weapons of mass destruction) once its regime collapsed. The surprising thing about the Soviet Union was not that it collapsed when it did, but rather that it somehow managed (with our "help"?) to survive as long as it did.

VII

It is not generally appreciated how much of a fluke the September Eleventh "successes" were. Any number of things could have gone "wrong," especially with so many people involved in the plot. It was particularly remarkable that so many conspirators should have been able to keep their rather complicated plans and activities so secret for years, suggesting thereby the ethnic, ideological, and other ties among them.

All of their plotting depended on the expectation that they could secure ready access to airliner cockpits, where they could convert airplanes into manned missiles. Once airliner cockpits were secured (or were *believed* to be secured) against such takeovers by anyone using primitive weaponry, it was no longer possible to plan as the September Eleventh perpetrators had done. This means, among other things, that most of the vast resources devoted to commercial airport security in this Country could be directed to far better uses, such as the detection of so-called suitcase nuclear bombs and the like.

Thus, a major concern among us should *not* be with the safety of commercial airliners, however sobering it can be to have one of them destroyed by explosives smuggled on board or by missiles fired from the ground. The costs of reducing completely (or almost completely) all the risks that may chance to threaten us are too great to be sensible. Here, as with our stupendous Cold War expenditures and as with the considerable Iraqi Intervention costs, much better uses can be made of our resources, uses that truly strengthen us at home and that earn us a useful respect abroad.

VIII

A recognition among us of an inevitable vulnerability can be salutary, a vulnerability that accompanies human life itself and that may be deepened by the kind of life we much prefer to have. After all, one man, perhaps acting alone, with, say, a rented truck filled with readily available fertilizer, can easily kill several hundred people. After all, also, natural catastrophes can suddenly kill tens of thousands of people far less equipped than we are to respond with restorative measures whenever *we* are afflicted.

In short, it is worth repeating that what is needed by us is *a sense of proportion* in assessing and responding to the dreadful things we are likely to encounter from time to time. Of course, such losses can seem even more threatening when deliberately done to us by other human beings.

But that is no reason for serving the purposes of evil men by crippling ourselves, in an ever more destructive manner, by how we respond to the wickedness we encounter.

The best defense, in the long run, is an informed awareness of our own virtue, an awareness that is not paralyzed in its effectiveness by an unbecoming apprehensiveness. That the United States is still able, despite all its shortcomings, to attract the rest of mankind is testified to by the efforts that have to be made by us to keep out multitudes of illegal immigrants. A properly informed, self-confident people can be particularly effective in exposing, by precept and by example, the wickedness and woeful ignorance that have always had to be reckoned with all over the world.

IX

It can be instructive to recall how the People of the United States allowed themselves to be misdirected and misused as they were during the Cold War. But it is also instructive to notice one critical difference this time around—and that is the fact that the freedom to discuss and criticize governmental measures remains substantially unabridged, except perhaps for some people in this Country identifiable as Middle Easterners. Vigorous criticisms can be, and are, leveled against all aspects of the way we went to war in Iraq and of how that war and the subsequent occupation (along with its incipient civil war) have been conducted.

These criticisms can include observations about the scandalous unwillingness of "the elites" who have taken us to war to devote either their sons or much of their treasure to the current campaign. Current criticisms can even include reminders of how some of our most hawkish leaders today were able to avoid combat service during the Vietnam War, a dubious war that they and their families were in favor of only if other people's sons were conscripted to fight it. So long as such, and more serious, criticisms may be made, the deeply rooted good sense of the American People can eventually be expected to assert itself properly in assessing what is being done and why.

It is such good sense that can consider properly how human mortality is to be understood. This consideration both encourages and permits us to identify what kind of life is truly worth having and how it might best be secured. It is thus, with a minimum of fearfulness, that we can put to the best possible use our natural desire for genuine self-preservation.

Appendix A

The Declaration of Independence (1776)

In CONGRESS, July 4, 1776.
A DECLARATION
By the REPRESENTATIVES of the
UNITED STATES OF AMERICA,
In GENERAL CONGRESS ASSEMBLED.

When in the Course of human Events, it becomes necessary for one People to dissolve the Political Bands which have connected them with another, and to assume among the Powers of the Earth, the separate and equal Station to which the Laws of Nature and of Nature's God entitle them, a decent Respect to the Opinions of Mankind requires that they should declare the causes which impel them to the Separation.

We hold these Truths to be self-evident, that all Men are created equal, that they are endowed by their Creator with certain unalienable Rights, that among these are Life, Liberty, and the Pursuit of Happiness—That to secure these Rights, Governments are instituted among Men, deriving their just Powers from the Consent of the Governed, that whenever any Form of Government becomes destructive of these Ends, it is the Right of the People to alter or to abolish it, and to institute new Government, laying its Foundation on such Principles, and organizing its Powers in such Form, as to them shall seem most likely to effect their Safety and Happiness. Prudence, indeed, will dictate that Governments long established should not be changed for light and transient Causes; and accordingly all Experience hath shewn, that Mankind are more dis-

Sources: See *The Declaration of Independence and the Constitution of the United States,* 96th Cong., 1st sess., House Document No. 96-143 (Washington, D.C.: Government Printing Office, 1979). See also, George Anastaplo, *The Constitution of 1787: A Commentary* (Baltimore: Johns Hopkins University Press, 1989), 235, 239–44. See, as well, George Anastaplo, *Abraham Lincoln: A Constitutional Biography* [preferred title, *Thoughts on Abraham Lincoln: A Discourse on Prudence*] (Lanham, Md.: Rowman & Littlefield, 1999), 1–38.

posed to suffer, while Evils are sufferable, than to right themselves by abolishing the Forms to which they are accustomed. But when a long Train of Abuses and Usurpations, pursuing invariably the same Object, evinces a Design to reduce them under absolute Despotism, it is their Right, it is their Duty, to throw off such Government, and to provide new Guards for their future Security. Such has been the patient Sufferance of these Colonies; and such is now the Necessity which constrains them to alter their former Systems of Government. The History of the present King of Great-Britain is a History of repeated Injuries and Usurpations, all having in direct Object the Establishment of an absolute Tyranny over these States. To prove this, let facts be submitted to a candid World:

He has refused his Assent to Laws, the most wholesome and necessary for the public Good.

He has forbidden his Governors to pass Laws of immediate and pressing Importance, unless suspended in their Operation till his Assent should be obtained; and when so suspended, he has utterly neglected to attend to them.

He has refused to pass other Laws for the Accommodation of large Districts of People, unless those People would relinquish the Right of Representation in the Legislature, a Right inestimable to them, and formidable to Tyrants only.

He has called together Legislative Bodies at Places unusual, uncomfortable, and distant from the Depository of their public Records, for the sole Purpose of fatiguing them into Compliance with his Measures.

He has dissolved Representative Houses repeatedly, for opposing with manly Firmness his Invasions on the Rights of the People.

He has refused for a long Time, after such Dissolutions, to cause others to be elected; whereby the Legislative Powers, incapable of Annihilation, have returned to the People at large for their exercise; the State remaining in the mean time exposed to all the Dangers of Invasion from without, and Convulsions within.

He has endeavoured to prevent the Population of these States; for that Purpose obstructing the Laws for Naturalization of Foreigners; refusing to pass others to encourage their Migrations hither, and raising the Conditions of new Appropriations of Lands.

He has obstructed the Administration of Justice, by refusing his Assent to Laws for establishing Judiciary Powers.

He has made Judges dependent on his Will alone, for the Tenure of their Offices, and the Amount and Payment of their Salaries.

He has erected a Multitude of new Offices, and sent hither Swarms of Officers to harass our People, and eat out their Substance.

He has kept among us, in Times of Peace, Standing Armies, without the consent of our Legislatures.

He has affected to render the Military independent of and superior to the Civil Power.

He has combined with others to subject us to a Jurisdiction foreign to our Constitution, and unacknowledged by our Laws; giving his Assent to their Acts of pretended Legislation:

For quartering large Bodies of Armed Troops among us:

For protecting them, by a mock Trial, from Punishment for any Murders which they should commit on the Inhabitants of these States:

For cutting off our Trade with all Parts of the World:

For imposing Taxes on us without our Consent:

For depriving us, in many Cases, of the Benefits of Trial by Jury:

For transporting us beyond Seas to be tried for pretended Offences:

For abolishing the free System of English Laws in a neighbouring Province, establishing therein an arbitrary Government, and engaging its Boundaries, so as to render it at once an Example and fit Instrument for introducing the same absolute Rule into these Colonies:

For taking away our Charters, abolishing our most valuable Laws, and altering fundamentally the Forms of our Governments:

For suspending our own Legislatures, and declaring themselves invested with Power to legislate for us in all Cases whatsoever.

He has abdicated Government here, by declaring us out of his Protection and waging War against us.

He has plundered our Seas, ravaged our Coasts, burnt our Towns, and destroyed the Lives of our People.

He is, at this Time, transporting large Armies of foreign Mercenaries to compleat the Works of Death, Desolation, and Tyranny, already begun with circumstances of Cruelty and Perfidy, scarcely paralleled in the most barbarous Ages, and totally unworthy the Head of a civilized Nation.

He has constrained our fellow Citizens taken Captive on the high Seas to bear Arms against their Country, to become the Executioners of their Friends and Brethren, or to fall themselves by their Hands.

He has excited domestic Insurrections amongst us, and has endeavoured to bring on the Inhabitants of our Frontiers, the merciless Indian

Savages, whose known Rule of Warfare, is an undistinguished Destruction, of all Ages, Sexes, and Conditions.

In every stage of these Oppressions we have Petitioned for Redress in the most humble Terms: Our repeated Petitions have been answered only by repeated Injury. A Prince, whose Character is thus marked by every act which may define a Tyrant, is unfit to be the Ruler of a free People.

Nor have we been wanting in Attentions to our British Brethren. We have warned them from Time to Time of Attempts by their Legislature to extend an unwarrantable Jurisdiction over us. We have reminded them of the Circumstances of our Emigration and Settlement here. We have appealed to their native Justice and Magnanimity, and we have conjured them by the Ties of our common Kindred to disavow these Usurpations, which, would inevitably interrupt our Connections and Correspondence. They too have been deaf to the Voice of Justice and of Consanguinity. We must, therefore, acquiesce in the Necessity, which denounces our Separation, and hold them, as we hold the rest of Mankind, Enemies in War, in Peace, Friends.

We, therefore, the Representatives of the UNITED STATES OF AMERICA, in General Congress, Assembled, appealing to the Supreme Judge of the World for the Rectitude of our Intentions, do, in the Name, and by Authority of the good People of these Colonies, solemnly Publish and Declare, That these United Colonies are, and of Right ought to be, Free and Independent States; that they are absolved from all Allegiance to the British Crown, and that all political Connection between them and the State of Great-Britain, is and ought to be totally dissolved; and that as Free and Independent States, they have full Power to levy War, conclude Peace, contract Alliances, establish Commerce, and to do all other Acts and Things which Independent States may of right do. And for the support of this Declaration, with a firm Reliance on the Protection of divine Providence, we mutually pledge to each other our Lives, our Fortunes, and our sacred Honor.*

[Signatures omitted.]

*Richard Henry Lee, of Virginia, had introduced in the Continental Congress, on June 7, 1776, the following resolution proposing the issuance of a declaration of independence and thereafter the adoption of articles of confederation:

"*Resolved*, That these United Colonies are, and of right ought to be, free and independent States, that they are absolved from all allegiance to the British Crown, and that all political connection between them and the State of Great Britain is, and ought to be, totally dissolved.

"That it is expedient forthwith to take the most effectual measures for forming foreign Alliances.

"That a plan of confederation be prepared and transmitted to the respective Colonies for their consideration and approbation."

Appendix B

The United States Constitution (1787)

The Constitution of the United States

We the People of the United States, in Order to form a more perfect Union, establish Justice, insure domestic Tranquility, provide for the common defence, promote the general Welfare, and secure the Blessings of Liberty to ourselves and our Posterity, do ordain and establish this Constitution for the United States of America.

Article. I.

Section. 1. All legislative Powers herein granted shall be vested in a Congress of the United States, which shall consist of a Senate and a House of Representatives.

Section. 2. The House of Representatives shall be composed of Members chosen every second Year by the People of the several States, and the Electors in each State shall have the Qualifications requisite for Electors of the most numerous Branch of the State Legislature.

No person shall be a Representative who shall not have attained to the Age of twenty five Years, and been seven Years a Citizen of the United States, and who shall not, when elected, be an Inhabitant of that State in which he shall be chosen.

Representatives and direct Taxes shall be apportioned among the several States which may be included within this Union, according to their respective Numbers, which shall be determined by adding to the whole Number of free Persons, including those bound to Service for a Term of

Sources: See *Documents Illustrative of the Formation of the Union of the American States*, 69th Cong., 1st sess., House Document No. 398 (Washington, D.C.: Government Printing Office, 1927). See also, George Anastaplo, *The Constitution of 1787: A Commentary* (Baltimore: Johns Hopkins University Press, 1989), 236, 266–79. See, on constitutionalism, George Anastaplo, *The Constitutionalist: Notes on the First Amendment* (Dallas: Southern Methodist University Press, 1971; Lanham, Md.: Lexington Books, 2005).

Years, and excluding Indians not taxed, three fifths of all other Persons. The actual Enumeration shall be made within three Years after the first Meeting of the Congress of the United States, and within every subsequent Term of ten Years, in such Manner as they shall by Law direct. The Number of Representatives shall not exceed one for every thirty Thousand, but each State shall have at Least one Representative; and until such enumeration shall be made, the State of New Hampshire shall be entitled to chuse three, Massachusetts eight, Rhode-Island and Providence Plantations one, Connecticut five, New-York six, New Jersey four, Pennsylvania eight, Delaware one, Maryland six, Virginia ten, North Carolina five, South Carolina five, and Georgia three.

When vacancies happen in the Representation from any State, the Executive Authority thereof shall issue Writs of Election to fill such Vacancies.

The House of Representatives shall chuse their Speaker and other Officers; and shall have the sole Power of Impeachment.

Section. 3. The Senate of the United States shall be composed of two Senators from each State, chosen by the Legislature thereof, for six Years; and each Senator shall have one Vote.

Immediately after they shall be assembled in Consequence of the first Election, they shall be divided as equally as may be into three Classes. The Seats of the Senators of the first Class shall be vacated at the Expiration of the second Year, of the second Class at the Expiration of the fourth Year, and of the third Class at the Expiration of the sixth Year, so that one third may be chosen every second Year; and if Vacancies happen by Resignation, or otherwise, during the Recess of the Legislature of any State, the Executive thereof may make temporary Appointments until the next Meeting of the Legislature, which shall then fill such Vacancies.

No Person shall be a Senator who shall not have attained to the Age of thirty Years, and been nine Years a Citizen of the United States, and who shall not, when elected, be an Inhabitant of that State for which he shall be chosen.

The Vice President of the United States shall be President of the Senate, but shall have no Vote, unless they be equally divided.

The Senate shall chuse their other Officers, and also a President pro tempore, in the Absence of the Vice President, or when he shall exercise the Office of President of the United States.

The Senate shall have the sole Power to try all Impeachments. When sitting for that Purpose, they shall be on Oath or Affirmation. When the

President of the United States is tried, the Chief Justice shall preside: And no Person shall be convicted without the Concurrence of two thirds of the Members present.

Judgment in Cases of Impeachment shall not extend further than to removal from Office, and disqualification to hold and enjoy any Office of honor, Trust or Profit under the United States: but the Party convicted shall nevertheless be liable and subject to Indictment, Trial, Judgment and Punishment, according to Law.

Section. 4. The Times, Places and Manner of holding Elections for Senators and Representatives, shall be prescribed in each State by the Legislature thereof; but the Congress may at any time by Law make or alter such Regulations, except as to the Places of chusing Senators.

The Congress shall assemble at least once in every Year, and such Meeting shall be on the first Monday in December, unless they shall by Law appoint a different Day.

Section. 5. Each House shall be the Judge of the Elections, Returns and Qualifications of its own Members, and a Majority of each shall constitute a Quorum to do Business; but a smaller Number may adjourn from day to day, and may be authorized to compel the Attendance of absent Members, in such Manner, and under such Penalties as each House may provide.

Each House may determine the Rules of its Proceedings, punish its Members for disorderly Behaviour, and, with the Concurrence of two thirds, expel a Member.

Each House shall keep a Journal of its Proceedings, and from time to time publish the same, excepting such Parts as may in their Judgment require Secrecy; and the Yeas and Nays of the Members of either House on any question shall, at the Desire of one fifth of those Present, be entered on the Journal.

Neither House, during the Session of Congress, shall, without the Consent of the other, adjourn for more than three days, nor to any other Place than that in which the two Houses shall be sitting.

Section. 6. The Senators and Representatives shall receive a Compensation for their Services, to be ascertained by Law, and paid out of the Treasury of the United States. They shall in all Cases, except Treason, Felony and Breach of the Peace, be privileged from Arrest during their Attendance at the Session of their respective Houses, and in going to and returning from the same; and for any Speech or Debate in either House, they shall not be questioned in any other Place.

No Senator or Representative shall, during the Time for which he was elected, be appointed to any civil Office under the Authority of the United States, which shall have been created, or the Emoluments whereof shall have been encreased during such time; and no Person holding any Office under the United States, shall be a Member of either House during his Continuance in Office.

Section. 7. All Bills for raising Revenue shall originate in the House of Representatives; but the Senate may propose or concur with Amendments as on other Bills.

Every Bill which shall have passed the House of Representatives and the Senate, shall, before it become a Law, be presented to the President of the United States; If he approve he shall sign it, but if not he shall return it, with his Objections to that House in which it shall have originated, who shall enter the Objections at large on their Journal, and proceed to reconsider it. If after such Reconsideration two thirds of that House shall agree to pass the Bill, it shall be sent, together with the Objections, to the other House, by which it shall likewise be reconsidered, and if approved by two thirds of that House, it shall become a Law. But in all such Cases the Votes of both Houses shall be determined by Yeas and Nays, and the Names of the Persons voting for and against the Bill shall be entered on the Journal of each House respectively. If any Bill shall not be returned by the President within ten Days (Sundays excepted) after it shall have been presented to him, the Same shall be a Law, in like Manner as if he had signed it, unless the Congress by their Adjournment prevent its Return, in which Case it shall not be a Law.

Every Order, Resolution, or Vote to which the Concurrence of the Senate and House of Representatives may be necessary (except on a question of Adjournment) shall be presented to the President of the United States; and before the Same shall take Effect, shall be approved by him, or being disapproved by him, shall be repassed by two thirds of the Senate and House of Representatives, according to the Rules and Limitations prescribed in the Case of a Bill.

Section. 8. The Congress shall have Power

To lay and collect Taxes, Duties, Imposts and Excises, to pay the Debts and provide for the common Defence and general Welfare of the United States; but all Duties, Imposts and Excises shall be uniform throughout the United States;

To borrow Money on the credit of the United States;

To regulate Commerce with foreign Nations, and among the several States, and with the Indian Tribes;

To establish an uniform Rule of Naturalization, and uniform Laws on the subject of Bankruptcies throughout the United States;

To coin Money, regulate the Value thereof, and of foreign Coin, and fix the Standard of Weights and Measures;

To provide for the Punishment of counterfeiting the Securities and current Coin of the United States;

To establish Post Offices and post Roads;

To promote the Progress of Science and useful Arts, by securing for limited Times to Authors and Inventors the exclusive Right to their respective Writings and Discoveries;

To constitute Tribunals inferior to the supreme Court;

To define and punish Piracies and Felonies committed on the high Seas, and Offences against the Law of Nations;

To declare War, grant Letters of Marque and Reprisal, and make Rules concerning Captures on Land and Water;

To raise and support Armies, but no Appropriation of Money to that Use shall be for a longer Term than two Years;

To provide and maintain a Navy;

To make Rules for the Government and Regulation of the land and naval Forces;

To provide for calling forth the Militia to execute the Laws of the Union, suppress Insurrections and repel Invasions;

To provide for organizing, arming, and disciplining, the Militia, and for governing such Part of them as may be employed in the Service of the United States, reserving to the States respectively, the Appointment of the Officers, and the Authority of training the Militia according to the discipline prescribed by Congress;

To exercise exclusive Legislation in all Cases whatsoever, over such District (not exceeding ten Miles square) as may, by Cession of particular States, and the Acceptance of Congress, become the Seat of the Government of the United States, and to exercise like Authority over all Places purchased by the Consent of the Legislature of the State in which the Same shall be, for the Erection of Forts, Magazines, Arsenals, dock-Yards, and other needful Buildings;—And

To make all Laws which shall be necessary and proper for carrying into Execution the foregoing Powers, and all other Powers vested by this

Constitution in the Government of the United States, or in any Department or Officer thereof.

Section. 9. The Migration or Importation of such Persons as any of the States now existing shall think proper to admit, shall not be prohibited by the Congress prior to the Year one thousand eight hundred and eight, but a Tax or duty may be imposed on such Importation, not exceeding ten dollars for each Person.

The Privilege of the Writ of Habeas Corpus shall not be suspended, unless when in Cases of Rebellion or Invasion the public Safety may require it.

No Bill of Attainder or ex post facto Law shall be passed.

No Capitation, or other direct, Tax shall be laid, unless in Proportion to the Census or Enumeration herein before directed to be taken.

No Tax or Duty shall be laid on Articles exported from any State.

No Preference shall be given by any Regulation of Commerce or Revenue to the Ports of one State over those of another: nor shall Vessels bound to, or from, one State, be obliged to enter, clear, or pay Duties in another.

No Money shall be drawn from the Treasury, but in Consequence of Appropriations made by Law; and a regular Statement and Account of the Receipts and Expenditures of all public Money shall be published from time to time.

No Title of Nobility shall be granted by the United States: And no Person holding any Office of Profit or Trust under them, shall, without the Consent of the Congress, accept of any present, Emolument, Office, or Title, of any kind whatever, from any King, Prince, or foreign State.

Section. 10. No State shall enter into any Treaty, Alliance, or Confederation; grant Letters of Marque and Reprisal; coin Money; emit Bills of Credit; make any Thing but gold and silver Coin a Tender in Payment of Debts; pass any Bill of Attainder, ex post facto Law, or Law impairing the Obligation of Contracts, or grant any Title of Nobility.

No State shall, without the Consent of the Congress, lay any Imposts or Duties on Imports or Exports, except what may be absolutely necessary for executing it's inspection Laws: and the net Produce of all Duties and Imposts, laid by any State on Imports or Exports, shall be for the Use of the Treasury of the United States; and all such Laws shall be subject to the Revision and Controul of the Congress.

No State shall, without the Consent of Congress, lay any Duty of

Tonnage, keep Troops, or Ships of War in time of Peace, enter into any Agreement or Compact with another State, or with a foreign Power, or engage in War, unless actually invaded, or in such imminent Danger as will not admit of delay.

Article. II.

Section. 1. The executive Power shall be vested in a President of the United States of America. He shall hold his Office during the Term of four Years, and, together with the Vice President, chosen for the same Term, be elected, as follows

Each State shall appoint, in such Manner as the Legislature thereof may direct, a Number of Electors, equal to the whole Number of Senators and Representatives to which the State may be entitled in the Congress: but no Senator or Representative, or Person holding an Office of Trust or Profit under the United States, shall be appointed an Elector.

The Electors shall meet in their respective States, and vote by Ballot for two Persons, of whom one at least shall not be an Inhabitant of the same State with themselves. And they shall make a List of all the Persons voted for, and of the Number of Votes for each; which List they shall sign and certify, and transmit sealed to the Seat of the Government of the United States, directed to the President of the Senate. The President of the Senate shall, in the Presence of the Senate and House of Representatives, open all the Certificates, and the Votes shall then be counted. The Person having the greatest Number of Votes shall be the President, if such Number be a Majority of the whole Number of Electors appointed; and if there be more than one who have such Majority, and have an equal Number of Votes, then the House of Representatives shall immediately chuse by Ballot one of them for President; and if no Person have a Majority, then from the five highest on the List the said House shall in like Manner chuse the President. But in chusing the President, the Votes shall be taken by States, the Representation from each State having one Vote; A quorum for this Purpose shall consist of a Member or Members from two thirds of the States, and a Majority of all the States shall be necessary to a Choice. In every Case, after the Choice of the President, the Person having the greatest Number of Votes of the Electors shall be the Vice President. But if there should remain two or more who have equal Votes, the Senate shall chuse from them by Ballot the Vice President.

The Congress may determine the Time of chusing the Electors, and the Day on which they shall give their Votes; which Day shall be the same throughout the United States.

No Person except a natural born Citizen, or a Citizen of the United States, at the time of the Adoption of this Constitution, shall be eligible to the Office of President; neither shall any Person be eligible to that Office who shall not have attained to the Age of thirty five Years, and been fourteen Years a Resident within the United States.

In Case of the Removal of the President from Office, or of his Death, Resignation, or Inability to discharge the Powers and Duties of the said Office, the Same shall devolve on the Vice President, and the Congress may by Law provide for the Case of Removal, Death, Resignation or Inability, both of the President and Vice President, declaring what Officer shall then act as President, and such Officer shall act accordingly, until the Disability be removed, or a President shall be elected.

The President shall, at stated Times, receive for his Services, a Compensation, which shall neither be encreased nor diminished during the Period for which he shall have been elected, and he shall not receive within that Period any other Emolument from the United States, or any of them.

Before he enter on the Execution of his Office, he shall take the following Oath or Affirmation:—"I do solemnly swear (or affirm) that I will faithfully execute the Office of President of the United States, and will to the best of my Ability, preserve, protect and defend the Constitution of the United States."

Section. 2. The President shall be Commander in Chief of the Army and Navy of the United States, and of the Militia of the several States, when called into the actual Service of the United States; he may require the Opinion, in writing, of the principal Officer in each of the executive Departments, upon any Subject relating to the Duties of their respective Offices, and he shall have Power to grant Reprieves and Pardons for Offences against the United States, except in Cases of Impeachment.

He shall have Power, by and with the Advice and Consent of the Senate, to make Treaties, provided two thirds of the Senators present concur; and he shall nominate, and by and with the Advice and Consent of the Senate, shall appoint Ambassadors, other public Ministers and Consuls, Judges of the supreme Court, and all other Officers of the United States, whose Appointments are not herein otherwise provided for, and which shall be established by Law: but the Congress may by Law vest the Appointment of such inferior Officers, as they think proper, in the President alone, in the Courts of Law, or in the Heads of Departments.

The President shall have Power to fill up all Vacancies that may happen during the Recess of the Senate, by granting Commissions which shall expire at the End of their next Session.

Section. 3. He shall from time to time give to the Congress Information of the State of the Union, and recommend to their Consideration such Measures as he shall judge necessary and expedient; he may, on extraordinary Occasions, convene both Houses, or either of them, and in Case of Disagreement between them, with Respect to the Time of Adjournment, he may adjourn them to such Time as he shall think proper; he shall receive Ambassadors and other public Ministers; he shall take Care that the Laws be faithfully executed, and shall Commission all the Officers of the United States.

Section. 4. The President, Vice President and all civil Officers of the United States, shall be removed from Office on Impeachment for, and Conviction of, Treason, Bribery, or other high Crimes and Misdemeanors.

Article. III.

Section. 1. The judicial Power of the United States, shall be vested in one supreme Court, and in such inferior Courts as the Congress may from time to time ordain and establish. The Judges, both of the supreme and inferior Courts, shall hold their Offices during good Behaviour, and shall, at stated Times, receive for their Services, a Compensation, which shall not be diminished during their Continuance in Office.

Section. 2. The judicial Power shall extend to all Cases, in Law and Equity, arising under this Constitution, the Laws of the United States, and Treaties made, or which shall be made, under their Authority;—to all Cases affecting Ambassadors, other public Ministers and Consuls;—to all Cases of admiralty and maritime Jurisdiction;—to Controversies to which the United States shall be a Party;—to Controversies between two or more States;—between a State and Citizens of another State;—between Citizens of different States,—between Citizens of the same State claiming Lands under Grants of different States, and between a State, or the Citizens thereof, and foreign States, Citizens or Subjects.

In all Cases affecting Ambassadors, other public Ministers and Consuls, and those in which a State shall be a Party, the supreme Court shall have original Jurisdiction. In all the other Cases before mentioned, the supreme Court shall have appellate Jurisdiction, both as to Law and Fact, with such Exceptions, and under such Regulations as the Congress shall make.

The Trial of all Crimes, except in Cases of Impeachment, shall be by Jury; and such Trial shall be held in the State where the said Crimes shall have been committed; but when not committed within any State, the Trial shall be at such Place or Places as the Congress may by Law have directed.

Section. 3. Treason against the United States, shall consist only in levying War against them, or in adhering to their Enemies, giving them Aid and Comfort. No Person shall be convicted of Treason unless on the Testimony of two Witnesses to the same overt Act, or on Confession in open Court.

The Congress shall have Power to declare the Punishment of Treason, but no Attainder of Treason shall work Corruption of Blood, or Forfeiture except during the Life of the Person attainted.

Article. IV.

Section. 1. Full Faith and Credit shall be given in each State to the public Acts, Records, and judicial Proceedings of every other State. And the Congress may by general Laws prescribe the Manner in which such Acts, Records and Proceedings shall be proved, and the Effect thereof.

Section. 2. The Citizens of each State shall be entitled to all Privileges and Immunities of Citizens in the several States.

A Person charged in any State with Treason, Felony, or other Crime, who shall flee from Justice, and be found in another State, shall on Demand of the executive Authority of the State from which he fled, be delivered up, to be removed to the State having Jurisdiction of the Crime.

No Person held to Service or Labour in one State, under the Laws thereof, escaping into another, shall, in Consequence of any Law or Regulation therein, be discharged from such Service or Labour, but shall be delivered up on Claim of the Party to whom such Service or Labour may be due.

Section. 3. New States may be admitted by the Congress into this Union; but no new State shall be formed or erected within the Jurisdiction of any other State; nor any State be formed by the Junction of two or more States, or Parts of States, without the Consent of the Legislatures of the States concerned as well as of the Congress.

The Congress shall have Power to dispose of and make all needful Rules and Regulations respecting the Territory or other Property belonging to the United States; and nothing in this Constitution shall be so construed as to Prejudice any Claims of the United States, or of any particular State.

Section. 4. The United States shall guarantee to every State in this Union a Republican Form of Government, and shall protect each of them against Invasion; and on Application of the Legislature, or of the Executive (when the Legislature cannot be convened) against domestic Violence.

Article. V.

The Congress, whenever two thirds of both Houses shall deem it necessary, shall propose Amendments to this Constitution, or, on the Application of the Legislatures of two thirds of the several States, shall call a Convention for proposing Amendments, which, in either Case, shall be valid to all Intents and Purposes, as Part of this Constitution, when ratified by the Legislatures of three fourths of the several States, or by Conventions in three fourths thereof, as the one or the other Mode of Ratification may be proposed by the Congress; Provided that no Amendment which may be made prior to the Year One thousand eight hundred and eight shall in any Manner affect the first and fourth Clauses in the Ninth Section of the first Article; and that no State, without its Consent, shall be deprived of it's equal Suffrage in the Senate.

Article. VI.

All Debts contracted and Engagements entered into, before the Adoption of this Constitution, shall be as valid against the United States under this Constitution, as under the Confederation.

This Constitution, and the Laws of the United States which shall be made in Pursuance thereof; and all Treaties made, or which shall be made, under the Authority of the United States, shall be the supreme Law of the Land; and the Judges in every State shall be bound thereby, any Thing in the Constitution or Laws of any State to the Contrary notwithstanding.

The Senators and Representatives before mentioned, and the Members of the several State Legislatures, and all executive and judicial Officers, both of the United States and of the several States, shall be bound by Oath or Affirmation, to support this Constitution; but no religious Test shall ever be required as a Qualification to any Office or public Trust under the United States.

Article. VII.

The Ratification of the Conventions of nine States, shall be sufficient for the Establishment of this Constitution between the States so ratifying the Same.

DONE in Convention by the Unanimous Consent of the States present the Seventeenth Day of September in the Year of our Lord one thousand seven hundred and Eighty seven and of the Independence of the United States of America the Twelfth. In witness whereof We have hereunto subscribed our Names,

[signatures omitted].

Appendix C

The Amendments to the
United States Constitution (1791–1992)

Articles in Addition to, and Amendment of, the Constitution of the United States, Proposed by Congress and Ratified by the Several States, Pursuant to the Fifth Article of the Original Constitution

Amendment I [1791]

Congress shall make no law respecting an establishment of religion, or prohibiting the free exercise thereof; or abridging the freedom of speech, or of the press; or the right of the people peaceably to assemble, and to petition the Government for a redress of grievances.

Amendment II [1791]

A well regulated Militia, being necessary to the security of a free State, the right of the people to keep and bear Arms, shall not be infringed.

Amendment III [1791]

No Soldier shall, in time of peace be quartered in any house, without the consent of the Owner, nor in time of war, but in a manner to be prescribed by law.

Sources: See *The Declaration of Independence and the Constitution of the United States,* 96th Cong., 1st sess., House Document No. 96-143 (Washington, D.C.: Government Printing Office, 1979). See also, George Anastaplo, *The Constitution of 1787: A Commentary* (Baltimore: Johns Hopkins University Press, 1989), 237, 288–97; George Anastaplo, *The Amendments to the Constitution: A Commentary* (Baltimore: Johns Hopkins University Press, 1996), 243, 375–84. The dates of ratification of the Amendments are provided in brackets. "Sec." is written here as "Section" in all Amendments.

Amendment IV [1791]

The right of the people to be secure in their persons, houses, papers, and effects, against unreasonable searches and seizures, shall not be violated, and no Warrants shall issue, but upon probable cause, supported by Oath or affirmation, and particularly describing the place to be searched, and the persons or things to be seized.

Amendment V [1791]

No person shall be held to answer for a capital, or otherwise infamous crime, unless on a presentment or indictment of a Grand Jury, except in cases arising in the land or naval forces, or in the Militia, when in actual service in time of War or public danger; nor shall any person be subject for the same offence to be twice put in jeopardy of life or limb; nor shall be compelled in any criminal case to be a witness against himself, nor be deprived of life, liberty, or property, without due process of law; nor shall private property be taken for public use, without just compensation.

Amendment VI [1791]

In all criminal prosecutions, the accused shall enjoy the right to a speedy and public trial, by an impartial jury of the State and district wherein the crime shall have been committed, which district shall have been previously ascertained by law, and to be informed of the nature and cause of the accusation; to be confronted with the witnesses against him; to have compulsory process for obtaining witnesses in his favor, and to have the Assistance of Counsel for his defence.

Amendment VII [1791]

In Suits at common law, where the value in controversy shall exceed twenty dollars, the right of trial by jury shall be preserved, and no fact tried by a jury, shall be otherwise re-examined in any Court of the United States, than according to the rules of the common law.

Amendment VIII [1791]

Excessive bail shall not be required, nor excessive fines imposed, nor cruel and unusual punishments inflicted.

Amendment IX [1791]

The enumeration in the Constitution, of certain rights, shall not be construed to deny or disparage others retained by the people.

Amendment X [1791]

The powers not delegated to the United States by the Constitution, nor prohibited by it to the States, are reserved to the States respectively, or to the people.

Amendment XI [1798]

The Judicial power of the United States shall not be construed to extend to any suit in law or equity, commenced or prosecuted against one of the United States by Citizens of another State, or by Citizens or Subjects of any Foreign State.

Amendment XII [1804]

The Electors shall meet in their respective states, and vote by ballot for President and Vice-President, one of whom, at least, shall not be an inhabitant of the same state with themselves; they shall name in their ballots the person voted for as President, and in distinct ballots the person voted for as Vice-President, and they shall make distinct lists of all persons voted for as President, and of all persons voted for as Vice-President, and of the number of votes for each, which lists they shall sign and certify, and transmit sealed to the seat of the government of the United States, directed to the President of the Senate;—The President of the Senate shall, in the presence of the Senate and House of Representatives, open all the certificates and the votes shall then be counted;—The person having the greatest number of votes for President, shall be the President, if such number be a majority of the whole number of Electors appointed; and if no person have such majority, then from the persons having the highest numbers not exceeding three on the list of those voted for as President, the House of Representatives shall choose immediately, by ballot, the President. But in choosing the President, the votes shall be taken by states, the representation from each state having one vote; a quorum for this purpose shall consist of a member or members from two-thirds of the states, and a majority of all the states shall be necessary to a choice. And if the House of Representatives shall not choose a President whenever the right of choice shall devolve upon them, before the fourth day of March next following, then the Vice-President shall act as President, as in the case of the death or other constitutional disability of the President.—The person having the greatest number of votes as Vice-President, shall be the Vice-President, if such number be a majority of the whole number of Electors appointed, and if no person have a majority, then from the two highest numbers on the list, the Senate shall choose the Vice-President; a quorum for the purpose shall consist of two-thirds of the whole number of Senators, and a majority of the whole number shall be necessary to a choice. But no person constitutionally ineligible to the office of President shall be eligible to that of Vice-President of the United States.

Amendment XIII [1865]

Section 1. Neither slavery nor involuntary servitude, except as a punishment for crime whereof the party shall have been duly convicted, shall exist within the United States, or any place subject to their jurisdiction.

Section 2. Congress shall have power to enforce this article by appropriate legislation.

Amendment XIV [1868]

Section 1. All persons born or naturalized in the United States, and subject to the jurisdiction thereof, are citizens of the United States and of the State wherein they reside. No State shall make or enforce any law which shall abridge the privileges or immunities of citizens of the United States; nor shall any State deprive any person of life, liberty, or property, without due process of law; nor deny to any person within its jurisdiction the equal protection of the laws.

Section 2. Representatives shall be apportioned among the several States according to their respective numbers, counting the whole number of persons in each State, excluding Indians not taxed. But when the right to vote at any election for the choice of electors for President and Vice President of the United States, Representatives in Congress, the Executive and Judicial officers of a State, or the members of the Legislature thereof, is denied to any of the male inhabitants of such State, being twenty-one years of age, and citizens of the United States, or in any way abridged, except for participation in rebellion, or other crime, the basis of representation therein shall be reduced in the proportion which the number of such male citizens shall bear to the whole number of male citizens twenty-one years of age in such State.

Section 3. No person shall be a Senator or Representative in Congress, or elector of President and Vice President, or hold any office, civil or military, under the United States, or under any State, who, having previously taken an oath, as a member of Congress, or as an officer of the United States, or as a member of any State legislature, or as an executive or judicial officer of any State, to support the Constitution of the United States, shall have engaged in insurrection or rebellion against the same, or given aid or comfort to the enemies thereof. But Congress may by a vote of two-thirds of each House, remove such disability.

Section 4. The validity of the public debt of the United States, authorized by law, including debts incurred for payment of pensions and bounties for services in suppressing insurrection or rebellion, shall not be questioned. But neither the United States nor any State shall assume or pay any debt or obligation incurred in aid of insurrection or rebellion against the United States, or any claim for the loss or emancipation of any slave; but all such debts, obligations and claims shall be held illegal and void.

Section 5. The Congress shall have power to enforce, by appropriate legislation, the provisions of this article.

Amendment XV [1870]

Section 1. The right of citizens of the United States to vote shall not be denied or abridged by the United States or by any State on account of race, color, or previous condition of servitude.

Section 2. The Congress shall have power to enforce this article by appropriate legislation.

Amendment XVI [1913]

The Congress shall have power to lay and collect taxes on incomes, from whatever source derived, without apportionment among the several States, and without regard to any census or enumeration.

Amendment XVII [1913]

The Senate of the United States shall be composed of two Senators from each State, elected by the people thereof, for six years; and each Senator shall have one vote. The electors in each State shall have the qualifications requisite for electors of the most numerous branch of the State legislatures.

When vacancies happen in the representation of any State in the Senate, the executive authority of such State shall issue writs of election to fill such vacancies: *Provided,* That the legislature of any State may empower the executive thereof to make temporary appointments until the people fill the vacancies by election as the legislature may direct.

This amendment shall not be so construed as to affect the election or term of any Senator chosen before it becomes valid as part of the Constitution.

Amendment XVIII [1919]

Section 1. After one year from the ratification of this article the manufacture, sale, or transportation of intoxicating liquors within, the importation thereof into, or the exportation thereof from the United States and all territory subject to the jurisdiction thereof for beverage purposes is hereby prohibited.

Section 2. The Congress and the several States shall have concurrent power to enforce this article by appropriate legislation.

Section 3. This article shall be inoperative unless it shall have been ratified as an amendment to the Constitution by the legislatures of the several States, as provided in the Constitution, within seven years from the date of the submission hereof to the States by the Congress.

Amendment XIX [1920]

The right of citizens of the United States to vote shall not be denied or abridged by the United States or by any State on account of sex.

Congress shall have power to enforce this article by appropriate legislation.

Amendment XX [1933]

Section 1. The terms of the President and Vice President shall end at noon on the 20th day of January, and the terms of Senators and Representatives at noon on the 3d day of January, of the years in which such terms would have ended if this article had not been ratified; and the terms of their successors shall then begin.

Section 2. The Congress shall assemble at least once in every year, and such meeting shall begin at noon on the 3d day of January, unless they shall by law appoint a different day.

Section 3. If, at the time fixed for the beginning of the term of the President, the President elect shall have died, the Vice President elect shall become President. If a President shall not have been chosen before the time fixed for the beginning of his term, or if the President elect shall have failed to qualify, then the Vice President elect shall act as President until a President shall have qualified; and the Congress may by law provide for the case wherein neither a President elect nor a Vice President elect shall have qualified, declaring who shall then act as President, or the manner in which one who is to act shall be selected, and such person shall act accordingly until a President or Vice President shall have qualified.

Section 4. The Congress may by law provide for the case of the death of any of the persons from whom the House of Representatives may choose a President whenever the right of choice shall have devolved upon them, and for the case of the death of any of the persons from whom the Senate may choose a Vice President whenever the right of choice shall have devolved upon them.

Section 5. Sections 1 and 2 shall take effect on the 15th day of October following the ratification of this article.

Section 6. This article shall be inoperative unless it shall have been ratified as an amendment to the Constitution by the legislatures of three-fourths of the several States within seven years from the date of its submission.

Amendment XXI [1933]

Section 1. The eighteenth article of amendment to the Constitution of the United States is hereby repealed.

Section 2. The transportation or importation into any State, Territory, or possession of the United States for delivery or use therein of intoxicating liquors, in violation of the laws thereof, is hereby prohibited.

Section 3. This article shall be inoperative unless it shall have been ratified as an amendment to the Constitution by conventions in the several States, as provided in the Constitution, within seven years from the date of the submission hereof to the States by the Congress.

Amendment XXII [1951]

Section 1. No person shall be elected to the office of the President more than twice, and no person who has held the office of President, or acted as President, for more than two years of a term to which some other person was elected President shall be elected to the office of the President more than once. But this Article shall not apply to any person holding the office of President when this Article was proposed by the Congress, and shall not prevent any person who may be holding the office of President, or acting as President, during the term within which this Article becomes operative from holding the office of President or acting as President during the remainder of such term.

Section 2. This article shall be inoperative unless it shall have been ratified as an amendment to the Constitution by the legislatures of three-fourths of the several States within seven years from the date of its submission to the States by the Congress.

Amendment XXIII [1961]

Section 1. The District constituting the seat of Government of the United States shall appoint in such manner as the Congress may direct:

A number of electors of President and Vice President equal to the whole number of Senators and Representatives in Congress to which the District would be entitled if it were a State, but in no event more than the least populous State; they shall be in addition to those appointed by the States, but they shall be considered, for the purposes of the election of President and Vice President, to be electors appointed by a State; and they shall meet in the District and perform such duties as provided by the twelfth article of amendment.

Section 2. The Congress shall have power to enforce this article by appropriate legislation.

Amendment XXIV [1964]

Section 1. The right of citizens of the United States to vote in any primary or other election for President or Vice President, for electors for President or Vice President, or for Senator or Representative in Congress, shall not be denied or abridged by the United States or any State by reason of failure to pay any poll tax or other tax.

Section 2. The Congress shall have power to enforce this article by appropriate legislation.

Amendment XXV [1967]

Section 1. In case of the removal of the President from office or of his death or resignation, the Vice President shall become President.

Section 2. Whenever there is a vacancy in the office of the Vice President, the President shall nominate a Vice President who shall take office upon confirmation by a majority vote of both Houses of Congress.

Section 3. Whenever the President transmits to the President pro tempore of the Senate and the Speaker of the House of Representatives his written declaration that he is unable to discharge the powers and duties of his office, and until he transmits to them a written declaration to the contrary, such powers and duties shall be discharged by the Vice President as Acting President.

Section 4. Whenever the Vice President and a majority of either the principal officers of the executive departments or of such other body as Congress may by law provide, transmit to the President pro tempore of the Senate and the Speaker of the House of Representatives their written declaration that the President is unable to discharge the powers and duties of his office, the Vice President shall immediately assume the powers and duties of the office as Acting President.

Thereafter, when the President transmits to the President pro tempore of the Senate and the Speaker of the House of Representatives his written declaration that no inability exists, he shall resume the powers and duties of his office unless the Vice President and a majority of either the principal officers of the executive department or of such other body as Congress may by law provide, transmit within four days to the President pro tempore of the Senate and the Speaker of the House of Representatives their written declaration that the President is unable to discharge the powers and duties of his office. Thereupon Congress shall decide the issue, assembling within forty-eight hours for that purpose if not in session. If the Congress, within twenty-one days after receipt of the latter written declaration, or, if Congress is not in session, within twenty-one days after Congress is required to assemble, determines by two-thirds vote of both Houses that the President is unable to discharge the powers and duties of his office, the Vice President shall continue to discharge the same as Acting President; otherwise, the President shall resume the powers and duties of his office.

Amendment XXVI [1971]

Section 1. The right of citizens of the United States, who are eighteen years of age or older, to vote shall not be denied or abridged by the United States or by any State on account of age.

Section 2. The Congress shall have power to enforce this article by appropriate legislation.

Amendment XXVII [1992]

No law varying the compensation for the services of the Senators and Representatives shall take effect until an election of Representatives shall have intervened.

Appendix D

Pericles, The Funeral Address (431 B.C.E.)

34. The same Winter the *Athenians,* according to their ancient custome, solemnized a public Funerall of the first slain in this Warre, in this manner. Having set up a Tent, they put into it the bones of the dead, three days before the Funerall, and every one bringeth whatsoever he thinkes good to his owne. When the day comes of carrying them to their buriall, certain Cypress Coffins are carried along in Carts, for every Tribe one, in which are the bones of the men of every Tribe by themselves. There is likewise borne an empty Hearse covered over, for such as appeare not, nor were found amongst the rest when they were taken up. The Funerall is accompanied by any that will, whether Citizen or Stranger; and the Women of their Kindred are also by at the buriall, lamenting and mourning. Then they put them into a publique Monument, which standeth in the fairest Suburbs of the Citie, (in which place they have ever interred all that dyed in the Warres, except those that were slain in the Fields of *Marathon;* who, because their vertue was thought extraordinary, were therefore buried there-right) and when the earth is throwne over them, some one, thought to exceede the rest in wisdome and dignity, chosen by the Citie, maketh an Oration, wherein hee giveth them such praises as are fit: which done, the Companie depart. And this is the forme of that Buriall; and for the

Sources: The best-known version of Pericles' Funeral Oration, in Athens (in 431 B.C.E.), is found in Thucydides, *The Peloponnesian War,* II, 34–46. (Compare, for example, Plato, *Menexenus.*) The text here of that oration is taken from Thomas Hobbes's translation (first published in 1629), which has been said by David Grene to be "by long odds the greatest translation of Thucydides in English."

The text of the oration drawn on in Essay Two of Part One of this volume is taken, however, from the translation by Susan D. Collins and Devin Stauffer. See George Anastaplo, ed., *Liberty, Equality & Modern Constitutionalism: A Source Book* (Newburyport, Mass.: Focus Publishing Company, 1999), 1:34. That translation is more reliable in its handling of the death-related terms discussed in the Essay. Also, it tends to avoid the modern tendency (seen in Hobbes and in others) to speak of the "state" when dealing with the Greek city of antiquity. The chapter divisions here (34–47) are those routinely used by modern scholars.

whole time of the Warre, whensoever there was occasion, they observed the same. For these first, the man chosen to make the Oration was *Pericles,* the son of *Xantippus,* who when the time served, going out of the place of buriall into a high Pulpit to be heard the further off by the multitude about him, spake unto them in this manner:

35. "Though most that have spoken formerly in this place, have commended the man that added this Oration to the Law, as honourable for those that dye in the Warres; yet to mee it seemeth sufficient, that they who have shewed their valour by action, should also by an action have their honour, as now you see they have, in this their sepulture performed by the State; and not to have the vertue of many hazarded on one, to be beleeved as that one shall make a good or bad Oration. For, to speake of men in a just measure, is a hard matter and though one do so, yet he shall hardly get the truth firmly beleeved; the favourable hearer, and hee that knowes what was done, will perhaps thinke what is spoken, short of what hee would have it, and what it was; and hee that is ignorant, will finde somewhat on the other side which hee will thinke too much extolled; especially if hee heare aught above the pitch of his owne nature. For to heare another man praised, findes patience so long onely, as each man shall thinke he could himselfe have done somewhat of that hee heares. And if one exceed in their praises, the hearer presently through envie thinkes it false. But since our ancestors have so thought good, I also, following the same ordinance, must endeavour to bee answerable to the desires and opinions of every one of you, as farre forth as I can.

36. "I will beginne at our Ancestours: being a thing both just and honest, that to them first be given the honour of remembrance in this kinde: For they, having been alwayes the inhabitants of this Region, by their valour have delivered the same to succession of posterity, hitherto, in the state of liberty: For which they deserve commendation; but our Fathers deserve yet more; for that besides what descended on them, not without great labour of their owne, they have purchased this our present Dominion, and delivered the same over to us that now are. Which in a great part also, wee ourselves, that are yet in the strength of our age here present, have enlarged; and so furnished the Citie with every thing, both for peace and warre, as it is now allsufficient in it selfe. The actions of Warre, whereby all this was attained, and the deedes of Armes both of our selves and our Fathers, in valiant opposition to the Barbarians, or Grecians, in their Warres against us, amongst you that are well acquainted with the

summe, to avoide prolixity I will passe over. But by what institutions wee arrived at this, by what forme of government and by what meanes we have advanced the State to this greatnesse, when I shall have laide open this, I shall then descend to these mens praises. For I think they are things both fit for the purpose in hand, and profitable to the whole company, both of Citizens and Strangers, to heare related.

37. "Wee have a forme of government, not fetched by imitation from the Lawes of our neighbouring States, (nay, wee are rather a patterne to others, then they to us) which, because in the administration, it hath respect, not to a few, but to the multitude, is called a Democracie. Wherein, though there bee an equality amongst all men in point of Law for their private controversies; yet in conferring of dignities, one man is preferred before another to publique charge, and that according to the reputation, not of his House, but of his vertue; and is not put backe through povertie, for the obscurity of his person, as long as hee can doe good service to the Common wealth. And we live not onley free in the administration of the State, but also one with another, voyd of jealousie, touching each others daily course of life; not offended at any man for following his owne humour, nor casting on any man censorious lookes, which though they bee no punishment, yet they grieve. So that conversing one with another for the private without offence, we stand chiefly in feare to transgresse against the publique; and are obedient always to those that governe, and to the Lawes, and principally to such Lawes as are written for protection against injurie, and such unwritten, as bring undeniable shame to the transgressours.

38. "Wee have also found out many wayes to give our mindes recreation from labour, by publike institution of Games and Sacrifices for all the dayes of the yeare, with a decent pompe and furniture of the same by private men; by the daily delight whereof wee expell sadnesse. Wee have this farther, by the greatnesse of our Citie, that all things, from all parts of the Earth are imported hither; whereby we no lesse familiarly enjoy the commodities of all other Nations, then our own.

39. "Then in the studies of Warre, wee excell our Enemies in this: wee leave our Citie open to all men; nor was it ever seene, that by banishing of strangers, we denyed them the learning or sight of any of those things, which, if not hidden, an enemie might reape advantage by; not relying on secret preparation and deceipt, but upon our owne courage in the action. They, in their discipline hunt after valour, presently from their youth, with laborious exercise; and yet wee that live remissely, undertake as great

dangers as they. For example; the Lacedæmonians invade not our dominion by themselves alone, but with the ayde of all the rest. But when wee invade our neighbours, though wee fight in hostile ground, against such as in their owne ground, fight in defence of their owne substance, yet for the most part wee get the victorie. Never Enemie yet fell into the hands of our whole Forces at once; both because wee apply our selves much to Navigation, and by Land also send many of our men into divers Countries abroad. But when fighting with a part of it, they chance to get the better, they boast they have beaten the whole; and when they get the worse, they say they are beaten by the whole. And yet when from ease, rather than studious labour, and upon naturall, rather than doctrinal valour, wee come to undertake any danger, wee have this oddes by it, that we shall not faint beforehand with the meditation of future trouble, and in the action wee shall appeare no less confident than they that are ever toyling,   ·

40. "procuring admiration to our Citie as well in this, as in divers other things. For we also give our selves to bravery, and yet with thrift; and to Philosophy, and yet without mollification of the minde. And we use riches rather for opportunities of action, then for verball ostentation: And hold it not ashame to confesse poverty, but not to have avoided it. Moreover there is in the same men, a care both of their owne, and the publique affaires; and a sufficient knowledge of State matters, even in those that labour with their hands. For we only think one that is utterly ignorant therein, to be a man not that meddles with nothing, but that is good for nothing. We likewise, weigh what we undertake, and apprehend it perfectly in our mindes; not accounting words for a hindrance of action, but that it is rather a hindrance to action, to come to it without instruction of words before. For also in this we excell others; daring to undertake as much as any, and yet examining what wee undertake; whereas with other men, ignorance makes them dare, and consideration, dastards; and they are most rightly reputed valiant, who though they perfectly apprehend both what is dangerous, and what is easie, are never the more thereby diverted from adventuring. Again, we are contrary to most men in matter of bounty. For we purchase our friends, not by receiving, but by bestowing benefits. And he that bestoweth a good turne, is ever the most constant friend; because hee will not lose the thankes due unto him, from him whom he bestowed it on. Whereas the friendship of him that oweth a benefit, is dull and flat, as knowing his benefit not to be taken for a favour, but for a debt. So that we onely do good to others, not upon computation of profit, but freenesse of trust.

41. "In summe, it may be said, both that the Citie is in generall a Schoole of the Grecians, and that the men here, have every one in particular, his person disposed to most diversity of actions, and yet all with grace and decency. And that this is not now, rather a bravery of words, upon the occasion, than reall truth, this power of the Citie, which by these institutions we have obtained, maketh evident. For it is the onely power now found greater in proofe, than fame; and the onely power, that neither grieveth the invader when he miscarries, with the quality of those he was hurt by, nor giveth cause to the subjected States to murmure, as being in subjection to men unworthy. For both with present and future Ages we shall be in admiration, for a power, not without testimony, but made evident by great arguments; and which needeth not either a Homer to praise it, or any other such, whose Poems may indeed for the present, bring delight, but the truth will afterwards confute the opinion conceived of the actions. For we have opened unto us by our courage, all Seas, and Lands, and set up eternal Monuments on all sides, both of the evil we have done to our enemies, and the good wee have done to our friends.

"Such is the city for which these men (thinking it no reason to lose it) valiantly fighting have died. And it is fit that every man of you that bee left, should bee like minded, to undergoe any travail for the same.

42. "And I have therefore spoken so much concerning the Citie in generall, as well to show you, that the stakes between us and them, whose Citie is not such, are not equall; as also to make known by effects, the worth of these men I am to speak of; the greatest part of their praises being therein already delivered. For what I have spoken of the Citie, hath by these and such as these beene achieved: Neither would praises and actions appear so levelly concurrent in many other of the Grecians, as they do in these: the present revolution of these mens lives seeming unto mee an argument of their vertues, noted in the first act thereof, and in the last confirmed. For even such of them as were worse than the rest, doe nevertheless deserve that for their valour showne in the Warres for defence of their Countrey, they should bee preferred before the rest. For having by their good actions abolished the memory of their evill, they have profited the State thereby, more than they have hurt it by their private behaviour. Yet there was none of these, that preferring the further fruition of his wealth, was thereby growne cowardly; or that for hope to overcome his poverty at length, and to attaine to riches, did for that cause withdraw himselfe from the danger. For their principall desire was not wealth, but revenge

on their Enemies; which esteeming the most honourable cause of danger, they made account through it, both to accomplish their revenge, and to purchase wealth withall; putting the uncertainty of successe, to the account of their hope; but for that which was before their eyes, relying upon themselves in the action; and therein chusing rather to fight and dye, than to shrinke and bee saved. They fled from shame, but with their bodies, they stood out the Battel; and so in a moment, whilst Fortune inclineth neither way, left their lives not in feare, but in opinion of victory.

43. "Such were these men, worthy of their Country; and for you that remaine, you may pray for a safer fortune; but you ought not to bee lesse venturously minded against the enemie; not weighing the profit by an Oration onely, which any man amplifying, may recount, to you that know as well as hee, the many commodities that arise by fighting valiantly against your enemies; but contemplating the power of the Citie in the actions of the same from day to day performed, and thereby becoming enamoured of it. And when this power of the Citie shall seeme great to you, consider then, that the same was purchased by valiant men, and by men that knew their duty, and by men that were sensible of dishonour when they were in fight; and by such men, as though they failed of their attempt, yet would not bee wanting to the Citie with their vertue, but made unto it a most honourable contribution. For having every one given his body to the Common-wealth, they receive in place thereof, an undecaying commendation, and a most remarkable Sepulcher; not wherein they are buried so much, as wherein their glory is laid up, upon all occasions, both of speech and action, to bee remembered for ever. For to famous men all the earth is a Sepulcher: and their vertues shall bee testified, not onely by the inscription in stone at home, but by an unwritten record of the minde, which more than of any Monument, will remaine with every one for ever. In imitation therefore of these men, and placing happiness in liberty, and liberty in valour, bee forward to encounter the dangers of Warre. For the miserable and desperate men, are not they that have the most reason to be prodigall of their lives; but rather such men, as if they live, may expect a change of fortune, and whose losses are greatest, if they miscarry in aught. For to a man of any spirit, Death, which is without sense, arriving whilst hee is in vigour and common hope, is nothing so bitter, as after a tender life to bee brought into misery.

44. "Wherefore I will not so much bewail, as comfort you the parents, that are present, of these men. For you know that whilst they lived, they

were obnoxious to manifold calamities, whereas whilst you are in griefe, they onely are happy, that dye honourably, as these have done: and to whom it hath been granted, not only to live in prosperity, but to dye in it. Though it be a hard matter to dissuade you from sorrow, for the losse of that, which the happiness of others, wherein you also when time was, rejoiced your selves, shall so often bring into your remembrance (for sorrow is not for the want of a good never tasted, but for the privation of a good we have been used to) yet such of you as are of the age to have children, may beare the losse of these, in the hope of more. For the later children will both draw on with some the oblivion of those that are slaine, and also doubly conduce to the good of the Citie, by population and strength. For it is not likely that they should equally give good counsell to the State, that have not children to bee equally exposed to danger in it. As for you that are past having of children, you are to put the former and greater part of your life, to the account of your gaine, and supposing the remainder of it will be but short, you shall have the glory of these for a consolation of the same. For the love of honour never groweth old, nor doth that unprofitable part of our life take delight (as some have said) in gathering of wealth, so much as it doth in being honoured.

45. "As for you that are the children or brethren of these men, I see you shall have a difficult taske of emulation. For every man useth to praise the dead; so that with oddes of vertue, you will hardly get an equall reputation, but still be thought a little short. For men envy their Competitors in glory, while they live; but to stand out of their way, is a thing honoured with an affection free from opposition. And since I must say somewhat also of feminine vertue, for you that are now Widdowes: I shall express it in this short admonition. It will bee much for your honour, not to recede from your Sexe, and to give as little occasion of rumour amongst the men, whether of good or evil, as you can.

46. "Thus also have I, according to the prescript of the Law, delivered in word what was expedient; and those that are here interred, have in fact beene already honoured; and further, their children shall bee maintained till they be at mans estate, at the charge of the Citie, which hath therein propounded both to these, and them that live, a profitable Garland in their matches of valour. For where the rewards of vertue are greatest, there live the worthiest men. So now having lamented every one his own, you may be gone."

47. Such was the Funerall made this Winter; which ending, ended the first yeere of this Warre. . . .

Appendix E

On Death and Dying: Ancient, Christian, and Modern

I. Aristotle: A Fine Death?

Those who attack rulers on account of love of honor and distinction are different from those talked about before. They are not like those who set upon rulers looking forward to great profits and to great offices as well as to honors for themselves.

Those who attack rulers primarily on account of honor and distinc-

---

Sources: This passage is taken from Book 5, Chapter 10, of Laurence Berns's translation of Aristotle's *Politics* (which is to be issued by the Focus Publishing Company). This passage (*Politics* 1312a21–38) is modified somewhat here in order to be immediately useful as an excerpt.

Professor Berns suggests that it can be instructive to consider as well here both Abraham Lincoln's Lyceum Address of January 27, 1838, and an observation made by Aristotle in the course of his discussion of courage in his *Nicomachean Ethics* (1117b10–13):

> The more a man possesses virtue in its entirety, the more happy he is, and the more will he be pained by death, for life is most worth living for such a man, and he will be deprived of the greatest goods knowingly, and this is painful.

The complications that can attend such actions by Dion as are referred to by Aristotle are suggested not only by the passage quoted from the *Ethics* but also by the following entry about Dion (in the *Oxford Classical Dictionary* [Oxford: Clarendon Press, 1949]), quoted here in its entirety:

> Dion (c. 408–354 B.C.) was a relative and minister of Dionysius I; but falling under the spell of Plato, he became opposed to tyranny. He tried to exert a liberalizing influence upon the young Dionysius II [of Syracuse], but like Plato himself he failed, and had to leave Syracuse (366). For many years he stayed in Greece, closely attached to the Academy [of Plato]. But the hostility of Dionysius grew, and Dion decided to attack him. With only a small force he succeeded in winning Syracuse, and other cities joined him. But he had internal enemies, being a haughty aristocrat and not a popular leader like his former friend Heraclides, who outstripped him by gaining a great naval victory over Dionysius' admiral Philistus. The intrigues against Dion increased, and he and his soldiers were expelled, only to be recalled soon after, when Syracuse was again attacked by Dionysius. Once more the city was liberated, but Heraclides' intrigues continued, and finally Dion had to allow his assassination. After his rather ideological attempt at a constitution according to Platonic ideas, he became "a tyrant in spite of himself." In 354 he was murdered by order of Callippus, a supposed friend and Platonist.

tion deliberately choose to face danger. They do what they do not in order to gain an office but rather glory. Those who set out for this reason are few in number, for one has to assume they take no concern for their own safety if their action should not succeed.

The seeker of honor should follow the judgment of Dion [of Syracuse], which is not easy for most men to do. He, with few men, attacked Dionysius, saying that in doing whatever they might be able to do, it was sufficient for him to share in the action that much, so that if after making one small step onto the land he should happen to die, this would be a fine death for him.

II. John Mason Neale: Ye Need Not Fear the Grave?

Good Christian men, rejoice with heart and soul, and voice;
Give ye heed to what we say: News! News! Jesus Christ is born today;
Ox and ass before Him bow; and He is in the manger now.
Christ is born today! Christ is born today!

Good Christian men, rejoice, with heart and soul and voice;
Now ye hear of endless bliss: Joy! Joy! Jesus Christ was born for this!
He has opened the heavenly door, and man is blest forevermore.
Christ was born for this! Christ was born for this!

Good Christian men, rejoice, with heart and soul and voice;
Now ye need not fear the grave: Peace! Peace! Jesus Christ was born to
   save!
Calls you one and calls you all, to gain His everlasting hall,
Christ was born to save! Christ was born to save!

Sources: It is reported that "Good Christian Men, Rejoice" was translated into English from the Latin by John Mason Neale in 1853. It is also reported that the music used for this hymn was a fourteenth-century German melody, "In Dulci Jubilo." It is reported as well that the German mystic Heinrich Seuse revealed that he learned the song from dancing angels.

III. William Shakespeare: Does Conscience
Make Cowards of Us All?

Hamlet: To be, or not to be, that is the question:
Whether 'tis nobler in the mind to suffer
The slings and arrows of outrageous fortune,
Or to take arms against a sea of troubles
And by opposing end them. To die, to sleep—
No more—and by a sleep to say we end
The heartache and the thousand natural shocks
That flesh is heir to. 'Tis a consummation
Devoutly to be wished. To die, to sleep;
To sleep, perchance to dream. Ay, there's the rub,
For in that sleep of death what dreams may come,
When we have shuffled off this mortal coil,
Must give us pause. There's the respect
That makes calamity of so long life.
For who would bear the whips and scorns of time,
The oppressor's wrong, the proud man's contumely,
The pangs of disprized love, the law's delay,
The insolence of office, and the spurns
That patient merit of th' unworthy takes,
When he himself might his quietus make
With a bare bodkin? Who would fardels bear,
To grunt and sweat under a weary life,
But that the dread of something after death,
The undiscovered country from whose bourn
No traveler returns, puzzles the will,
And makes us rather bear those ills we have
Than fly to others that we know not of?
Thus conscience does make cowards of us all;
And thus the native hue of resolution
Is sicklied o'er with the pale cast of thought,

Sources: This speech is taken from William Shakespeare, *The Tragedy of Hamlet, Prince of Denmark*, III, I, 57–91. See David Bevington, ed., *The Complete Works of Shakespeare* (New York: Longman, 1997), 1087.

And enterprises of great pitch and moment
With this regard their currents turn awry
And lose the name of action.—Soft you now,
The fair Ophelia. Nymph, in thy orisons
Be all my sins remembered.

Appendix F

Patrick Henry, Give Me Liberty or Give Me Death (1775)

The morning of the 23d March [1775] was opened, by reading a petition and memorial from the assembly of Jamaica to the king's most excellent majesty: whereupon it was—"Resolved, That the unfeigned thanks and most grateful acknowledgments of the convention be presented to that very respectable assembly, for the exceeding generous and affectionate part they have so nobly taken, in the unhappy contest between Great Britain and her colonies; and for their truly patriotic endeavours to fix the just claims of the colonists upon the most permanent constitutional principles:—that the assembly be assured, that it is the most ardent wish of this colony (and they were persuaded of the whole continent of North America,) to see a speedy return of those halcyon days, when we lived a free and happy people."

These proceedings were not adapted to the taste of Mr. [Patrick] Henry; on the contrary, they were "gall and wormwood" to him. The house required to be wrought up to a bolder tone. He rose, therefore, and moved the following manly resolutions:—

"Resolved, That a well-regulated militia, composed of gentlemen and yeomen, is the natural strength and only security of a free government; that such a militia in this colony would for ever render it unnecessary for the mother-country to keep among us, for the purpose of our defence, any standing army of mercenary soldiers, always subversive of the quiet, and

Sources: This is based upon the account of Patrick Henry's March 23, 1775, resolutions and speech in William Wirt, *Sketches of the Life and Character of Patrick Henry* (3rd ed., Philadelphia: James Webster, 1818), 115–25, and (9th ed., Philadelphia: Desilver, Thomas and Co., 1836), 134–44. This account reports a meeting of the Second Revolutionary Convention of Virginia, at Richmond, Virginia. See also, Moses Coit Tyler, *Patrick Henry* (New York: Frederick Ungar Publishing Company, 1898), 140–51. (The complete text of the Wirt account of the speech is provided here.)

dangerous to the liberties of the people, and would obviate the pretext of taxing us for their support.

"That the establishment of such militia is, *at this time,* peculiarly necessary, by the state of our laws, for the protection and defence of the country, some of which are already expired, and others will shortly be so: and that the known remissness of government in calling us together in legislative capacity, renders it too insecure, in this time of danger and distress, to rely that opportunity will be given of renewing them, in general assembly, *or making any provision to secure our inestimable rights and liberties, from those further violations with which they are threatened.*

"Resolved, therefore, *That this colony be immediately put into a state of defence, and that [some members be designated] a committee to prepare a plan for embodying, arming, and disciplining such a number of men, as may be sufficient for that purpose."*

The alarm which such a proposition must have given to those who had contemplated no resistance of a character more serious than petition, non-importation, and passive fortitude, and who still hung with suppliant tenderness on the skirts of Britain, will be readily conceived by the reflecting reader. The shock was painful. It was almost general. [Patrick Henry's] resolutions were opposed as not only rash in policy, but as harsh and well nigh impious in point of feeling. Some of the warmest patriots of the convention opposed them. Richard Bland, Benjamin Harrison, and Edmund Pendleton, who had so lately drunk of the fountain of patriotism in the continental congress, and Robert C. Nicholas, one of the best as well as ablest men and patriots in the state [of Virginia], resisted them with all their influence and abilities.

They urged the late gracious reception of the congressional petition by the throne. They insisted that national comity, and much more filial respect, demanded the exercise of a more dignified patience. That the sympathies of the parent country were now on our side. That the friends of American liberty in parliament were still with us, and had, as yet, had no cause to blush for our indiscretion. That the manufacturing interests of Great Britain, already smarting under the effects of our non-importation, co-operated powerfully towards our relief. That the sovereign himself [George III] had relented, and showed that he looked upon our sufferings with an eye of pity. "Was this a moment," they asked, "to disgust our friends, to extinguish all the conspiring sympathies which were working in our favour, to turn their friendship into hatred, their pity into revenge?

And what was there, they asked, in the situation of the colony, to tempt us to this? Were we a great military people? Were we ready for war? Where were our stores—where were our arms—where our soldiers—where our generals—where our money, the sinews of war? They were nowhere to be found. In truth, we were poor—we were naked—we were defenceless. And yet we talk of assuming the front of war! of assuming it, too, against a nation, one of the most formidable in the world! A nation ready and armed at all points! Her navies riding triumphant in every sea; her armies never marching but to certain victory! What was to be the issue of the struggle we were called upon to court? What *could* be the issue, in the comparative circumstances of the two countries, but to yield up *this country* an easy prey to Great Britain, and to convert the illegitimate right which the British parliament now claimed, into a firm and indubitable right *by conquest*? The measure might be brave; but it was the bravery of madmen. It had no pretension to the character of prudence; and as little to the grace of genuine courage. It would be time enough to resort to measures of *despair,* when every well-founded *hope* had entirely vanished."

To this strong view of the subject, supported as it was by the stubborn fact of the well-known helpless condition of the colony, the opponents of those resolutions [by Patrick Henry] superadded every topic of persuasion which belonged to the cause.

"The strength and lustre which we derived from our connexion with Great Britain—the domestic comforts which we had drawn from the same source, and whose value we were now able to estimate by their loss—that ray of reconciliation which was dawning upon us from the east, and which promised so fair and happy a day:—with this they contrasted the clouds and storms which the measure now proposed was so well calculated to raise—and in which we should not have even the poor consolation of being pitied by the world, since we should have so needlessly and rashly drawn them upon ourselves."

These arguments and topics of persuasion were so well justified by the appearance of things, and were moreover so entirely in unison with that love of ease and quiet which is natural to man, and that disposition to hope for happier times, even under the most forbidding circumstances, that an ordinary man, in Mr. Henry's situation, would have been glad to compound with the displeasure of the house, by being permitted to withdraw his resolutions in silence.

Not so Mr. Henry. His was a spirit fitted to raise the whirlwind, as well as to ride in and direct it. His was that comprehensive view, that un-erring prescience, that perfect command over the actions of men, which qualified him not merely to guide, but almost to create the destinies of nations.

He rose at this time with a majesty unusual to him in an exordium, and with all that self-possession by which he was so invariably distinguished. "No man," he said, "thought more highly than he did of the patriotism, as well as abilities, of the very worthy gentlemen who had just addressed the house. But different men often see the same subject in different lights; and, therefore, he hoped it would not be thought disrespectful to those gentlemen, if, entertaining as he did, opinions of a character very opposite to theirs, he should speak forth *his* sentiments freely, and without reserve. This," he said, "was no time for ceremony. The question before this house was one of awful moment to this country. For his own part, he considered it as nothing less than a question of freedom or slavery. And in proportion to the magnitude of the subject, ought to be the freedom of the debate. It was only in this way that they could hope to arrive at truth, and fulfill the great responsibility which they held to God and their country. Should he keep back his opinions at such a time, through fear of giving offence, he should consider himself as guilty of treason toward his country, and of an act of disloyalty toward the majesty of Heaven, which he revered above all earthly kings."

"Mr. President," said he, "it is natural to man to indulge in the illu-sions of hope. We are apt to shut our eyes against a painful truth—and listen to the song of that syren, till she transforms us into beasts. Is this," he asked, "the part of wise men, engaged in a great and arduous struggle for liberty? Were we disposed to be of the number of those, who having eyes, see not, and having ears, hear not, the things which so nearly concern their temporal salvation? For his part, whatever anguish of spirit it might cost, *he* was willing to know the whole truth; to know the worst, and to provide for it."

"He had," he said, "but one lamp by which his feet were guided; and that was the lamp of experience. He knew of no way of judging of the future but by the past. And judging by the past, he wished to know what there had been in the conduct of the British ministry for the last ten years, to justify those hopes with which gentlemen had been pleased to solace themselves and the house? Is it that insidious smile with which our peti-tion has been lately received? Trust it not, sir; it will prove a snare to your

feet. Suffer not yourselves to be betrayed with a kiss. Ask yourselves how
this gracious reception of our petition comports with those warlike preparations which cover our waters and darken our land. Are fleets and armies
necessary to a work of love and reconciliation? Have we shown ourselves
so unwilling to be reconciled, that force must be called in to win back our
love? Let us not deceive ourselves, sir. These are the implements of war
and subjugation—the last arguments to which kings resort. I ask gentlemen, sir, what means this martial array, if its purpose be not to force us to
submission? Can gentlemen assign any other possible motive for it? Has
Great Britain any enemy in this quarter of the world, to call for all this
accumulation of navies and armies? No, sir, she has none. They are meant
for us: they can be meant for no other. They are sent over to bind and rivet
upon us those chains which the British ministry have been so long forg-
ing. And what have we to oppose to them? Shall we try argument? Sir, we
have been trying that for the last ten years. Have we any thing new to offer
upon the subject? Nothing. We have held the subject up in every light of
which it is capable; but it has been all in vain. Shall we resort to entreaty
and humble supplication? What terms shall we find, which have not been
already exhausted? Let us not, I beseech you, sir, deceive ourselves longer.
Sir, we have done every thing that could be done, to avert the storm which
is now coming on. We have petitioned—we have remonstrated—we have
supplicated—we have prostrated ourselves before the throne, and have
implored its interposition to arrest the tyrannical hands of the ministry
and parliament. Our petitions have been slighted; our remonstrances have
produced additional violence and insult; our supplications have been disregarded; and we have been spurned, with contempt, from the foot of
the throne. In vain, after these things, may we indulge the fond hope of
peace and reconciliation. *There is no longer any room for hope.* If we wish to
be free—if we mean to preserve inviolate those inestimable privileges for
which we have been so long contending—if we mean not basely to abandon the noble struggle in which we have been so long engaged, and which
we have pledged ourselves never to abandon, until the glorious object of
our contest shall be obtained—we must fight!—I repeat it, sir, we must
fight!! An appeal to arms and to the God of Hosts, is all that is left us!"

[Note: "Imagine to yourself," says my correspondent, (Judge Tucker,)
"this sentence delivered with all the calm dignity of Cato of Utica—imagine to yourself the Roman senate, assembled in the capitol, when it was
entered by the profane Gauls, who, at first, were awed by their presence, as

if they had entered an assembly of the gods!—imagine that you heard that Cato addressing such a senate—imagine that you saw the hand writing on the wall of Belshazzar's palace—imagine you heard a voice as from heaven uttering the words, '*We must fight*,' as the doom of fate, and you may have some idea of the speaker, the assembly to whom he addressed himself, and the auditory, of which I was one."]

"They tell us, sir," continued Mr. Henry, "that we are weak—unable to cope with so formidable an adversary. But when shall we be stronger? Will it be the next week or the next year? Will it be when we are totally disarmed, and when a British guard shall be stationed in every house? Shall we gather strength by irresolution and inaction? Shall we acquire the means of effectual resistance by lying supinely on our backs, and hugging the delusive phantom of hope, until our enemies shall have bound us hand and foot? Sir, we are not weak, if we make a proper use of those means which the God of nature hath placed in our power. Three millions of people armed in the holy cause of liberty, and in such a country as that which we possess, are invincible by any force which our enemy can send against us. Besides, sir, we shall not fight our battles alone. There is a just God who presides over the destinies of nations, and who will raise up friends to fight our battles for us. The battle, sir, is not to the strong alone, it is to the vigilant, the active, the brave. Besides, sir, we have no election. If we were base enough to desire it, it is now too late to retire from the contest. There is no retreat but in submission and slavery! Our chains are forged. Their clanking may be heard on the plains of Boston! The war is inevitable—and let it come!! I repeat it, sir, let it come!!!

"It is vain, sir, to extenuate the matter. Gentlemen may cry, peace, peace—but there is no peace. The war is actually begun! The next gale that sweeps from the north will bring to our ears the clash of resounding arms! Our brethren are already in the field! Why stand we here idle? What is it that gentlemen wish? What would they have? Is life so dear, or peace so sweet, as to be purchased at the price of chains and slavery? Forbid it, Almighty God!—I know not what course others may take; but as for me," cried he, with both his arms extended aloft, his brows knit, every feature marked with the resolute purpose of his soul, and his voice swelled to its boldest note of exclamation—"give me liberty, or give me death!"

He took his seat. No murmur of applause was heard. The effect was too deep. After the trance of a moment, several members started from their seats. The cry, "to arms!" seemed to quiver on every lip, and gleam from every eye! Richard H. Lee arose and supported Mr. Henry, with his usual spirit and elegance. But his melody was lost amid the agitations of that ocean, which the master-spirit of the storm had lifted up on high. That supernatural voice still sounded in their ears, and shivered along their arteries. They heard, in every pause, the cry of liberty or death. They became impatient of speech—their souls were on fire for action.

The [Henry] resolutions were adopted; and Patrick Henry, Richard H. Lee, Robert C. Nicholas, Benjamin Harrison, Lemuel Riddick, George Washington, Adam Stevens, Andrew Lewis, William Christian, Edmund Pendleton, Thomas Jefferson, and Isaac Zane, esquires, were appointed a committee to prepare the plan called by the last resolution.

The constitution of this committee proves, that in those days of genuine patriotism there existed a mutual and noble confidence, which deemed the opponents of a measure no less worthy than its friends to assist in its execution. A correspondent [Thomas Jefferson], who bore himself a most distinguished part in our revolution, in speaking of the gentlemen whom I have just named as having opposed Mr. Henry's resolutions, and of Mr. Wythe who acted with them, says—"These were honest and able men, who had begun the opposition on the same grounds, but with a moderation more adapted to their age and experience. Subsequent events favoured the bolder spirits of Henry, the Lees, Pages, Mason, &c., with whom I went in all points. Sensible, however, of the importance of unanimity among our constituents, although we often wished to have gone on faster, we slackened our pace, that our less ardent colleagues might keep up with us; and they, on their part, differing nothing from us in principle, quickened their gait somewhat beyond that which their prudence might, of itself, have advised, and thus consolidated the phalanx which breasted the power of Britain. By this harmony of the bold with the cautious, we [in Virginia] advanced, with our constituents, in undivided mass, and with fewer examples of separation than perhaps existed in any other part of the union."

Appendix G

Abraham Lincoln, The Gettysburg Address (1863)

Four score and seven years ago our fathers brought forth on this continent, a new nation, conceived in Liberty, and dedicated to the proposition that all men are created equal.

Now we are engaged in a great civil war, testing whether that nation, or any nation so conceived and so dedicated, can long endure. We are met on a great battle-field of that war. We have come to dedicate a portion of that field, as a final resting place for those who here gave their lives that that nation might live. It is altogether fitting and proper that we should do this.

But, in a larger sense, we can not dedicate—we can not consecrate—we can not hallow—this ground. The brave men, living and dead, who struggled here, have consecrated it, far above our poor power to add or detract. The world will little note, nor long remember what we say here, but it can never forget what they did here. It is for us the living, rather, to be dedicated here to the unfinished work which they who fought here have thus far so nobly advanced. It is rather for us to be here dedicated to the great task remaining before us—that from these honored dead we take increased devotion to that cause for which they gave the last full measure of devotion—that we here highly resolve that these dead shall not have died in vain—that this nation, under God, shall have a new birth of freedom—and that government of the people, by the people, for the people, shall not perish from the earth.

Sources: See George Anastaplo, *The Constitution of 1787: A Commentary* (Baltimore: John Hopkins University Press, 1989), 300. See also George Anastaplo, *Abraham Lincoln: A Constitutional Biography* [preferred title: *Thoughts on Abraham Lincoln: A Discourse on Prudence*] (Lanham, Md.: Rowman and Littlefield, 1999), 229.

Appendix H

George Anastaplo, On the *Ultron* and the Foundations of Things (1974)

What seems to be missing in the current scientific enterprise is a systematic inquiry into its presuppositions and purposes. That is, the limits of modern science do not seem to be properly recognized. Bertrand Russell has been quoted as saying, "Physics is mathematical not because we know so much about the physical world, but because we know so little: it is only its mathematical properties that we can discover." But the significance of this observation is not generally appreciated—as one learns upon trying to persuade competent physicists to join one in presenting a course devoted to a careful reading of Aristotle's *Physics* [where, among other things, an extended examination of the meaning of *cause* can be found]. Is there any reason to doubt that physicists will, if they continue as they have in the Twentieth Century, achieve again and again "decisive breakthroughs" in dividing subatomic "particles"? But what future, or genuine understanding, is there in *that*? I believe it would be fruitful for physicists—that is, for a few of the more imaginative among them—to consider seriously the nature of what we can call the "ultron." What must this ultimate particle be like (if, indeed, it *is* a particle and not an idea or a principle)? For is not an "ultron" implied by the endeavors of our physicists, by their recourse to more and more ingenious (and expensive) equipment and experiments? Or are we to assume an infinite regress (sometimes called progress) and no standing place or starting point? Or, to put this question still another way, what is it that permits the universe to be and *to be* (if it *is*) *intelligible*?

Sources: See George Anastaplo, *The Artist as Thinker: From Shakespeare to Joyce* (Athens: Ohio University Press, 1983), 252–55, 474. See also, George Anastaplo, *The Bible: Respectful Readings* (Lanham, Md.: Lexington Books, 2008), 332–33. Is recourse to the *ultron* an echo of the ancient Greek reliance on the *atom*?

Appendix I

Life, Death, and the Systematic Perversions of Law
(2000)

A: How old were you when you left Lithuania [for Germany]? **B:** I must have been twenty. I was born in 1924. Without background, my story doesn't make any sense. There was a secret protocol between Molotov and Ribbentrop, the 23rd of August [1939]. What's very important about the secret protocol is what I have underlined in this document. **A:** "The Northern Boundary of Lithuania," it says here, "shall represent the boundary of the spheres of influence of Germany and the USSR." **B:** This means that Lithuania is included in the German territories, while Estonia and Latvia are subject to the Soviet influence. But that's not what happened in real life. **A:** Maybe we can talk about that when I have had a chance to look at this document myself. **B:** You'll look at it later on.

Sources: This is the opening conversation (of March 23, 2000) in an eight-hundred-page transcript of thirteen recorded conversations (in 2000–2001) between George Anastaplo (A) and Simcha Brudno (B), *Simply Unbelievable: Conversations with a Holocaust Survivor.* This opening recorded conversation is supplemented here by a few pages from the next recorded conversation (March 30, 2000). There had been earlier exploratory conversations that were not recorded, but which are drawn on in the recorded conversations. (The tapes of these conversations were transcribed by Adam Reinherz, who was then a student in the Loyola University Chicago School of Law.)

Simcha Brudno (1924–2006), a recognized mathematician, lived in Siauliai, Lithuania, until he was deported (by way of Memel, Lithuania) to Dachau, Germany, in 1944. After the war he lived in Israel before settling in the United States. See, on the Brudno-Anastaplo encounter, "The Holocaust and the Divine Ordering of Human Things," in George Anastaplo, *The Bible: Respectful Readings* (Lanham, Md.: Lexington Books, 2008), 319–25.

The Second World War began, in Europe, with the German invasion of Poland in September 1939. Thereafter Russia occupied the Baltic States (Estonia, Latvia, and Lithuania). Germany invaded Russia in June 1941, at which time the German occupation of the Baltic States began. That occupation continued until the German retreat from Russia in 1944, at which time the Russians returned to the Baltic States. (The spellings used in this transcript of the names of persons and places in Lithuania could not always be confirmed.)

I have to give this background because it is unusually important. Anyway, the 28th of September [1939] there was another agreement by which Lithuania went over to the influence of Russia. On the 28th of September everything changed. Why is it so important to me personally? In the factory that we worked [in Siauliai] the blue collar workers were Lithuanians, while the engineers and the foreman and the chemists were all Germans. **A:** Were they Lithuania-born Germans or had they come in from Germany? **B:** It doesn't matter, it doesn't matter. I don't want to distinguish. **A:** They were both kinds? **B:** Yes. For example, take the neighbor that I am very interested in, Garborg. He was a German soldier who came in the First World War to Lithuania. He was, as a matter of fact, an officer who fell in love with a Lithuanian girl, married her, and they settled in Lithuania. The other Germans must have been native Lithuanians. The Germans are those who built the cities in Latvia, Estonia, and Lithuania. Butrika, they built; Klipidow, which is in Mammal, they built; Koenigsberg, they built—all these cities. They developed the country. Now, why am I telling you this? There was one German who had been a chemist in the place where my mother worked, a glue factory. When you cut the skins, in the leather factory that my father ran, the inner layer has fat, and this fat can be turned into glue. The glue factory did that and my mother was basically the boss in that factory. She worked with a chemist, a German, Schroeder, and he is very important to our story. Schroeder had been one of the soldiers who defended the Winter Palace [in Russia] against the Bolsheviks in 1917. He said the Bolsheviks tricked them, because the Bolsheviks had claimed that there were many more of them than there were in real life. If they had known how few the Bolsheviks were in numbers, they would not have turned over the Winter Palace to them. That's history. **A:** He was a German? **B:** Yes. **A:** He was there under whose command at the Winter Palace? **B:** I have no idea. He never said. He was defending the Czar. That much is obvious.

   A: You thought he was in the Czar's army? **B:** Most probably. He's very important to my whole story. He got very friendly to my mother and, of course, he would play tricks on us. He would cut out any newspaper article about the Kristallnacht and leave it on her table. He didn't say anything, just like that. **A:** From what newspaper? **B:** It doesn't matter. **A:** It could have been a local newspaper? **B:** Yes, Kristallnacht was famous all over the world. **A:** That was in 1938? **B:** 1938. I am just telling you how good relations were. **A:** Why would he leave such a newspaper article for your mother to look at? **B:** Why are you asking me? I will give you only the facts, you translate them which way you want. **A:** Well, how did she understand it? **B:** It meant nothing but a trick on his part, but it's completely on the level. He didn't say a word about it, he just left it on her table. **A:** So what *was* that supposed to mean? **B:** Are you asking *me*? **A:** Well, what did your mother think it meant? **B:** It meant that he wants her to feel bad because that's— **A:** To feel bad? **B:** —to feel bad because she didn't know *that* about him. **A:** Was he friendly to her otherwise? **B:** He was friendly, he was friendly. He was friendly with me, too. **A:** You were fourteen years old then? **B:** No! I was a little boy, nothing! **A:** 1938. You were fourteen years old? **B:** Maybe I *was* fourteen. **A:** That's Kristallnacht you're talking about? **B:** Yes. Earlier he was the only German who had been invited to my bar mitzvah. **A:** And did he come? **B:** Of course, he came, and he drank a lot. **A:** Did his wife come? **B:** No, he was a bachelor. But he did have a child, so he couldn't have been a bachelor, but he lived all by himself. What he liked very much was to go hunting. But he was well informed; that's the most important point that I have to underline. He told my mother, in the beginning of the war, that Lithuania would belong to Germany. How could he know it, by any stretch of the imagination, when it was so secret everywhere? How could he know it? Here's my interpretation and it is very important about Hitler, why he won so much the trust of his nation. Hitler did not play the game of other leaders. He identified with the German people and he shared with them. He shared with some German organizations the most secret agreements. The German government shared with plain Germans even such a secret agreement. Therefore why shouldn't they love a leader that is on their side? **A:** Yes. **B:** That's a very important point that I have to underline. He told my mother that Lithuania would belong to Germany and so he was quite surprised when the Russians entered. He was surprised because that was not according to the agreement. I found out later that the agreement had been changed on the 28th of September. That's basically what I have to underline, that Hitler shared with a nation that he was on their side. The German nation felt, "Hitler is one of us, he defends us." And, of course, I see this repeated elsewhere. Why is Milosevic so appreciated by the Serbs? Because they feel he doesn't play games: he is not on the side of the leaders; he is on the Serbs' side, right or wrong. He defends the Serbs' interest, he is on the Serbs' side, and therefore they love him, true love. This episode, I had to tell you, is very important to me, because I am the only eyewitness to such a thing. **A:** You are an eyewitness in the sense that he had said what he did to you— **B:** He said very clearly that the Germans will enter Lithuania, beyond any shade of doubt. **A:** Yes, but he was wrong about that, wasn't he? **B:** That was the agreement and he knew about it. What do I care? **A:** Well, what he really knew is a question. He may have known— **B:** He knew the agreement. **A:** —or he may have guessed it to be one or the other. **B:** No, no, no guessing! Please don't be so nice and polite, no guessing. He knew. **A:** After all, it was going to be either one or the other, you know. **B:** No! **A:** It was going to be the Russians or the Germans. **B:** No. **A:** He said the Germans, but it happened to be the Russians. **B:** He knew about the agreement. Don't try to be so wishy-washy about such important things. He knew when the Germans entered Memel [in Lithuania]. **A:** Let me ask you, why is it so important to you that he knew? **B:** That Hitler shared with the nation is very important to me. **A:** I see. But he didn't share the change in the agreement. **B:** No, he didn't share with them the change. **A:** Why didn't he share that if he was so big on sharing? **B:** It was to his shame. They lost. **A:** He shared some things and didn't share others? **B:** Victories he shared. Victories he shared.

A: Now, shall we go on to 1944? You're twenty years old. **B:** Yes. **A:** The Germans have occupied Lithuania for how many years? **B:** Three years. **A:** They entered when? **B:** 26th of June 1941. **A:** So they entered Lithuania in June 1941. It is now three years later. You've seen them around, you've gotten used to them. **B:** I never did get "used to them." I assumed that this was a temporary thing. **A:** Would you have assumed that it was temporary if the Germans had won the war? **B:** I didn't assume that they would win the war. **A:** If they had won the war, would they have stayed on? **B:** I don't know. **A:** Did you believe they might? **B:** I don't know. I had all kind of little illusions that even if they won, that twenty years later there will be another war and they will lose, that it will go in a see-saw—all kinds of illusions. **A:** So the Germans had been there for three years. **B:** I had other illusions also which I used, such as the technique that I am not here. Or I am here, but I am a journalist, who is here only to observe what is going on—I am not involved. **A:** You're a foreign correspondent? **B:** Yes. **A:** Stationed in Lithuania? **B:** Yes. I am not involved, I cannot accept it. You want the truth. To this day I cannot accept it. **A:** Now, by 1944 the Germans had been there three years. **B:** Before 1944 a lot of things had happened. **A:** I want to talk about this particular part of it, not the other parts, so that I can carry it through systematically. The earlier parts we can take care of separately. By 1944 the Germans had been there three years. **B:** Okay, you want 1944, I will give you 1944. **A:** You are twenty years old; by this time your father has died. **B:** My father is already three years dead. **A:** Yes, and your mother is doing what? **B:** She is working in the factory. **A:** She is still working in the factory? **B:** You see me now, I look old, so you assume that my mother was old, but at that time my mother was fifty-two, fifty-three. **A:** She was working still. **B:** At fifty-three women work. **A:** By that time your sister is gone, of course. **B:** My sister is in America since 1937. **A:** So you are the only one left there, besides your mother, from your family? **B:** Yes. **A:** And you are still living where? **B:** In the ghetto. **A:** In the house you had been living in? **B:** No! No! **A:** You had to move out of there? **B:** We had been kicked out into the ghetto. **A:** Where did you move to in the ghetto? **B:** A house in the ghetto. **A:** Whose house? **B:** It must have belonged previously to Lithuanians. **A:** Lithuanians in the ghetto were moved out? **B:** Of course. **A:** The area was designated as the ghetto by the Germans and they said that the Lithuanians had to leave. **B:** No, the thing was arranged much more cleverly. **A:** Okay, how was it done? **B:** The Jewish houses that were in the city were given to the Lithuanians who left the ghetto. So it was for them a bargain. **A:** Because the Jewish houses were better? **B:** Yes. **A:** So they moved the Lithuanians out of the ghetto? **B:** Besides there were more Jewish houses in the city than Lithuanian houses in the ghetto. **A:** Did the Lithuanians have a choice about whether they left the ghetto or not? **B:** I don't think they had a choice. **A:** They had to leave? They were told by the Germans— **B:** They were told by the Germans or by the Lithuanians, the local people. I think they were told by the Germans. But they got a good bargain. **A:** They got better houses? **B:** They got better houses. **A:** And so you moved into a house, but you could not move your furniture? **B:** We moved the furniture. **A:** You did move your furniture? **B:** Yes. **A:** Now you were in the ghetto. How far was that, your house in the ghetto, from the factory? **B:** Only a few hundred meters. **A:** So you still were close by? **B:** Very. **A:** Because the ghetto is on the edge of the factory property? **B:** The ghetto is special-made for us to walk to the factory. **A:** One ghetto only in the town? **B:** There were two ghettos, but one was eliminated. **A:** Eliminated when? **B:** In '43. **A:** So originally two ghettos were created. The ghettos were created when? **B:** In 1941, the 20th of August. **A:** Okay, 1941. And there were two of them, created at the same time? **B:** Yes. **A:** And, within a very short time, all the Jews or virtually all the Jews [of Siauliai] were in those two ghettos? **B:** Right. **A:**

And it remained that way so long as the Germans were there, so long as they remained in the town. Is that right? **B:** Yes. **A:** Were you free to come and go out of the ghetto? **B:** No! **A:** At all? **B:** No! **A:** You *could* go to the factory. **B:** Under the guide of a Lithuanian guard. **A:** You could go to the factory? **B:** Yes. **A:** And you could shop in the ghetto? **B:** No shops, what are you talking about? There was only one cooperative. **A:** Well, where would you get your food, drink? **B:** From the cooperative, and we got it not for money, but for coupons. **A:** And clothing and things like that, where would you get those? **B:** Oh, God! **A:** You must have had— **B:** God have mercy! **A:** Did you ever have to buy clothing at all? **B:** No clothes. Stop! **A:** No clothing? **B:** No clothing. **A:** Other things beside food? Did you ever have to buy anything besides food? **B:** Nothing. **A:** Only food was available in the cooperative? **B:** Only food, using coupons. **A:** Suppose you had to get something else for the house, a spoon or something, where would you get it? **B:** Forget it. **A:** A pencil. **B:** No. **A:** A piece of paper; could you buy it? **B:** No. See, even you cannot accept it. **A:** I'm just trying to find out how closed off it was. So you could not get anything? **B:** Not anything. Money was not allowed for Jews to have. **A:** If somebody died in the ghetto, what happened to him? **B:** He was buried in the cemetery. **A:** Was the cemetery in the ghetto, or out of the ghetto? **B:** It was next to the second ghetto. **A:** Which one were you living in? **B:** I was first living in Caukaz, then I moved over to Drakua. **A:** You moved when the Caukaz ghetto was closed? **B:** Yes. **A:** Where was the cemetery for the Jews? **B:** It was bordering the Caukaz ghetto. **A:** Synagogues were in the ghetto too? **B:** You really kill me. You really— **A:** Were there synagogues in the ghetto? **B:** No. How can there be synagogues in the ghetto? **A:** I have no idea. Were there houses of worship in the ghetto? **B:** No. **A:** Well, where did Jews go for worship? **B:** There was a private apartment and people made a congregation there and prayed. **A:** I'm just trying to see what it was like to live in the ghetto. **B:** I can see that you really don't understand. **A:** You must assume that I'm quite ignorant. **B:** I do assume that. **A:** That's not hard to assume, is it? **B:** [*Chuckles.*] That's the usual assumption about anyone. It's very important, because people don't realize how bad it was in the ghetto. **A:** That's what I'm trying to find out. **B:** So now I am telling you. **A:** Okay, all right. **B:** No worship house?

A: The Germans created the ghettos in June 1941. Right? **B:** August 1941. **A:** They entered in June 1941? **B:** The Germans entered my hometown then. **A:** In August 1941 the ghettos, two ghettos, were created? **B:**

Yes. **A:** How long after the ghettos were created were the Jews moved in? I mean how long did it take? **B:** We were the first ones to enter, my family. It didn't take long. **A:** Would you say it took days, weeks, months? **B:** Weeks. **A:** In a few weeks? **B:** Yes. **A:** All the Jews were then in the ghettos? **B:** Yes. **A:** How many Jews were there at this time? **B:** I don't know. **A:** Roughly? **B:** They said about forty-five hundred. One Jew was allowed to live outside of the ghetto. **A:** Who was that? **B:** Davidav was his name, he had a factory for all kinds for pills and there were skins from cats and everything. **A:** And because he had his factory outside, he had to be there at it, is that it? **B:** Yes, he was allowed. **A:** Now within a few weeks after the Germans came you're in the ghetto. At that time you were still very young. You were what, seventeen years old? **B:** Yes. **A:** When you moved into the ghetto, was your father dead yet? **B:** No, he died in the ghetto. **A:** And you moved into a house in the ghetto? **B:** Yes. **A:** A smaller house than you lived in before— **B:** No! No! No! No! Into *a room.* **A:** Into a single room? **B:** With two families per room. **A:** I see. **B:** Now you will begin to see why there was no place for prayer or worship or anything, with two families per room. **A:** And was that standard? **B:** Yes. **A:** And that means a bedroom? **B:** That doesn't mean anything. The cooking and the sleeping and the reading—everything was in the same room. **A:** You moved into a house, right? How big a house was it? Roughly, I don't want precision; this is not mathematics. **B:** I don't know. **A:** Well, was it one floor or two floors? **B:** One floor. **A:** The house was one floor? **B:** Yes. **A:** Was the kitchen in the house? **B:** In each room there was a stove. **A:** There was a stove put into each room? **B:** Not "put," it was originally there. **A:** It couldn't have been there "originally." If a family had been living there before— **B:** Please, don't make me angry. There was, there was. **A:** No. **B:** You don't believe it? **A:** No, I don't believe it. I don't believe that you are saying what you mean to say. **B:** No, I mean it. Why don't you believe that a family lived there before in one room, poor Lithuanians. Why don't you buy that? **A:** What I'm wondering about is this— **B:** Why don't you buy it? **A:** Because that may be true of some of the houses, but it cannot be true of all of the houses. **B:** I don't care about all of the houses, I am again very personal. I speak only about— **A:** But you must have gone to other houses while you were there. You didn't just stay in your house in the ghetto, right? **B:** I am telling you that was the situation. **A:** Okay. You moved into your house. How many families moved into that house? **B:** The whole house was only two rooms, so we were four families. **A:** Before that there had been two

Lithuanian families in there? **B:** I don't know. **A:** Well? **B:** Most probably, yes. Therefore there was a stove in each room. **A:** There was a stove in each room, but that was also the bedroom? **B:** Most probably. **A:** And it was that for you. **B:** Me and my mother and another family! **A:** Yes, but as far as your family—you are talking about you, your mother, and your father? **B:** Me and my father and mother and also another family, two women and a child. **A:** In the same room? **B:** In the same room. **A:** How did you divide the room? **B:** We didn't divide the room; when you are in such a situation you don't divide anything. **A:** Well, you put beds in there right? **B:** Yes. We had beds. **A:** Now, were the beds on one side for one family and on the other side for the other family? **B:** Yes. **A:** One stove. You shared the stove. **B:** It goes without saying. **A:** What kind of stove was that? **B:** It was the kind that you put coal into. **A:** Coal or wood? **B:** Yes. **A:** Not gas, obviously. **B:** No, not gas. **A:** Not electricity, obviously. **B:** Not electricity. **A:** So you moved in and you had your beds? **B:** Yes. **A:** And then people would go to bed, right? **B:** Yes. **A:** Would they all have to go to bed at the same time? **B:** No. **A:** Well, would they leave lights on when one family went to bed? Was there a way of dividing the room? **B:** No, no! They didn't have any space for dividing. Every centimeter counted. **A:** I was just wondering what the arrangements were. **B:** Very bad. **A:** So if you want to go to bed— **B:** So, go to bed. **A:** But if the other ones didn't want to go to bed? **B:** So they'd stay up. **A:** And would they have their lights on? **B:** There's only one bulb in the whole room. **A:** And when did that go off? **B:** Somebody shuts it off, by mutual consent. There was never a non-agreement about it. You ask about an outhouse— **A:** I haven't asked yet. **B:** Okay, but I am telling you about it. The outhouse was outside; it did not belong to the building. Therefore everyone went outside whenever he felt like it. **A:** One outhouse for the building or one outhouse for several buildings? **B:** One outhouse for each building. **A:** The other family was a mother— **B:** A mother, a sister and her boy. **A:** How long were you all together in that house? **B:** Till my father died and then we exchanged. We went into the next room. **A:** Why did you exchange? **B:** I don't know. **A:** Who made the exchange. **B:** We decided amongst ourselves. **A:** Among yourselves? You had altogether four families inside this house. You knew each other before? **B:** Three of the families worked in the same factory. **A:** So you had known each other before? **B:** Yes. **A:** Now, all this time your mother of course is continuing to work in the glue works? **B:** Yes.

A: Where were you working at the beginning of the three years? Were you working when you first moved into the house? **B:** No, we moved into the ghetto and of course I was not working. **A:** You are seventeen years old? **B:** Yes. I can't go out. I am basically closed in the ghetto. That's not to my liking, I am not the type. **A:** You could go out in the ghetto? **B:** In the ghetto, yes; in the ghetto, freedom. You could do whatever you liked. **A:** How large an area was that? **B:** I really don't know. I have somewhere a map showing how big it was. **A:** Well, is it as big as Hyde Park [here in Chicago]? **B:** I don't know how big Hyde Park is. **A:** Well, do you have any kind of idea how long or wide it was, any sense at all? Do you know how big the campus of the University of Chicago is across? **B:** I always assume everything to me is a square kilometer. I think the ghetto and the cemetery were as big as the factory. **A:** Yes, and then how big was the factory? **B:** I told you, a square kilometer. **A:** So it's a square kilometer that you can move around in? **B:** Yes. **A:** You don't need permission to move around in it? **B:** No, no, no. It's a Jewish state. **A:** It's a Jewish state? **B:** Yes. Jewish police. **A:** The Jews themselves policed it? **B:** Yes. **A:** Did they have their own government in the ghetto? **B:** There were three representatives. **A:** What do you mean, three representatives? Was it a council that ran the ghetto? **B:** These three are responsible to the Germans directly. **A:** And did they run things in the ghetto? **B:** Yes. **A:** And how were they chosen? Did the Germans pick them? **B:** No, no, no! **A:** The Jews among themselves picked the three? **B:** Yes. **A:** And who were the three, do you remember? **B:** Yes. One was Boris Captoun, he had before this a linen factory. I knew him personally because I was studying with one of his sons. The children already had been taken away right away when the war started and killed, so he was with his wife. Then there was Rubinshtein and the third one was Katz. **A:** Were they all businessmen? **B:** Captoun and I think Rubenshtein were businessman. Katz was only a guy who always deals in public— **A:** Public affairs, public matters? **B:** Yes. **A:** Okay, so they're the representatives. **B:** Yes. **A:** You yourself, as a seventeen year old, could move around in the ghetto? **B:** Oh, yes. **A:** And you did? **B:** Of course. **A:** Was there any kind of theater or movie house or anything like that in the ghetto? **B:** God have mercy! **A:** Was there anywhere at all to which people went in order to amuse themselves? **B:** Nothing. **A:** They didn't try to do anything like that? **B:** Nope. **A:** Could they have? **B:** I don't know. What they did try to do, at first, was a school for little children. **A:** Only for the little ones. **B:** For little ones that don't go out to work. **A:** But not for you? **B:** Oh, no. I was already grown up. I had already gone to work. I had already finished high school. **A:** So you were just waiting for something to happen. What would you have done if the war hadn't come? **B:** I don't know because I made my last exams, and the next day, the war broke out. **A:** But when you were studying in high school, what were you thinking about? **B:** The plan was that I was going to university. **A:** You probably would have gone to the university. **B:** Yes, in Vilna. My city didn't have a university. **A:** You were a good student? **B:** Just because I insist on the truth. I was very good in mathematics, geography, and history—in all of these things I was very good. In languages I was very bad. I am not good at writing till this day. My worst language was Latin. **A:** What would you do when you moved around in the ghetto? Where would you go, when you left your house? **B:** We would roam around the ghetto, a square kilometer is a lot. **A:** Would you go to your friends' rooms? **B:** Yes, friends' rooms. **A:** Visit them? **B:** Visit them, yes. **A:** But you wouldn't leave the ghetto? **B:** It was guarded.

A: Was there a fence around it? **B:** Yes. **A:** What kind of fence? **B:** Barbed wire. **A:** Who put it up? **B:** Matter of fact, the Jews themselves. **A:** The Jews themselves did it? **B:** Yes, they were forced to do it. **A:** Did you yourself work on the barbed wire fence? **B:** Yes. **A:** How long did it take to put up? **B:** I don't know. I was the first one who started the barbed wire wall and I'll just tell you the truth. I was in the factory and in the factory my father was king. In order to make the first holes in which to put the fence posts we needed a shtanger. I don't know what you call this in English? **A:** Some kind of thing to dig holes? **B:** Yes, so I took it from the factory. **A:** You took it? You volunteered it? **B:** Yes. Because I was a boss in the factory. Nobody in the factory interfered with me. **A:** How did you know that you had to put the fence up? **B:** There was an order. **A:** From the Germans? **B:** I don't know. **A:** Or from the three representatives? **B:** No! No! No! No! This was before everything. I didn't even know about the representatives. I was usually taken to forced labor. Also, I volunteered because I like to know what is going on. I was curious. So one day I am going to the forced labor and I am assigned to build the barbed wire fence. **A:** The Germans came in June and this is August? **B:** Yes. **A:** They had only been there two months when this happened? **B:** Yes. **A:** So you understood that they wanted this barbed wire fence put up around the ghetto, right? **B:** I didn't even know it would be a ghetto, honest to God. **A:** Well, what did you think they were putting the fence up for? **B:** I didn't think at all. Wait a minute. There were guys, Jewish guys, who assumed that this would be an enclave for Russian prisoners of war. **A:** So that's what you believed? **B:**

Isn't it reasonable? **A:** I don't know. **B:** You can believe anything. **A:** Well, is that what you were told? **B:** No, we weren't told anything, just build it, that's all. **A:** But some of you thought or believed that it was for Russian prisoners of war? **B:** Yes. **A:** And you didn't mind building it for that purpose? **B:** I had absolutely nothing to say. **A:** Well, presumably some uses would be better than others, right? **B:** There were some Jewish people who were making jokes and saying that they build it for the Russians, but in the reality it would be for German prisoners of war when the Russians came back. **A:** I see, but they did not think it was for them? **B:** But after awhile we knew it would be a ghetto. Building a fence takes time. It took several weeks. **A:** It took several weeks of putting a fence all the way around? **B:** Yes, a fence around one ghetto and then around the other. **A:** Did you work on both of them? **B:** No, I worked on Caukaz and then I got fed up so I didn't go to work there. I stayed in the factory. **A:** It took several weeks to build the fence? **B:** Yes. **A:** Who supervised the building? **B:** Nobody. **A:** Of course, somebody supervised. You all didn't just go out and start putting holes in the ground just anywhere, somebody must have— **B:** People who know how to build, that's all. **A:** But who determined where it was to be built, where the line was going to be? **B:** I don't know. It had already been decided. **A:** So, when you came to work there, it had been decided where it was going to go? **B:** I just put in the first holes. They started from the Jewish cemetery. That's all. **A:** So you started putting the holes in, others came along and put the posts in? **B:** Yes. **A:** Barbed wire was already there? **B:** Then people brought barbed wire. **A:** Coils of barbed wire? **B:** Yes. **A:** The Germans supplied that? **B:** I don't know. **A:** Was there barbed wire in Lithuania before this? **B:** Obviously. **A:** Did it grow there? **B:** The factory was surrounded by barbed wire. **A:** So you had experience with barbed wire before? **B:** Oh, yes. **A:** You are putting it in and it takes several weeks. How many entrances were there to the ghetto? **B:** In this Caukaz ghetto at first there were two entrances and then it became one. One was towards the factory and one was towards the city. And then they closed the one towards the factory. **A:** How high was the fence? **B:** Not so high. **A:** As high as a man? **B:** A little higher. **A:** A little higher. How far apart would the wires be? **B:** If you really wanted, you could sneak through. **A:** You could crawl through. **B:** Oh, yes. It was not a concentration camp. There were no guards standing with machine guns. **A:** Just a guard at the entrance? **B:** At the door. **A:** Armed guards? **B:** I guess so. **A:** One or two? **B:** Two, of course. **A:** Germans or Lithuanians?

B: Lithuanians! Lithuanians! Lithuanians! **A:** No Germans involved? **B:** No Germans involved. **A:** So the Lithuanians are standing guard? **B:** Yes. **A:** Did you know the Lithuanians who were standing guard? **B:** I didn't, but people knew them. Some of them had worked in the factory before. **A:** So there were two such entrances? **B:** Yes.

    A: What were the entrances for? People couldn't leave? **B:** People were taken to work and back from work. **A:** That was the purpose of the entrance? **B:** The only purpose. **A:** If somebody got ill, what would happen, if you had to go to a doctor, a hospital? **B:** Tough luck. **A:** Tough luck? **B:** Yes. The Jews themselves made a hospital in the cemetery. **A:** Within the cemetery? **B:** Yes. **A:** They set up a room? **B:** The Jewish law is that you have to clean a dead man, you have to wash him before you bury him. So there is a little building. **A:** And they turned that into a hospital? **B:** They turned it into a hospital. **A:** And there were doctors, of course. **B:** Jewish doctors, yes. **A:** What about medicine, drugs? Did you get any of those? **B:** [*Pause.*] It was illegal to give Jews drugs or anything. **A:** But there were some? **B:** There were some, because Jewish doctors worked as doctors in the city. **A:** They could leave to go out and work as doctors? **B:** Yes, as doctors. **A:** So some people *could* leave the ghetto, beside going to the factory, I mean? **B:** Yes, there were some people. At first, many could go out; then they were cut down. **A:** So some doctors could practice medicine elsewhere in the city? **B:** In the hospital. **A:** And their patients would be Lithuanians? Not Jews? **B:** Yes, Lithuanians and Germans. Not Jews. **A:** Not Jews. Jews they had to treat back at the cemetery? **B:** Yes. **A:** And when they went out in this way they would sometimes bring medicines back if they could? **B:** Yes. **A:** Or bandages? **B:** Stealing them, of course. **A:** Stealing them? **B:** They didn't steal from somebody else. They stole their own property. **A:** Who else could leave to go out besides doctors? **B:** The police. The Jewish police. **A:** Where would they go when they went out? **B:** I don't know, wherever they were sent. **A:** They were working as police in the city? **B:** No. They were working as police in the ghetto. **A:** Who could go out of the ghetto is what I'm trying to find out. Some people could go out to the factory to work. Doctors could go out and work in the hospitals? **B:** Yes. There were also other little factories that the Jews still worked in, in the beginning. **A:** And they could go there? Could they go by themselves? **B:** By themselves nobody could go. **A:** Including the doctors when they went to the hospitals? **B:** I think the doctors might have. **A:** By themselves? How about courts? Were there any courts that Jews would go to? **B:** That is a very good question. I didn't know that there were courts in the ghetto, but later on I read that there were courts in the ghetto. **A:** For Jews? **B:** For the Jews, among the Jews. **A:** Among the Jews? **B:** And they had moral authority and they imposed judgments. But while I was in the ghetto I didn't know about that. I tried to avoid the ghetto like the plague. It's very personal to me. **A:** What do you mean, you tried to avoid it? You were living in it. **B:** Till Yom Kippur, I was, unfortunately— **A:** Yom Kippur? **B:** 1941. **A:** So you only slept in the ghetto? **B:** Basically I only went to sleep there. **A:** But you didn't work every day? **B:** Six days a week. Is this enough? **A:** And on the seventh day? **B:** On the Sunday— **A:** You wouldn't sleep all day, would you? **B:** No. **A:** You would go out in the ghetto and walk around? **B:** Or visit friends. **A:** Now, did you ever go out of the ghetto to any place besides your factory work? **B:** Never. **A:** You never slipped out to go somewhere to visit somebody outside, a Lithuanian friend, nobody outside, you never went out to go walk in the country or something? **B:** [*Laughs.*] **A:** Nothing like that? Well, did anybody in the ghetto ever do this? Were there any young men who had girlfriends elsewhere who slipped out? None of them ever had things outside that they would slip out to do? You *could* slip out? **B:** In reality, yes. **A:** But very few did, you said, because? **B:** Because it was illegal, period. **A:** But that meant what? Would there be punishment for doing that, or what would happen? **B:** Obviously there would be some punishment, but I don't remember anyone being caught.

A: All right, you're there, you're working in a factory, you have one day a week in which you can walk around in the ghetto, visit with your friends. There's a worship service available in some of the houses or in one house somewhere in some room? **B:** Yes. **A:** Occasionally? **B:** Yes. **A:** There's no school for anybody beyond the early grades? **B:** That's right. **A:** And of course all this time you were very much aware of what was happening in the rest of Lithuania? **B:** I wouldn't say so. No. **A:** You were not? **B:** No. **A:** You got the news regularly about the war? **B:** I read the German paper. **A:** That was available in the ghetto? **B:** No it wasn't. It was illegal. **A:** To have a German paper? **B:** Yes. It was illegal for a Jew to read the German paper. **A:** Illegal, why was that? **B:** What, are you asking *me*? **A:** Did it occur to you to wonder why? **B:** The Germans said that Jews should not know any news. The Germans took away all the radios. Did I tell you that? **A:** They confiscated all the radios? **B:** Yes. **A:** But there were some radios still? **B:** No. **A:** Some people must have hidden their radios.

B: No. **A:** Of course, somebody did. **B:** No. Not at all. **A:** You mean there were four thousand people there and no one had managed to keep a radio? **B:** No, not even one. **A:** Was there a Yiddish press in the ghetto? **B:** What are you talking about? **A:** I am talking about a Yiddish press. **B:** How? **A:** I don't know. That's why I am trying to find out. **B:** Obviously, no. **A:** There was nobody printing anything? **B:** No. **A:** No piece of paper with information on it that was being written by Jews and distributed? **B:** No. **A:** All right, so there were forty-five hundred people there and they had no paper, they had no radio, they had some idea of what was happening elsewhere by way of German newspapers which it was illegal to have and which you didn't altogether trust anyway— **B:** I trusted them, 100 percent. **A:** What they said? **B:** Yes. **A:** You did trust what they said? **B:** I did trust what they said. **A:** You were following the war by way of German newspapers which were illegal? **B:** Which were illegal. **A:** All right, and this went on for— **B:** In reality, nobody got punished for reading German newspapers. In reality, nobody would know. **A:** Where would you get the papers? **B:** Every kiosk outside of the ghetto was selling them. **A:** Did you have kiosks? **B:** No! Outside of the ghetto, I made it very clear to you. **A:** Well, how did you get papers from outside of the ghetto if you couldn't go outside of the ghetto? **B:** In the factory, we worked together with non-Jews. **A:** So you got the German newspapers in the factories and brought them home? **B:** Yes. **A:** This went on for three years for you? **B:** Yes. **A:** You worked in the factory for three years almost and your mother kept working there all the time you were working there? **B:** Yes. Of course, she lost her good job and she had to go work at another job, but she still worked there. **A:** Was there any kind of organization of Jews in the ghetto? **B:** There was an organization, an underground organization. I applied and was not accepted. **A:** You applied to whom? **B:** A guy that belonged to the organization. **A:** And what kind of organization was this? **B:** Supposedly an underground to fight the Germans. **A:** To fight against them? **B:** Yes. **A:** And did they fight against them? **B:** No, it was only talk. **A:** What do you mean that it was only talk? **B:** From time to time it would gather together and say that we had to defend ourselves and there would be big speeches about Masada. Do you know about Masada? **A:** Yes. **B:** Big speeches that we have to behave like the heroes of Masada, only talk. **A:** But they *would* talk about Masada? **B:** Oh, yes. Talk is cheap. **A:** But nobody ever did anything? **B:** No. There were some people that ran away to the real partisans. **A:** There *were* some partisans? **B:** Yes. **A:** Where were the partisans hiding? **B:** They were not hiding. **A:** Well, where were they? They were not in the city streets of Lithuania, were they? **B:** They were in the woods. **A:** They were hiding in the woods? **B:** But very few. The general Lithuanian population was against the Russians. **A:** And *for* the Germans? **B:** Against the Russians. **A:** Only that, and not *for* the Germans? **B:** For the Germans only as far as Jews are concerned. That's all. **A:** They shared the Germans' view about the Jews? **B:** About Jewish property. **A:** It was property primarily that they wanted? **B:** Property only. That's my own analysis. **A:** They didn't have any personal feelings about the Jews themselves, besides about their property? **B:** The Jews were a matter of principle. **A:** They were what? **B:** A matter of principle. **A:** What was a matter of principle? **B:** To hate the Jews. **A:** To hate the Jews? **B:** "They crucified our God." They didn't need any other excuse.

A: All right, so all this continued for three years? **B:** Yes. **A:** You were a teenager? **B:** Yes. **A:** Was there any kind of entertainment for you? **B:** No. **A:** I don't mean theater. I mean was there— **B:** No entertainment. **A:** —amusements? Were there sports in the ghetto? **B:** No. **A:** Games that people would play? **B:** The people could play cards till doomsday, if they wanted to. **A:** What about the boys? Card-game playing is not their thing. And what did the girls do in the ghetto? **B:** They worked like men, what do you want, for God's sake? **A:** They would go out? **B:** Out to work exactly, like men. **A:** Like men. You had a fairly good idea what was happening in the war? **B:** Yes. **A:** You had an idea that the Germans were in trouble in Russia? **B:** Yes. **A:** You did know that? **B:** Oh, yes, they were very open about it. That's another reason why he won over the German nation. He was open. **A:** Hitler, that is? **B:** Hitler and the newspapers. The German newspapers were open about it. I remember two places they lost, one near Leningrad, another on the Black Sea. They had written that they had to retreat. They also had written when there were great attacks from Leningrad, that they had to defend themselves. **A:** And these were in the German newspapers? **B:** In the German newspapers. **A:** Where were those German newspapers printed? **B:** Riga [in Latvia]. **A:** Riga, and distributed all over this area, is that it? **B:** Latvia, Estonia, and Lithuania became one country: Austland. The entire thing was Deustertzire in Austland. **A:** The Eastland, is that it? **B:** Yes. **A:** So they would distribute the paper out of Riga? **B:** Yes. **A:** The Germans would distribute it themselves? **B:** Yes. **A:** How would it be distributed? **B:** I don't know. **A:** Trucks? **B:** I don't know. **A:** Tanks? **B:** No! No! **A:** Trains? **B:** Whatever the usual transportation was. **A:** You had a fairly good idea about the war? **B:** A very good idea about the war.

A: Now what did you think was going to happen to you? **B:** I thought we would all be killed. That was my own personal diagnosis. **A:** You thought that from the beginning? **B:** Around September I came to that conclusion. **A:** September of 1941? **B:** Yes. **A:** You began to believe that— **B:** We would all be killed, we were lost, finished. **A:** That you would be killed, not just allowed to die? **B:** Physically killed. **A:** They would be going after you? The Germans would do it? **B:** Whoever, who cares, we will be killed. Why? Because that's what all the German papers were about—the Jews, the Jews, the Jews, the Jews. **A:** You mean the German papers that you were reading? **B:** Yes, the only papers that there were. **A:** They had a lot in them about the Jews? **B:** Not a lot, not a lot. They would mention them from time to time. **A:** And what would they say about the Jews? **B:** Only bad things. **A:** Such as what? **B:** That the Jews wanted the war. **A:** They wanted the war? **B:** Yes. What is unifying the British and Americans plutocracies with Communist Russia? The Jews. A very simple answer. How can they both work together? The Jew. **A:** The Jew is the link between them? **B:** The Jew is the link. **A:** I see. **B:** The Jew wants the war. If not for the Jew, there would have been peace long ago. **A:** Did the Germans want peace? **B:** Officially everyone wants peace. Don't you know that? **A:** But did they talk in the papers about wanting peace? **B:** No. They worshiped war. But everybody talks about peace. I mean even now, all the newspapers— **A:** Well, what else would they say about the Jews, besides the fact that they— **B:** Oh, a very interesting thing is about the Karaims, you know the Karaims? **A:** No. **B:** A Jewish sect, the Karaims. Have you never heard about them? **A:** Karaims? **B:** Karaims. **A:** What about them? **B:** This was a Jewish sect that separated from Judaism in the eighth century. **A:** Oh, do you mean the Kuzars? **B:** No! No! No! **A:** No, not them? **B:** Karaims. Karaims. **A:** Okay. How is that spelled, you think? **B:** I don't know. K-A-R-A-I-M-S. **A:** Eighth century, you say? **B:** In the eighth century they separated. **A:** Where were they living when they separated? **B:** They were then in Mesopotamia, in Iraq, Babylonia. **A:** Oh, down there. All right. Then what happened? **B:** They don't believe in the Talmud at all. The Talmud is superfluous; they believe only in the Bible. So they have different customs and everything. The Jews and the Karaims didn't mix. Although I know my mother once had a friend who told her that he's not a Jew, he's a Karaim, but of course he was a Jew and spoke Yiddish and everything. Savage was his name. What I remember in the German paper, and I was very impressed, it was in the beginning of the war—is that a group of Karaims on horses welcomed the German army. And there was a picture with the Karaims sitting on the horses. And the Karaim religion was called a mixture of the Christian, Muslim, and Jewish religions. **A:** Where was this? **B:** In Lithuania. **A:** They were living in Lithuania? **B:** They were living in Lithuania. **A:** Did you know any Karaims? **B:** No. **A:** They weren't living in your town? **B:** No. **A:** Where had they been living, that they could welcome Germans? **B:** I think near Truck, near Trako. **A:** There was a little group of them there? **B:** Yes. And they survived the war. You never heard about them? **A:** No. They survived the war? **B:** Yes. **A:** Did they go to concentration camps? **B:** No. **A:** They were allowed to live there? **B:** Yes. **A:** Because they were not thought of as Jews? **B:** Not thought of as Jews. There was a huge controversy, and only after the war I found out what the controversy was. At a certain point Hitler decided he needed Muslim allies. So the Karaim had been included as Muslim allies. There were several refuges of these Karaims in France, in Paris, and there was a question as to how to deal with them and then there had been the decision that they were Muslims. Therefore they were to be treated nicely. **A:** Okay. **B:** You didn't know about them? **A:** No. So they were declared to be Muslims. **B:** Yes. **A:** And would you spell that name again? **B:** Karaims. K-A-R-A-I-M-S. S is the plural. **A:** Karaims, all right. **B:** They dressed like non-Jews. They were completely non-Jews. **A:** How did the Jews dress? **B:** The Jews dressed like the average person. **A:** Like an average person? **B:** Yes.

A: Your town itself [Siauliai, Lithuania] was how large? **B:** Thirty thousand. **A:** Thirty thousand. If a Jew was walking outside the ghetto— **B:** No! He was not walking outside the ghetto. **A:** If he did— **B:** I don't know *if*— **A:** Well, there must have been somebody that walked outside the ghetto sometimes. The doctors did when they went to the hospital, you already told me that. **B:** I forgot to tell you a little detail. **A:** Yes? **B:** No Jew was allowed to walk on the sidewalk. **A:** Okay. **B:** So a Jew had to walk along the sidewalk where the horses were going in the middle of the street. **A:** How could you tell a Jew from a non-Jew? **B:** The star. **A:** The yellow star? **B:** Yes. **A:** Everybody wore one? **B:** Everybody wore one. **A:** And you never had to wear that before? **B:** No! The Jews lived in Lithuania like the Jews in America. So it was very good. **A:** When did the star come? When did Jews start wearing the stars? **B:** I don't know. I think sometime in July. **A:** Shortly after the Germans came? **B:** Yes. **A:** Where did the stars come from? **B:** I don't know. Every Jew had to provide his own material for the star. The government didn't issue material for the star. **A:** It did not? **B:** No. **A:** But you had to have one. **B:** Everyone had to have two, front and back. **A:** How large were they? **B:** I don't remember. **A:** Well, were they as big as your fist? **B:** Bigger. **A:** As big as your head? **B:** No, I think about ten centimeters. **A:** Same size front and back? **B:** Yes. **A:** Was there anything else that would be distinctive, besides the star? **B:** That's enough. **A:** What about hair? **B:** Who cares about hair? **A:** I don't know. I am wondering. **B:** Nobody cares. **A:** So Jews were not distinctive looking? **B:** Jews had brown eyes. It was the only Mediterranean race that went that far north. No Italians, no Greeks, no Spaniards. I never saw a non-Jew that has brown eyes; maybe some Germans have brown eyes; Lithuanians are all blue eyes—all of them. **A:** Are you suggesting that a Jew would be fairly easy to identify? **B:** For the Lithuanians, not for the Germans. **A:** For the Lithuanians to identify? **B:** Oh, yes. **A:** So you lived there for three years? **B:** Wait! Wait! Wait! Wait! **A:** Oh, I'm sorry. **B:** There were Jewish people at first—you know we are all smart alecs—who put the yellow star on so that you could take it off for the moment, and they would take off the yellow star and walk on the sidewalk. I know of two cases where the German police caught them, they were taken to German police headquarters, and they had to pay a fine for walking on the sidewalk. These Jews kept this little piece of paper from the police to show their grandchildren. But they did not survive. **A:** What else could the Jew not do when he was out of the ghetto? He could not walk on the sidewalk and he could be outside the ghetto for only limited purposes. Is that it? **B:** But there were Jews who risked everything. I know Jews who dared to go to the synagogue. **A:** You mean your friends, young friends? **B:** I don't know. There were people that worked in the factory who went to the synagogue. **A:** And did anything happen to them? **B:** They were never caught. But they were twice in danger, because in the end the Germans needed people to work in Germany, so outside of the cinemas they would catch all the males and send them to Germany. **A:** You mean they would wait there until they came out? **B:** Yes. **A:** And they could tell they were Jews? **B:** Not Jews, Lithuanians! Jews were not allowed in the cinema. Lithuanians were caught and sent to Germany. **A:** When they came out of the cinema? **B:** Out of the cinema. You never heard about that? **A:** No, I never heard about that. **B:** Till now? **A:** Yes. **B:** And they were sent to work in Saxonia. **A:** Well, that must not have been very popular. **B:** And the Lithuanians called it Saxophonia. They didn't even call it Saxonia, Saxophonia, that gives it. The Lithuanians, in the end, were not happy with the Germans.

A: So you have three years with the Germans in Lithuania? **B:** It is not a continuous thing, the three years, that's what I am trying to tell you. It's getting worse and worse. **A:** But you *were* three years in the ghetto. **B:** I hated the ghetto. I hate it till this day. **A:** Well, what other restrictions were there after the initial ones? **B:** At first, we were paid money. **A:** To work? **B:** Yes. Not as much as the non-Jews. **A:** Then after a while they stopped paying you money? **B:** Yes. **A:** And gave you coupons instead? **B:** Yes. **A:** Which you could use only in the cooperative? **B:** Yes. **A:** Was there any way of leaving the country? **B:** Where to? **A:** I don't know. Was there any way of leaving the country? **B:** Absolutely no chance. What are you saying! **A:** No chance? **B:** No chance. **A:** If somebody asked you to come to Palestine, for example. **B:** What are you saying, "If somebody asked"? There was no chance. **A:** If somebody sent a ticket to you, could you leave? **B:** Jews were not allowed anything. **A:** Could people come to visit the ghetto from outside? **B:** Some non-Jews wanted and came. **A:** Lithuanians? **B:** Yes. **A:** How about people from outside of Lithuania? Did you ever have any Jews come to visit you? **B:** Even Jews from another Lithuanian ghetto were not allowed to visit. Once a truck came to the factory from the Vilna ghetto and Jews tried to smuggle letters to their relatives in Vilna. They were caught, they had the hell beaten out of them. One of the scenes was very important to me. I remember a guy and his father: the German foreman took his stick and beat his father up and that guy stood there and he couldn't help even his own father and it breaks my heart until this day, the scene was so horrible. **A:** A German who was beating up his father, and what was he doing? **B:** He could do nothing; he had to look, that's all. These are the horrible scenes that I remember, that you couldn't even help your own father. This is horrible. **A:** So the restrictions got harder and harder over the three years? **B:** Yes, and then the lawlessness got more and more. Finally the Jews stopped worrying about the law at all. **A:** Within the ghetto? **B:** Everywhere. There was no use listening to the law about what a Jew is allowed or is not allowed to do. You do what you have to do. It didn't make any sense. There was no relation between the punishment and the crime, absolutely no relation.

A: What about the health of the people in the ghetto? **B:** The doctors tried very much to keep the health up. **A:** And did they? **B:** They tried.

There was an outbreak of typhus and it was very important that nobody should know, because the assumption was that if the Germans found out that there was typhus in the ghetto, they would destroy the whole ghetto. So it was kept a secret. Those with typhus went to the hospital; I don't know what was done to them; and they came back, healed from the typhus. Yes, the doctors were working very hard, very hard. **A:** Were there rabbis? **B:** They had to work like anybody else. There was no distinction. **A:** No distinction? **B:** No distinction. The original rabbi from my home town was taken to jail right away. I knew the rabbi because I had visited him. It was assumed that I was a gifted child. So I went to the rabbi; he wanted to talk to me, and he was talking to me and I realized that he didn't know what world he was living in. Before the First World War, a rabbi was a very important personage. Even for non-Jews the rabbi was considered an honest man and so on. I didn't have the heart to tell him that I knew he was living in an illusionary world and, sure enough, when the Germans came, he was put in jail. He thought that he would say that he was the rabbi and that that would help him. When he was in jail he said, "I am the rabbi." So they harnessed him on a buggy instead of a horse and beat the hell out of him. **A:** They made him pull the buggy? **B:** Yes. **A:** By himself? **B:** By himself. And finally they killed him by beating him. **A:** Out there in the street? **B:** Not in the street, in jail. Harav Bachts, that's his name, Aron Bachts. He didn't know what world he was living in. Most of the Jews in Lithuania did not know in what world they were. They had no idea what was going to happen or how deep the anti-Semitism was or anything. The number of people that had open eyes was very small.

   A: What happened to the three Jewish representatives—Katz and the other two? **B:** Very good. Now I have got you. The 5th of November 1943 the Germans took away all the children and the sick people and this could be a whole story in itself, the 5th of November. These representatives went to the German commandant and asked him, "Where are you taking these people?" **A:** Women and children? **B:** No! **A:** Just the children? **B:** Women were working like men. **A:** Okay, so they took away all of the children. **B:** The children up until sixteen and all of the sick people. If a child was fourteen and he looked grown up, they let him alone. So these representatives went to the German commandant; they were very brave, and they asked him "Where are you taking these people?" And the commandant says, "You want to know? Go with them." And two went. You've never heard this kind of story? **A:** No. **B:** And two went. Captoun and Katz went and the only one that stayed was Rubinshtein, he was very old. So they went and the Jews believed that these representatives would return to tell them where the children had been taken. They were idiots to believe this. The Germans said that after three days they would come back and report. So people counted three days, and then a week, but they never came back. **A:** I see. **B:** So, why shouldn't I be proud of such representatives? **A:** Don't you think they were too trusting? **B:** What do you mean "too trusting"? **A:** At least, you could be proud of them that they were trying to find out something about their people? **B:** I am very proud of them that they didn't separate themselves from their people. **A:** Now, they were replaced— **B:** Yes, they were replaced. **A:** By two others? **B:** Not two others, one guy. Arizal was a Jew who was married to a German woman. An interesting story, this Arizal. He came from Mamalan with his Aryan wife and two children. So when the time came to go to the ghetto, the Germans suggested to her that she say that these two children were bastards and she should not have to go with her husband. But she prepared to go with her husband in the ghetto. This is a good story. This is one you might write when you write my stories, because I do have good stories. **A:** So she went into the ghetto with her husband and two children. What happened to her? **B:** Very good. He managed to become head of the ghetto. Then he managed, when he learned that we Jews would be transported to Germany, to join the Germans and so he did not go to a concentration camp. He managed to get by as a German. He was a soldier in the German army in the First World War and so on, and he was very loyal to Germany. He was a German for all practical purposes. So he survived to be a witness at a postwar trial. **A:** And his wife and children survived? **B:** Yes. **A:** Okay. So there you have the representatives, who try to do something, sent off and are never heard of again? **B:** Yes. **A:** Probably they were killed? **B:** They were sent to one of those horrible places that I don't want to mention. **A:** So they were sent there and therefore they were very likely killed? **B:** Certainly, not "very likely."

A: In the meantime, you are seeing this happen and you are getting close to twenty years old. **B:** I am nineteen, yes. **A:** And it's getting worse. **B:** Getting worse. **A:** Did you think about running away to Russia? **B:** Where is Russia? It is far away to the east. Every Lithuanian will turn me in. That is the whole problem: the local population was not on our side. Not the Russians, not the Germans, nobody. The local population was against us. Twice I made attempts to run away. Both times I failed miserably, so I gave up. **A:** When did you try? **B:** One day I worked in the factory. The factory I worked in had transports. I went on them to all kinds of places outside, even sometimes on a highway. So I came to a place where I asked a farmer for food. He had a very nice garden and carrots were growing there. He says, "Go and pick as many carrots as you want." Obviously I grabbed the carrots. I must have worked very hard because the farmer said, "Stay with me and you will work for me." So I told him, "I have a mother in the ghetto, can she come, too?" He said no. Now there were cases where people faced this trick: they worked for Lithuanians and then, come fall, Lithuanians would bring them back to the ghetto for running away. Being in the ghetto was punishment enough. **A:** So you worked for how long for this man? **B:** What man? **A:** The man with the carrots. **B:** Never! It was one day. **A:** One day, and the other time you ran away? **B:** I didn't. The other time is in the last day that the ghetto existed, the last day when we were told that we were going to Germany. I went to my mother and I say, "Mama, all these four years I have waited for this moment." I went to my neighbors who lived in the same factory, who know me and my mother— **A:** Lithuanians? **B:** Lithuanians. And I went to them and I say to them, "Look, during all these three years I never asked you for anything." These neighbors never treated me like a Jew, but like a neighbor all these three years. "Now is the moment, please hide us." And this woman says—her husband was a drunk so he didn't count—and she says, "I will not hide you, but if you and your mother try to run away I will not turn you in. The other Jews I will." She didn't have to add this last sentence. She didn't have to add it, but it hurts me till this day. Ah, I mean that's life. **A:** Now why did it make a difference what she did? **B:** She wouldn't turn me in. **A:** Well, was she in charge of you some way? **B:** Nobody was in charge of anything. A Lithuanian thought it was his duty to turn in Jews, for God's sake. **A:** Well, I know, but— **B:** She told me that if I and my mother tried to run away she would not turn us in. **A:** I see. **B:** She knew we were decent people. **A:** She wasn't going to help you hide but she would let you— **B:** She will not turn us in. **A:** But she was not doing anything to help you, was she? **B:** No. **A:** I see. Would she have known that you had run away if you had done it? **B:** The factory had barbed wire around and people see you. You cannot leave the factory without being seen by people. **A:** And she would have known you were gone? **B:** Yes.

    A: So, you say, they were closing down the ghetto? **B:** Yes. **A:** They told you that they were closing it down? **B:** No! One day I was working in the factory and all of a sudden there was a rumor that we were being taken away to Germany. A rumor. **A:** That who was being taken away? **B:** All of the Jews, all of the ghetto. **A:** All the Jews in the ghetto? **B:** Yes. **A:** So you went home? **B:** I didn't go home. My mother worked in a factory, I worked in a factory. **A:** So what did you do? **B:** I took my mother and went to the neighbors and failed. **A:** Trying to get a hiding place, you mean? You couldn't get a hiding place? **B:** I couldn't get a hiding place. **A:** If you had had a hiding place, what would you have done? **B:** I would go hiding. What kind of question is that? **A:** For how long, for how long? **B:** It was only a matter of at most two weeks before the Russians entered. **A:** The Russians entered in 1944. You mean that the Germans knew the Russians were coming? **B:** That's why they evacuated us. **A:** They didn't want any Jews there? **B:** No, they needed the workforce. Don't kid yourself one moment about any other reasons, for them. In the end the Germans were desperate; they really needed a workforce. **A:** Whom were they going to take out of the town? **B:** The Jews. **A:** Well, all the Jews who could work, you mean? **B:** All Jews worked. Those who didn't work had been killed already. **A:** So all that was left by 1944 in the ghetto were working Jews? **B:** Yes. **A:** The children were gone? **B:** Gone. **A:** The old people were gone? **B:** Gone. **A:** The sick people were gone? **B:** Gone. **A:** So all that's left is— **B:** Slave labor. **A:** And how many of you were left at the time, do you estimate, of the four thousand originally? There were four thousand? **B:** Forty-five hundred. **A:** How many of them would have been left by this time? **B:** I don't know, even then I still thought it was about four thousand, but I don't know. I believed that they took us to kill us, but that was my own personal opinion. I didn't know how desperate they were— **A:** In Germany? **B:** In Germany. **A:** Okay. But why hadn't they taken them out before? **B:** Taken whom? **A:** The Jews, to work. **B:** We worked in the leather factory. We were useful for the German war effort. **A:** So you were doing the work there? **B:** Yes. **A:** In the factory one day, a rumor came to you? **B:** Yes. **A:** That you were all going to be moved out? **B:** Yes. Yes. **A:** All that had survived were to be moved out. How long after? **B:** I think two weeks after. **A:** Everybody you know was moved? **B:** All the Jews from the ghetto. **A:** Including your mother? **B:** She moved, with me, of course. **A:** They were moved, they were all moved? **B:** Yes.

A: How were you moved? **B:** That's another story. **A:** We'll talk about it, maybe next time. **B:** If you wish, next time. We were moved in railway carriages. **A:** From the town itself? **B:** From the town itself we had to walk about twenty kilometers because the railway was already cut off by the Russians. So you had to go twenty kilometers to another railway branch. **A:** They walked you over there? **B:** Yes. **A:** All together? **B:** Yes. **A:** All four thousand of you? **B:** Not all four thousand. Many of them were already taken by rail transport. But at the last there was no rail connection. **A:** That's when you went, when you were with your mother? **B:** With my mother. And we stayed together until the concentration camp. In the concentration camp they separated us. **A:** I see. And so you went to this place twenty kilometers away where they could put you on a train? **B:** Yes. Wait, wait, wait. I'll have to tell this story, but I don't know if it's true. The story is that the Jewish heads of the ghetto made arrangement with the heads of the train station that there should not be rail carriages for us to be carried out. They made an agreement with them. That's a story, that's a rumor. **A:** That there should be no rail carriages? **B:** There should be no rail carriages for us to be taken to Germany. **A:** So how were you going to go? **B:** Wait a minute. That's the rumor. I don't know if it's true. **A:** Okay. **B:** There were no rail carriages to carry us. So we walked twenty kilometers, where there were rail carriages. **A:** So they thought that they were doing you a favor, but they weren't? **B:** Who is "they"? **A:** The representatives. **B:** They planned that there should be no railway carriages. **A:** Yes, but the only result of that was that you had to walk twenty kilometers further. **B:** Yes, that was the result. **A:** So that was not a good thing? **B:** How do you know that it was not a good thing? **A:** I don't know. That's what I am asking. **B:** They played for time. **A:** How long did it take to walk the twenty kilometers? **B:** I don't know. **A:** Well, a day? **B:** We went out, I think, at noon and I think we got there in the evening. **A:** How were you walking? Were you all walking together? How were you walking? **B:** Walking on the street. **A:** Were the Germans with you? **B:** There were German guards on both sides. **A:** Front, back? **B:** Yes. **A:** Along the sides too? **B:** Yes. **A:** German soldiers? **B:** Yes. **A:** In uniform? **B:** Of course, in uniform. **A:** Armed? **B:** Armed, of course. **A:** And did they make sure that everybody stayed together? **B:** They tried their best. **A:** And how big a group was it, in terms of space when you were walking? **B:** I don't remember. Several hundred. **A:** Several hundred people? **B:** Yes. **A:** Over how large an area were they spread? **B:** I don't know. **A:** Well? **B:** Please. I don't know. **A:** Were they a mile long, a kilometer long? **B:** I don't know. **A:** Yes, you know that. **B:** I don't. How could I know, you think I was really measuring? **A:** No, but could you see the beginning or the end of it all as you were walking? **B:** I don't know.

I never looked back or anything, I looked forward, I really never looked back. **A:** Well, how wide was the column? **B:** Not wide, not wide. **A:** Were there three or four of you abreast, or how many? **B:** The usual thing I think was five abreast. That's the German army. **A:** They weren't marching you, were they? **B:** No, we were not lined up. **A:** You weren't marching 1, 2, 3, 4? **B:** No, we were not marching like that. **A:** And you were talking as you were going? **B:** Oh, yes. **A:** Singing? **B:** What are you saying? **A:** No singing? **B:** No, you are killing me. **A:** No singing, some talking. No effort to get away? **B:** I looked left and right to see if I had a chance. I didn't see any chance. **A:** So you *were* looking for a place to run, to get away? **B:** Of course. At one point we stopped for people to relieve themselves and I thought maybe this was the opportunity. But it was not an opportunity. **A:** They were watching you? **B:** They were watching. **A:** How many places did they have like that, for relief stops? **B:** Once. **A:** In twenty kilometers? **B:** Yes. **A:** I see. **B:** And people right away started talking about the bad morals that men and women were pissing together and shitting together, how can you become an animal like that. **A:** And were they together, the men and the women? **B:** What choice have we got? **A:** I don't know. That's why I'm asking. **B:** Yes. **A:** So you all moved together. Did you have any food? It *was* half a day. **B:** I had enough to take with me. I took bread on reserve for the half day.

A: So you got to the railroad. **B:** No, no. We got to a place that was before a factory. We went there and we slept over there a whole night. Only in the morning did the trains come. **A:** They came to where you were sleeping? **B:** Yes. **A:** These were Lithuanian trains, German trains? **B:** I don't know. There were railway carriages that were ready to take us away. **A:** So the next morning, they took you? **B:** Yes. **A:** How early? **B:** I don't know. **A:** Well, was it dark or light? **B:** It was light, of course. And we got good food, we got a box of meat and bread. **A:** From whom? **B:** From the Germans. **A:** They had it waiting for you? **B:** They had prepared it. It was all prepared. **A:** So you all got on the train? **B:** Yes. **A:** How many of you were in the cars, in the carriages? **B:** A very good question. Twenty. **A:** Only twenty? **B:** Only twenty. **A:** Did you have seats to sit in? **B:** It was a freight car. **A:** Would they count you on? **B:** They let only twenty on, because at that point they still needed our good will. **A:** They needed your good will? **B:** Yes, that we shouldn't panic and try to jump from the train and so on. They were still feeding us all kinds of stories, even the guards. We are being taken to work in Germany? **A:** Well, that was true, wasn't it? **B:** Kind of. And they were skilled in treating us fair. Twenty people for each car. We made a separate place for shitting and pissing. **A:** Where, in the train? **B:** In the carriage. And everything was still families together. **A:** And these are all Jews? **B:** Yes. **A:** No Lithuanians? **B:** No Lithuanian soldiers. **A:** None of the Lithuanians from the cinema or anyone else who had been taken? **B:** No. Some Lithuanians *were* running away for their lives with their own free will. **A:** But the Jews were certainly not doing that? **B:** The Jews were forced. **A:** And most of the Lithuanians? **B:** They would wait for the Russian occupation. **A:** Now, how long after you left did the Russians come into your town? **B:** I think only one day, at most two days. **A:** So they got you out just in time? **B:** When we walked we could not carry all of our luggage and our things. They told us to take just food. I took my father's golden watch. The rest, they said, should be put into sacks and trucks will come and pick them up and bring them up to us. **A:** That was very good? **B:** Very good. Except what they did was that they came with flamethrowers and burned the whole ghetto and everything. **A:** They burned it all? **B:** Yes. **A:** They didn't even loot it? **B:** No, no, they didn't loot it. **A:** Why not, do you think? **B:** Don't ask me why. Maybe they didn't have the time. They had to run away. **A:** Because the Russians were coming? **B:** Yes. **A:** I see. Why were they burning the ghetto? **B:** Perhaps a Jew had tried to hide there or something. **A:** So even though the Jews were gone— **B:** They burned the whole ghetto down. **A:** They didn't say to the Lithuanians, "Go ahead and take it, now that the Jews are gone"? **B:** Nothing. They burned it with flamethrowers. **A:** Meanwhile you are on the train going to Germany? **B:** We are still not on the train. We are twenty kilometers from there, but then the rumor came that the ghetto had been burnt down. **A:** So you are not expecting your sacks anymore? **B:** No, no, I did not believe one moment all the stories. I was sure that they wanted to kill us and that's it. When I saw other people crying when they lost their belongings, I thought, "What are they talking about? Their lives are in danger and they are talking about belongings?" **A:** So they put you on a train the next morning? **B:** Yes. **A:** And they gave you some food? **B:** Some good food. **A:** Good food? **B:** Yes, it was very good. **A:** And then how long were you on the train? **B:** Five days.

    A: Could you get off at all, to walk around? **B:** There is a good story about that— I forgot to tell you. **A:** Yes? **B:** On the way we stopped before, while still in Lithuania. We found another train, with Lithuanian refugees, who were also going to Germany. **A:** Lithuanians? **B:** Lithuanians. What's more is that some of them knew some of us, and we even exchanged greetings. **A:** But you didn't change places at all? **B:** [*Laughs.*] **A:** You didn't try to go into that train? **B:** Please, of course not. **A:** Were they also twenty per carriage? **B:** No! They were like human beings. **A:** Well, how many would there have been? **B:** I don't know. They had railway carriages like human beings. **A:** Oh, they had seats. **B:** Chairs and seats. **A:** You didn't have seats at all, did you? **B:** No, no. **A:** Just an empty carriage, right? **B:** An empty carriage. **A:** A freight car? **B:** Yes. **A:** Did anybody try to hide in the Lithuanian carriage? **B:** No, we talked through the window. We said "Hi" only through the window. **A:** Did you see people you knew? **B:** Some people did. I didn't see people that I knew. **A:** So you and they could look out the window? **B:** They looked out and called each other by name. **A:** It's summer time. In summer time the windows are open? **B:** Yes. **A:** There was no air conditioning in those days? **B:** The people in the other train are standing outside; they are walking along the train. **A:** You could talk to them? **B:** Yes. And they are running from the Russians. **A:** To Germany? **B:** To Germany. **A:** These are Lithuanians? **B:** Lithuanians. **A:** Why were *they* running? **B:** Because they didn't want to be under Russian occupation. **A:** Were these people political people or just ordinary people? **B:** The average Lithuanian does not want to be under Russian rule, to this day. **A:** Yes. But most Lithuanians did not leave Lithuania then? **B:** Most, no. **A:** So why were these people leaving? Who were these people? Were they special? You don't know? **B:** No. **A:** So you saw them there? This was not at Memel, but earlier? **B:** Earlier. And they even talked to us. **A:** A brief encounter? **B:** A brief encounter. **A:** And then you were all running on the same railroad line? **B:** Parallel tracks; yes, the same railroad. **A:** Two parallel lines and the two trains are both going the same direction? **B:** Yes, but we stopped our train, and their train stopped for some reason. **A:** So this route you're taking had two sets of tracks? **B:** I don't know if it had two sets of tracks all the way. **A:** But it did have two sets of tracks at this point? **B:** At this point, yes. **A:** Okay, so you visited with each other a little bit. **B:** We talked. **A:** You compared notes about— **B:** The head of the factory, the Lithuanian head of the factory, was one of them. **A:** You saw him? **B:** Yes. I forget his name. **A:** But you recognized him. Did he see you? **B:** He didn't have to see me, he saw others that he knew. **A:** I see. **B:** It was like friends talking among themselves. **A:** Yes. But there was no sense about what the difference was going to be for each? **B:** There was a very good sense of that. We are in railway carriages like pigs and they are in railway carriages like human beings. **A:** And did they say anything about that? **B:** They didn't say anything, just "Hi!" The whole atmosphere looked strange to me then and still does, like it's a joyous occasion, like people are going to a picnic. **A:** On the part of? **B:** On both parts. It's excitement, you know; trains are going— **A:** But there was no sense, on the part of the Lithuanians you talked to, of sympathy for your situation? **B:** No sense, no, nothing. **A:** No sense of, "Gee, this is awful, what they are doing to you"? **B:** No, no. **A:** Nothing like that? **B:** Nothing like that. That's what bothers me more than anything— **A:** Yes. That's why I want to— **B:** — that they did not have any pity for us. **A:** That *is* very intriguing. **B:** That's the thing that bothers me. **A:** Yes. They saw what condition you were in? **B:** Yes. **A:** There was no question about that, right? **B:** They see what kind of railway carriages we are in— **A:** That's what I mean, they see how you are traveling. **B:** They see, and we wave to them, and they wave to us. **A:** And you recognized some of them? **B:** Yes. **A:** And yet, as far as you know, may they have been afraid to express pity? Do you think— **B:** They didn't give a damn about us, it's clear. **A:** They didn't care at all about— **B:** Of course, they didn't. And they were trying to save their own lives, their own hides. **A:** Even though some of them were old friends? **B:** "Old friends" is an exaggeration, but okay. **A:** Old acquaintances? **B:** Old acquaintances. **A:** Fellow workers? **B:** Yes, fellow workers, no doubt. **A:** Some of them had been working for your father? **B:** No, no, no, no. **A:** No, never? **B:** No. This factory had been a huge factory, it had about five departments, five factories, in effect. **A:** So they wouldn't have been with your father? All right, so you are there, you see these people, you greet them. **B:** Yes, as if nothing was wrong. I feel that we are condemned to die, and they are saving their own lives. This was my own personal feeling. **A:** And at the same time that you feel you are condemned to die, and although you have several days during which to do it, you don't jump out of the carriage to try to take your chances. **B:** To go where? [*Stomps down.*] Where can I go? **A:** But you are quite clear in your mind that if you kept going on this trip you are going to get killed? **B:** That was my own personal opinion. **A:** But you don't take any measures to get away from the trip? **B:** I'm fatalistic. Finished. **A:** Okay, you get to Memel. **B:** So I was surprised. [They brought us] coffee, like we were German soldiers.

Appendix J

Cases and Other Materials Drawn On

Cases

Brown v. *Board of Education*, 347 U.S. 483 (1954).
Buck v. *Bell*, 274 U.S. 200 (1927).
Burr, United States v., 8 U.S. 455 (1807).
Bush v. *Gore*, 531 U.S. 98 (2000).
Church of the Lukumi Babalu Aye, Inc. v. *City of Hialeah*, 508 U.S. 520 (1993).
Coker v. *Georgia*, 433 U.S. 584 (1977).
Cruzan v. *Director, Missouri Department of Health*, 497 U.S. 261 (1990).
Doe v. *Bolton*, 410 U.S. 179 (1973).
Dred Scott v. *Sandford*, 60 U.S. 393 (1857).
Edwards v. *Aguillard*, 482 U.S. 578 (1987).
Enmund v. *Florida*, 458 U.S. 782 (1982).
Epperson v. *Arkansas*, 393 U.S. 97 (1968).
Erie Railroad Company v. *Tompkins*, 304 U.S. 64 (1938).
Ford v. *Wainwright*, 477 U.S. 399 (1986).
Furman v. *Georgia*, 408 U.S. 238 (1972).
Gibbons v. *Ogden*, 22 U.S. 1 (1824).
Gideon v. *Wainwright*, 372 U.S. 335 (1963).
Gillette v. *United States*, 401 U.S. 437 (1971).
Gonzales v. *Oregon*, 546 U.S. 243 (2006).
Gonzales v. *Raich*, 545 U.S. 1 (2005).
Gregg v. *Georgia*, 428 U.S. 153 (1976).
Griswold v. *Connecticut*, 381 U.S. 479 (1965).
Jacobson v. *Massachusetts*, 197 U.S. 11 (1905).
Kitzmiller v. *Dover Area School District*, 400 F. Supp.2d 707 (2005).
Lochner v. *New York*, 198 U.S. 45 (1905).
Lopez, United States v., 514 U.S. 549 (1995).
Marbury v. *Madison*, 1 Cranch (5 U.S.) 137 (1803).

McCleskey v. *Kemp*, 481 U.S. 279 (1987).
Minersville School District v. *Gobitis*, 310 U.S. 586 (1940).
Missouri v. *Holland*, 252 U.S. 416 (1920).
Olmstead v. *United States*, 277 U.S. 438 (1928).
Planned Parenthood v. *Casey*, 505 U.S. 833 (1992).
Powell v. *Alabama*, 287 U.S. 45 (1932).
Ramdial and Others v. *Emperor*, AIR 1914 All. 249 (14 Cri. L.J. 634)
    (1914).
Reynolds v. *United States*, 98 U.S. 145 (1878).
Roe v. *Wade*, 410 U.S. 113 (1973).
Sacco and Vanzetti v. *Massachusetts*, 158 N.E. 167 (1927); 275 U.S. 574
    (1927).
Schenck v. *United States*, 249 U.S. 47 (1919).
Scopes v. *State of Tennessee*, 278 S.W. 57 (1925).
Seeger, United States v., 380 U.S. 163 (1965).
Texas v. *Johnson*, 491 U.S. 397 (1989).
Union Pacific Railroad Company v. *Botsford*, 141 U.S. 250 (1891).
Vacco v. *Quill*, 521 U.S. 793 (1997).
Washington v. *Glucksberg*, 521 U.S. 702 (1997); 79 F.3d 790 (1996).
Welch v. *United States*, 398 U.S. 333 (1970).
West Virginia State Board of Education v. *Barnette*, 319 U.S. 624 (1943).
Wickard v. *Filburn*, 317 U.S. 111 (1942).
Wisconsin v. *Yoder*, 406 U.S. 205 (1972).

Other Materials

Aeschylus. Plays.
Anastaplo, George. *Abraham Lincoln: A Constitutional Biography* [pre-
    ferred title: *Thoughts on Abraham Lincoln: A Discourse on Prudence*].
    Lanham, Md.: Rowman and Littlefield, 1999.
———. *The Amendments to the Constitution: A Commentary.* Baltimore:
    Johns Hopkins University Press, 1995.
———. *The American Moralist: On Law, Ethics, and Government* (Essays
    on capital punishment; the abolition of television; the Moral Major-
    ity). Athens: Ohio University Press, 1992.
———. *The Bible: Respectful Readings.* Lanham, Md.: Lexington Books,
    2008.
———. Bibliography. In *Leo Strauss and His Legacy: A Bibliography,* ed.

John A. Murley. Lanham, Md.: Lexington Books, 2005, 29, 733–855, 871.

——. *But Not Philosophy: Seven Introductions to Non-Western Thought.* Lanham, Md.: Lexington Books, 2002.

——. *The Constitution of 1787: A Commentary.* Baltimore: Johns Hopkins University Press, 1989 (Chinese-language edition, 2008).

——. "Constitutional Comment." Afterword for Gera-Lind Kolarik, *Freed to Kill: The Story of Larry Eyler* (Chicago: Chicago Review Press, 1990), 367–79 (on the Exclusionary Rule).

——. "Constitutionalism and the Good: Explorations," 70 *Tennessee Law Review* 757, 796–98 (2003) (an exchange with B. F. Skinner).

——. *The Constitutionalist: Notes on the First Amendment.* Dallas: Southern Methodist University Press, 1971; Lanham, Md.: Lexington Books, 2005.

——. "Did Anyone 'in Charge' Know What He Was Doing? The Thirty Years' War of the Twentieth Century." In *Campus Hate-Speech Codes, Natural Right, and Twentieth Century Atrocities.* Lewiston, New York: Edwin Mellen Press, 1999, 49.

——. *Human Being and Citizen: Essays on Virtue, Freedom, and the Common Good.* Chicago: Swallow Press; Athens: Ohio University Press, 1975.

——. "In re Antonin Scalia." 28 *Perspectives in Political Science* 22 (1999).

——, ed. *Liberty, Equality and Modern Constitutionalism: A Source Book.* 2 vols. Newburyport, Mass.: Focus Publishing Company, 1999.

——. *Reflections on Constitutional Law.* Lexington: University Press of Kentucky, 2006.

——. *Reflections on Freedom of Speech and the First Amendment.* Lexington: University Press of Kentucky, 2007.

——. "September Eleventh, The ABCs of a Citizen's Responses: Explorations," 29 *Oklahoma City University Law Review* 165–382 (2004) (supplemented by collections of periodic assessments in 4 *International Law Review* [Loyola University of Chicago], 135–65 [2006], and in a forthcoming issue of the *Oklahoma City University Law Review*).

——. "Yearnings for the Divine and the Natural Animation of Matter" (included in Anastaplo, *The Bible: Respectful Readings* [2008], and in Anastaplo, *Reflections on Religion, the Divine, and Constitutionalism* [in course of preparation]). (This Essay is available, with commentary, on the Internet.)

Aristotle. *Nicomachean Ethics.*

———. *Politics.*

Arnhart, Larry. "Conservatives, Darwin and Design." *First Things* (November 2000): 23, 31.

———. *Darwinian Natural Right: The Biological Ethics of Human Nature.* SUNY Press, 1998.

Augustine, Saint. *The City of God.*

Bergher, Daniel. "Death in the Family." *New York Times Magazine,* December 2, 2007, 38.

Bible.

Bunyan, John. *The Pilgrim's Progress.*

Chapman, Steve. "Drop in Abortion Rate Shows Society Changing, Not the Law." *Chicago Tribune,* January 20, 2008, sec. 2, p. 7.

Chaucer, Geoffrey. *The Canterbury Tales.*

Clark, Ramsey. "The Lawyer's Duty of Loyalty: To the Client or to the Institution?" 16 *Loyola University Chicago Law Journal* 459–69 (1985).

Compassionate Use Act of 1996 (California).

Confederate Constitution of 1861–1865 (reprinted in Anastaplo, *Reflections on Constitutional Law*).

"Conservatives, Darwin and Design." *First Things* (November 2000).

Constitution of the United States and Amendments (Appendices B and C of this volume).

Dante Alighieri. *Divine Comedy.*

Declaration of Independence (Appendix A of this volume).

Dostoyevsky, Fyodor. *Crime and Punishment.*

———. *The Brothers Karamazov.*

Encyclopedia of the American Constitution. New York: Macmillan, 1986, 2000.

Euripides. Plays.

Everyman.

Federal Assisted Suicide Funding Restriction Act (1997).

Ford, John C. "The Morality of Obliteration Bombing," *Theological Studies* 5 (1944): 261. Reprinted, in part, in Anastaplo, ed., *Liberty, Equality & Modern Constitutionalism,* 2:199–214.

Hawthorne, Nathaniel. *The Scarlet Letter.*

Hobbes, Thomas. *Leviathan.*

Homer. *Iliad.*

———. *Odyssey.*

Johnston, David, and Neil A. Lewis. "[Department of Justice Is] Ending Raids of Dispensers of Marijuana for Patients." *New York Times,* March 19, 2009, A18.

Joyce, James. *Ulysses.*

Kass, Leon R. "Appreciating the Phenomenon of Life." *Graduate Faculty Philosophy Journal* (The New School) 23 (2001): 1–2.

Lewis, C. S. *A Preface to Paradise Lost.* London: Oxford University Press, 1942.

Lincoln, Abraham. *The Political Speeches and Writings.* Ed. Joseph R. Fornieri. Washington, D.C.: Regnery Publishing Company, 2009.

Magna Carta (reprinted in Anastaplo, *Reflections on Constitutional Law*).

Mayer, Milton S. *What Can a Man Do?* Chicago: University of Chicago Press, 1964.

McReavy, Lawrence L. "Appalling Insinuations." *Theological Studies,* 6 (1945): 140. Reprinted in Anastaplo, ed., *Liberty, Equality & Modern Constitutionalism,* 2:214–16.

Mill, John Stuart. *On Liberty.*

Milton, John. *Areopagitica.*

———. *Paradise Lost.*

———. *Paradise Regained.*

Mishima, Yukio. "Patriotism." In *Death in Midsummer and Other Stories.* New York: New York Directions, 1966.

Murley, John A., ed. *Leo Strauss and His Legacy: A Bibliography.* Lanham, Md.: Lexington Books, 2005.

Newton, Isaac. *Principia Mathematica.*

Nuremberg Trial Record, 1945–1946.

Oxford Classical Dictionary. Oxford: Clarendon Press, 1949.

Page, Clarence. "Is It Reefer Madness?" *Chicago Tribune,* March 11, 2009, sec. 1, p. 29.

Pape, Robert A. *Dying to Win: The Strategic Logic of Suicide Terrorism.* New York: Random House, 2005.

Plato. *Dialogues.*

Proust, Marcel. *Remembrance of Things Past.*

Publius. *The Federalist.*

Shakespeare, William. *The Complete Works of William Shakespeare.* Ed. David Bevington. New York: Longman, 1997.

Smith, Adam. *The Wealth of Nations.*

Strauss, Leo. *The City and Man.* Chicago: Rand McNally, 1964.

Thoreau, Henry. *Essay on Civil Disobedience.*
Thucydides. *The Peloponnesian War.*
The Time Almanac 2000. Boston, Mass.: Family Education Company, 1949.
Virginia Statute of Religious Freedom (1786). (Reprinted in Anastaplo, *Reflections on Freedom of Speech and the First Amendment*).

Index

There are appended to this Index rosters of documents and cases considered in George Anastaplo, *Reflections on Constitutional Law* (University Press of Kentucky, 2006), and Anastaplo, *Reflections on Freedom of Speech and the First Amendment* (University Press of Kentucky, 2007).

Rosters of Documents and Cases Considered in George Anastaplo, *Reflections on Constitutional Law*, and Anastaplo, *Reflections on Freedom of Speech and the First Amendment*

I. There are, in George Anastaplo, *Reflections on Constitutional Law* (University Press of Kentucky, 2006), considerations of these documents: the Articles of Confederation (1776–1789), the Bill of Rights (1791), the Confederate Constitution (1861–1865), the Declaration of Independence (1776), the Emancipation Proclamation (1862–1863), *The Federalist* (1787–1788), the Gettysburg Address (1863), Magna Carta (1215), the Northwest Ordinance (1787), the Petition of Right (1628), and the United States Constitution and its Amendments (1787, 1791–1992).

Also, there are, in George Anastaplo, *Reflections on Constitutional Law*, considerations of these cases: *Baker* v. *Carr* (1962), *Barron* v. *Baltimore* (1833), *Black and White Taxicab Company Case* (1928), *Bolling* v. *Sharp* (1954), *Brown* v. *Board of Education* (1954–1955), *Bush* v. *Gore* (2000), *Calder* v. *Bull* (1798), *Carey* v. *South Dakota* (1919), *Civil Rights Cases* (1883), *Cohen* v. *California* (1971), *Colegrove* v. *Green* (1946), *Corfield* v. *Coryell* (1823), *Dean Milk Company* v. *City of Madison* (1951), *Dred Scott* v. *Sandford* (1857), *Erie Railroad Company* v. *Tompkins* (1938), *Gibbons* v. *Ogden* (1824), *Gratz* v. *Bollinger* (2003), *Hammer* v. *Dagenhart* (1918), *Hirabayashi Case* (1943), *H.P. Hood & Sons* v. *DuMond* (1949), *Kassel* v. *Consolidated Freightways Corporation* (1981), *Korematsu Case* (1944), *Kuhn* v. *Fairmont Coal Company* (1910),

Langbridge's Case (1345), *Lochner* v. *New York* (1905), *Lucas* v. *Forty-fourth General Assembly* (1964), *Marbury* v. *Madison* (1803), *Martin* v. *Hunter's Lessee* (1816), *M'Culloch* v. *Maryland* (1819), *Missouri* v. *Holland* (1920), *Plessy* v. *Ferguson* (1896), *Regents of the University of California* v. *Bakke* (1978), *Roe* v. *Wade* (1973), *San Antonio Independent School District* v. *Rodriguez* (1973), *Shelley* v. *Kramer* (1948), *Slaughter-House Cases* (1872), *Somerset* v. *Stewart* (1771–1772), *Southern Pacific Company* v. *Arizona* (1945), *Steel Seizure Case* (1952), *Swift* v. *Tyson* (1842), *United States* v. *Lopez* (1995), and *Wickard* v. *Filburn* (1942).

II. There are, in George Anastaplo, *Reflections on Freedom of Speech and the First Amendment* (University Press of Kentucky, 2007), considerations of these documents: the Articles of Confederation (1776–1789), the Bill of Rights (1791), the Confederate Constitution (1861–1865), the Declaration of Independence (1776), *The Federalist* (1787–1788), Habeas Corpus Acts (1641, 1679), Magna Carta (1215), the Northwest Ordinance (1787), the Virginia Resolutions (1798), the Virginia Statute of Religious Freedom (1786), and the United States Constitution and its Amendments (1787, 1791–1992).

Also, there are, in Anastaplo, *Reflections on Freedom of Speech and the First Amendment,* considerations of these cases: *Abrams* v. *United States* (1919), *Bar Admission Cases* (1961), *Barron* v. *Mayor and City of Baltimore* (1833), *Bates* v. *State Bar of Arizona* (1977), *Brandenburg* v. *Ohio* (1969), *Brown* v. *Board of Education* (1954), *Buckley* v. *Valeo* (1976), *Cohen* v. *California* (1971), *Communist Party of the United States* v. *Subversive Activities Control Board* (1961), *Debs* v. *United States* (1919), *Dennis* v. *United States* (1951), *Dred Scott* v. *Sandford* (1857), *Erie Railroad Company* v. *Tompkins* (1938), *FW/PBS, Inc.* v. *City of Dallas* (1990), *Gertz* v. *Robert Welch Inc.* (1974), *Gitlow* v. *New York* (1925), *Jacobellis* v. *Ohio* (1964), *Korematsu* v. *United States* (1944), *Marbury* v. *Madison* (1803), *Miller* v. *California* (1973), *Near* v. *Minnesota* (1931), *New York Times* v. *Sullivan* (1964), *New York Times* v. *United States* (1971), *Paris Adult Theatre I.* v. *Slaton* (1973), *Pentagon Papers Case* (1971), *United States* v. *Progressive Magazine* (1979), *Randall* v. *Sorrell* (2006), *Regina* v. *Hicklin* (1868), *Rosenberg* v. *United States* (1953), *Schenck* v. *United States* (1919), *Somerset* v. *Stewart* (1772), *Spies* v. *Illinois* (1887), *Texas* v. *Johnson* (1989), *Tinker* v. *Des Moines Independent Community School District* (1969), *Virginia State Board of Pharmacy* v. *Virginia Citizens Council* (1976), *Whitney* v. *California* (1927), *Wickard* v. *Filburn* (1942), *Yarbrough, Ex parte* (1884), and *Zenger, Case of John Peter* (1735).

About the Author

George Anastaplo was born in St. Louis, Missouri, in 1925, and grew up in Southern Illinois. After serving three years as an aviation cadet and flying officer during and just after the Second World War, he earned A.B., J.D., and Ph.D. degrees from the University of Chicago. He is currently Lecturer in the Liberal Arts at the University of Chicago (in the Basic Program of Liberal Education for Adults), Professor of Law at Loyola University of Chicago, and Professor Emeritus of Political Science and of Philosophy at Dominican University.

His publications include more than a dozen books and two dozen book-length collections in law reviews. His scholarship was reviewed in seven articles in the 1997 volume of the *Political Science Reviewer.* A two-volume Festschrift, *Law and Philosophy,* was issued in his honor in 1992 by the Ohio University Press. Between 1980 and 1992 he was nominated annually for a Nobel Peace Prize by a Chicago-based committee that had as its initial spokesman Malcolm P. Sharp (1897–1980), professor emeritus of the University of Chicago Law School.

Professor Anastaplo's career is assessed in a chapter in *Leo Strauss, The Straussians, and the American Regime* (Lanham, Md.: Rowman and Littlefield, 1999). It is assessed as well in the cover story of the November 26, 2000, issue of the *Chicago Tribune Magazine.* A bibliography of his work is included in the Anastaplo Festschrift, *Law and Philosophy,* 2:1073–1145. See also, "George Anastaplo: An Autobiographical Bibliography (1947–2001)," 20 *Northern Illinois University Law Review* 581–710 (2000); "George Anastaplo: Tables of Contents for His Books and Published Collections (1950–2001)," 39 *Brandeis Law Journal* 219–87 (2000–2001). See, as well, the massive bibliography in political philosophy compiled by John A. Murley, *Leo Strauss: A Bibliographical Legacy* (Lanham, Md.: Lexington Books, 2005), 733–855, 871. The initial volumes of the Anastaplo *Reflections* series are assessed in the seven book reviews noticed in the preface to this volume.